Death in America

Philippe Ariès

Ann Douglas

Stanley French

Jack Goody

Patricia Fernández Kelly

Mary Ann Meyers

Lewis O. Saum

David E. Stannard

DEATH
IN
AMERICA

EDITED, WITH AN INTRODUCTION,
BY DAVID E. STANNARD

University of Pennsylvania Press
1975

CONTENTS

INTRODUCTION

IT HAS BEEN A COMMON PRACTICE THROUGHOUT HISTORY FOR MEN TO personify death in a great variety of ways. As well as the literal identification of a specific spirit of death in most of the world's religions, there are the more popular images of death as the Grim Reaper, the Pale Horseman, the Destroying Angel, the King of Terrors, and so on. It is now twenty years since the English anthropologist Geoffrey Gorer, in a brief essay published in *Encounter*, suggested that another name might be added to this pantheon. Although he did not actually use the term, Gorer in effect pointed out that in the modern West death possessed the characteristics of the emperor who wore no clothes. And, as happened in that famous children's tale, once Gorer spoke the forbidden words identifying death as the "new pornography" about which nothing should be said in polite company, he was joined by a rousing and rising chorus of echoing voices.

Since that time, with ever-increasing frequency, the reading public has been deluged with all manner of writings on the problem of death in the modern West, and particularly in modern America. One of the striking things about this recent literature on death and dying is that at first glance the themes pursued most often seem curiously contradictory. On the one hand there is the popular social criticism, exemplified by Jessica Mitford's *The American Way of Death*, focusing on the excesses of the funeral industry and its largely successful effort to construct its own "grotesque cloud-cuckoo-land where the trappings of Gracious Living are transformed, as in a nightmare, into the trappings of Gracious Dying."[1] On the other hand there is the more scholarly sociological analysis of the common fate of most Americans who now die in hospitals and rest homes, deserted by their families and friends, and faced with doctors and nurses so intent on maintaining their professional demeanor that they avoid personal contact with the dying at every turn—so lonely that they are forced into such pathetic stratagems as removing their bedside telephones from the hook in order to at least hear a human voice.[2]

Under closer scrutiny, however, what becomes clear is that each of these responses—the extravagant masquerade of death, and the determined

---

[1] *The American Way of Death* (New York: Simon and Schuster, 1963), p. 16.
[2] Elisabeth Kubler-Ross, *On Death and Dying* (New York: Macmillan, 1969), p. 44. Cf. Barney G. Glaser and Anselm L. Strauss, *Awareness of Dying* (Chicago: Aldine, 1965); and Jeanne C. Quint, *The Nurse and the Dying Patient* (New York: Macmillan, 1967).

avoidance of the dying—are reactions with a common source. For the phenomenon of death has become something of an acute embarrassment to modern man: in a technological world that has effectively ruled out of order explanations of a mystical nature, man is brought up short in his inability to understand or give meaning to death. The answers of the past are no longer appropriate; the answers of the present are insufficient. Death is thus avoided as much as possible, and when it is no longer possible—when a body must be confronted and dealt with—it is turned over to professionals who provide their own special skills in the effort of denial. The dead are transformed in appearance with the aid of such products as Nature-Glo "the ultimate in cosmetic embalming"; they are provided with "Beautyrama Adjustable Soft Foam Bed Caskets," and are placed in "slumber rooms" for viewing by the bereaved; and, if circumstances are sufficiently favorable, they may even be fortunate enough to spend the future in a Forest Lawn crypt outfitted with air conditioning and piped-in music.

Forest Lawn, of course, is by no means a *typical* American cemetery. Neither, perhaps, are all of the other approaches described above typical of every American funeral. They are, however, vivid exemplars of the general direction funeral customs have taken in America during the twentieth century.

It also may not be typical for the dying individual to reach for his bedside telephone merely to be afforded the privilege of hearing a voice. But if it is not typical, it is not so in large measure because the dying are generally not capable of such activity—for the great majority of deaths now occur in hospitals where the dying individual has long been sedated into unconsciousness. One 1967 study of approximately two hundred and fifty deaths in California hospitals, for example, reported that barely a dozen subjects had been conscious when death took place, and none of these had been engaged in conversation at the time.[3] Indeed, the term "social death" is now well established in the sociological lexicon as describing that point when an individual is sedated into a pre-death comatose state and effectively regarded from then on as a corpse; this affords the hospital staff the convenience of adequate time to make preparations for the occurrence of actual death, allowing them to see to it, for example, that the individual's eyes are properly closed, as this is a more difficult task to perform once death has taken place.[4]

Perhaps in part as a response to these earlier works, still another type of literature on death and dying has recently emerged. This latest literature can perhaps best be described, with no flippancy intended, as of the "how-

[3]David Sudnow, *Passing On: The Social Organization of Dying* (Englewood Cliffs, N.J.: Prentice-Hall, 1967), p. 89.
[4]Ibid., p. 74.

to-do-it" variety, instructing survivors on the most dignified and rational ways of coping with the deaths of loved ones and of preparing for their own eventual demise. Along with the recent proliferation of societies dedicated to the ideal of simplicity and gracefulness in the face of death, and of hospital seminars on the most humane ways of treating the dying, it may well be that we are in the midst, or at least on the verge of major changes in the modern American attitude and approach to death. But if this very personal approach is the most recent variation on the contemporary literature on death, it is also the one with the deepest roots in the traditions of Western man. And it is also the best example of modern man's treatment of death not only as a response to the secularization of the religious universe, but also as a consequence of the modern ordering of social structure. For whether we look to the hedonistic advice of Siduri the wine maiden in the ancient Mesopotamian *Epic of Gilgamesh,* to the harrowing block-prints of the medieval *Ars Moriendi,* or to the sentimental poetry on death in nineteenth century school books, it is evident that few eras in human history have been without some sort of advice literature on the best way of making a good end. What is most striking about these historical precursors, however, is not their mere presence, but the fact that they have varied so much in the advice they have had to offer—and that this advice has been a reflection of the specific culture's way of life as much as it has been a reaffirmation of the profound disquietude the prospect of death has always brought to the mind of man.

The physical residue of death is the most valuable material archaeologists have had to work with in understanding the life of prehistoric man, for the earliest evidence of uniquely human-like behavior among our ancestors—pre-dating even the crudest cave paintings by at least tens of thousands of years, and perhaps even preceding the development of the ability to express abstract ideas in language—are the remains of the ritualized binding and coloring of the dead by Paleolithic man. Such coloring, almost invariably with a red ochre substance, is generally interpreted as suggestive of a new life for the dead, while the binding, usually with the corpse in a pre-natal position, has been variously interpreted either as indicating a belief in rebirth or as an attempt at constraining the dead from returning to haunt the living. Recently, speculations have even been made concerning Neanderthal attitudes toward children, cripples, and the aged, based on detailed analysis of Neanderthal grave sites.[5] But whatever the specific findings may be, the

[5]Ralph M. Rowlett and Mary Jane Schneider, "The Material Expression of Neanderthal Child Care," in Miles Richardson, ed., *The Human Mirror: Material and Spatial Images of Man* (Baton Rouge: Louisiana State University Press, 1974), pp. 41–58. For estimates of the early stages of man's development when engagement in burial ritual first appeared, see (among many sources) Johannes Maringer, *The Gods of Prehistoric Man* (New York: Knopf, 1960), p. 37; and V. Gordon Childe, "Directional Changes in Funerary Practices During 50,000 Years," *Man,* 45 (1945).

important point is that the physical remains of prehistoric man's burial rituals are the earliest real evidence we have of man's ability to carry out and respond to abstract thought.

With the rise of modern anthropology and the sociology of religion in the nineteenth century, scholars recognized in the rituals surrounding death what Jack Goody has termed "the kernel of their studies."[6] Death has since often been regarded as the source of all religion and even, as Goody notes, as the origin of Greek tragedy and of the Olympic games.[7] But if there is disagreement on some of this, one general connection between death and the organization of human culture that has been repeatedly observed and analyzed since the turn of the present century is the tie between attitudes toward death and the sense of community purpose and meaning a people may or may not enjoy.

Writing in 1907 Robert Hertz, a young student of Emile Durkheim, noted that in virtually all cultures the death of an important leader brought on a significant response by the society at large, while that of someone less critical to the functioning of the community was often barely noticed. He made the elementary but seminal point that if sociologists and anthropologists were to make any sense of this they would have to recognize that every individual in a society possesses not only a biological being, but also a "social being" that is "grafted onto him" by other members of the society.[8] The death of an important individual thus brings with it serious damage to the social fabric, and a natural and spontaneous effort is then made by the society to compensate for the loss. This is particularly evident in the dramatic funerary rites of smaller, more unified societies where, as Robert Blauner has more recently written, "much 'work' must be done to restore the social system's functioning."[9]

Such smaller, more unified, simpler societies were the rule in America until at least the early years of the nineteenth century. Prior to then, and in small scattered pockets since then, death generally brought with it a substantial disorganization of the community's structure and ongoing functions. Whether or not the family was a more cohesive unit in the past—a question of some continuing debate among social historians—in virtually all American communities of the seventeenth and eighteenth centuries the family was well-integrated into the web of *community* cohesiveness. Death had a great deal of meaning for the individual, meaning that admittedly differed substantially from time to time and from place to place, and it had

[6]*Death, Property, and the Ancestors* (Stanford: Stanford University, 1962), p. 13.
[7]Ibid.
[8]Robert Hertz, "The Collective Representation of Death" [1907], in Hertz, *Death and the Right Hand,* translated by R. and C. Needham (Glencoe, Ill.: The Free Press, 1960), p. 76.
[9]Robert Blauner, "Death and Social Structure," *Psychiatry,* 29 (1966), 387.

a great deal of meaning for the community; but because its meaning was diffused throughout the community at large, its burden was lightened somewhat from the shoulders of the immediate family whose sense of bereavement was widely shared.

We are now well into the closing years of the twentieth century. The tides of secularization in religion, specialization and diversification in commerce, and individualism and mobility in social relations have long swept over the civilization of our time. Few individuals can any longer, when faced with death, find solace in the promise of a spiritual paradise, or can locate a sense of genuine importance for themselves in either their work or their community. When they face death they must often do so with a sense of its meaninglessness, and of their own insignificance; and when their small circle of intimates are forced to provide the meaning that is absent, they must often turn to the only source available—the commercial funerary establishment.

* * *

None of the essays in this volume were written with a single theme in mind, other than that they should address the problem of death. They were written by historians, anthropologists, literary scholars and art historians—each with his or her own choice of chronological, geographical, and conceptual focus—and they can and should be read primarily with their individual concerns in mind. There are, however, a good many overlapping and complementary themes. The relationship between death and childhood, death and religion, death and social class, death and cultural expression are only a few such common denominators. It was intended that this collection would help fill a prominent gap in the contemporary literature on death by providing historical background for what has almost invariably been a parochial concern for the present. But in assembling these writings it became clear that each in its own different way was also a building block toward a general history and perhaps at least a partial explanation for the disturbing turns the concept of death has taken in modern American society.

The brief opening comment by Jack Goody introduces some of the recent scholarship on death in a variety of social settings and suggests certain reasons for its continuing importance to those who would seek to understand the many levels of organized human culture. Despite the fact that, as he puts it, "only the bare bones of death are seen today in Western societies," Goody demonstrates ways in which modern studies of traditional cultures—from the work of anthropologists in Africa and Asia to that of the *Annales* school of French social historians—can assist in understanding the contemporary cultural suppression of death.

My own essay on childhood and death in Puritan New England focuses on
a problem treated at least in passing in the later articles by Saum, Douglas,
Kelly and Ariès. Taking issue with some recent interpretations of the
meaning of childhood in early American society, I suggest that the Puritans' concerns and fears of death had their roots in the imposition, on the
child's naive sense of reality, of a vision of death beset with theological
pessimism and internal contradiction. Death often had terrifying meaning
for the Puritan, but such meaning, I argue, can only be grasped by understanding the world-view of the relatively closed society in which the Puritan
lived.

In a sense, the early Mormon movement can also be characterized as a
closed society, but one in which the picture of the world of the living and the
world of the dead differed fundamentally from that of the Puritan. Mary
Ann Meyers points out that a sense of continuing, evolutionary "progress"
marked the thought of the founders of Mormonism, with the result that
death did not bring with it the stunning changes traditionally perceived in
the Christian cosmological scheme. Nor, as a consequence, did the
Mormon suffer the deep-seated apprehension in the face of death so common to Christianity in general and so exaggerated in the Puritan context.

But in the eventual mainstream of American culture, Puritans and Mormons alike were something of an anachronism. Their contrasting visions of
death suggest some of the ways the elasticity of Christian dogma can
provide approaches to the problem that vary even to the point of opposition.
But with the dawning of the nineteenth century and the emergence of
cultural Romanticism, a broader gauge "American" vision of death began
settling in. One of the earliest pieces of evidence attesting to this new sentimentalized attitude toward death was the construction, in 1796, of New
Haven's Grove Street Cemetery. As Stanley French indicates, the new rural
cemetery movement of the early nineteenth century—exemplified finally by
Boston's Mount Auburn Cemetery, built in 1831—carried with it strong
currents of Romanticism, but also the seeds of a rising ethic of possessive
individualism.

If, as French concludes, the rural cemetery movement was at least in
part an effort at "cultural uplift . . . during the Age of the Common Man,"
so too was much of the literary outpouring on death that marked that era.
At a time when religion was increasingly becoming the province of women
and children, as Ann Douglas vividly demonstrates, death (like religion)
took on new meaning. Schoolbook poetry and popular consolation
literature spread wide the message that death was a thing to be desired and
hoped for with all one's heart: it meant deliverance from this mundane
world, and glorious reunion with loved ones in the dazzling palaces of
heaven. Death was indeed so marvelous, wrote one popular author of the

time, that God had found it necessary to implant in man a natural apprehension of it, in order to "keep his children from rushing uncalled into his presence, leaving undone the work which he has given them to do.[10] Heaven literally became home to much of nineteenth century America.

But not to all of it. Lewis O. Saum's combing of various state and local archives for evidence of attitudes toward death among less urban and less urbane Americans during roughly the same period as that studied by French and Douglas has turned up strikingly different results. Far from spiritualism and sentimentality, Saum found an attitude of frankness and openness, a "seeming insouciance"; and far from envisioning in death the splendor of "the golden stair" to heaven, the subjects of Saum's inquiry saw death as, at best, "escape from the world's sadness." It was, he writes, "a qualified, even a negative vision. But for people whose quotient of delight had had severe limitations, it seems to have been heaven enough."

Patricia Fernandez Kelly's essay on death in Mexican folk culture provides an instructive comparison which can help in understanding the fundamental differences among nineteenth century Americans in their attitudes toward death—as well as extending the boundaries of this volume beyond the restriction of viewing the United States as all that is "American." Despite the centuries of forced immersion of Mexican folk life in a powerful solution of European Christianity, Kelly shows that the resulting syncretistic cultural fusion has been characterized by much retention of traditional beliefs and attitudes. The tenacity of folk culture has been such, for example, that the idea of the Resurrection—so central to the Christian metaphysic—is largely ignored in contemporary Mexican folk religion. Although it is, of course, vastly different from either of the approaches to death described by Douglas or Saum, in its openness and its absence of romanticization the attitude toward death of Kelly's subjects seems conceptually closer to that of the "common" people described in Saum's essay than to that expressed by the consolation literature that is at the core of Douglas' study.

One tentative conclusion that might be drawn from this parallel—a conclusion that is underscored by some of the more recent theoretical work that has been done on death and social structure[11]—is that, in contrast to those nineteenth century Americans who wrote and read the volumes of sentimental literature on death and who celebrated Mt. Auburn and its many subsequent imitators as a charming "dormitory" for the deceased, the provincial and folk cultures of the United States and Mexico were better

[10]John Pierpont, *The Garden of Graves* (Dedham, Mass.: H. Mann, 1841), p. 7.
[11]E.g., Blauner, "Death and Social Structure"; and Le Roy Bowman, *The American Funeral: A Study in Guilt, Extravagance, and Sublimity* (Washington, D.C.: Public Affairs Press, 1959).

able to maintain a sense of communal unity and integrity, were less affected by the socially alienating forces of modernism, and thus had less of a need to create an *artificial* meaning for the experience of death. In these societies death continued to have the significant disruptive effect on the social fabric described by Hertz more than half a century ago, and its meaning remained clear both for the individual anticipating death and for those who would survive. In the more urban, cosmopolitan world that is the subject of French and Douglas' essays—a world witnessing the emergence of commercial specialization and social isolation and mobility—this "natural" social disruption occasioned by death was rapidly losing its force; sentimentalization and the locating of heaven as the real "home" for all men was one way of re-creating the sense of community that was thus lost, and of re-establishing meaning in the experience of death that waned with the lessened cohesiveness of the social structure.

But such efforts were doomed to eventual failure. For as their central premise they had a widely-felt and literally conceived religious world-view, a world-view that had become essentially anachronistic before the middle of the twentieth century. The search for meaning in death became no less demanding—if anything, it was intensified—but if it was to be found it would have to be located in a world of increasing secularization. As Philippe Ariès points out in his concluding essay, avoidance and denial on the one hand, and commercial exploitation on the other, seem to have been the inevitable result.[12]

Moving back well beyond the Puritan experience which marks the chronological beginning of this collection, Ariès views contemporary American attitudes toward death in the context of developments having their roots in the early Middle Ages. With the shifting pattern of family life at the heart of his analysis, Ariès sees the modern concern with death as a reversal of certain structural themes that marked the medieval era, a reversal intimately bound up with what he calls the modern "crisis of individuality." But Ariès is careful to avoid the "moralistic and polemical" tone of social criticism that he notes has marked so many of the recent treatments of modern American funerary ritual; indeed, he views the contemporary American approach to death as an almost heroic attempt to devise new rituals to fit new conditions. And in so doing he implicitly supports the contention stated earlier that the two most striking and seemingly contradictory characteristics of our culture's response to death and dying—avoidance and ostentation—are merely variations derived from a common source. Each is a necessary, and yet by itself inadequate, response to a world in which religion has lost much of its power to explain, and to a so-

[12]I have developed some of these themes more fully in the closing chapter of a forthcoming study, *The Puritan Way of Death: A Study in Religion, Culture, and Social Change.*

ciety in which the death of an individual touches deeply only a small handful of intimates.

It is in opposition to these tendencies toward avoidance and ostentation that the new literature on death, the hospital seminars on the treatment of the dying, and the societies committed to openness in the face of death have arisen. But, as all of the essays in this volume suggest, the success of such endeavors is dependent upon major changes in the world-view and social structure of the society at large. For if any single theme dominates the entirety of this work, it is that the way a people look at death and dying is invariably and inevitably a direct concomitant of the way they look at life.

DEATH AND THE INTERPRETATION OF CULTURE: A BIBLIOGRAPHIC OVERVIEW

JACK GOODY

THE FACT OF DEATH PROVIDES A CENTRAL FOCUS AROUND WHICH HUMAN cultures develop in two main ways. Firstly, there is what we may loosely call the conceptual aspect of death; secondly, the organizational. Or to put it another, and not altogether overlapping, way, there is the anticipation of death and the actuality of death, the ideology and the interment.

The first of these clusters of meaning lies at the core of much religious and indeed philosophical activity, and from it perhaps stems the whole mesh of religious beliefs. The inevitable fact of death needs to be reckoned with and accounted for; it has to be explained and to be included in a wider scheme of representations, a belief system, a religion, an ideology. In a recent volume on "the origins of a sense of God," J. Bowker argues that religion has failed to disappear because of the great "constraint" of death; the role of religion is to find a way through this limitation to human existence.[1] The theme echoes Malinowski and the many scholars of previous centuries who, taking a cue from the actors themselves, stressed the link between the journey of the soul (death, survival, immortality and passage to the other world), the dualistic concept of the human being (body and spirit/soul), and the existence of *spiritual* beings.

The theme requires little elaboration. It characterizes Euhemerist explanations of the origin of religion, and runs through the evolutionary schemas of 19th century scholars like Herbert Spencer and E. B. Tylor.[2] Indeed it is enshrined in the latter's minimum definition of religion.[3] But such specula-

---

[1]*The Sense of God: Sociological, Anthropological and Psychological Approaches to the Origin of the Sense of God* (Oxford: Clarendon Press, 1973).

[2]For a fuller account see the opening chapter of Jack Goody, *Death, Property and the Ancestors* (Stanford: Stanford Univ. Press, 1962).

[3]For a recent comment, see Gillian Ross, "Neo-Tylorianism: A Reassessment," *Man,* 6 (1971), 105–16.

tions about origins, whether from the pen of theologians, sociologists or historians, are backed by little evidence. Historically the elaborations of human burials in the Upper Palaeolithic strongly suggest the existence of a symbolic and ideological halo around the physiological facts of death, specifically in the use of red ochre, of special burial positions, and other funerary rituals. Such a set of beliefs would clearly require the elaboration of a complex system of communication which permitted the reference to "concepts" that were not physically present to the actors, in other words, a language. But whether these forms of disposing of the dead constituted in any way an "origin" of the whole complex of religious beliefs must remain guesswork, though one that fits with an acceptable logical model.

But when we come to deal with the religious activities of specific societies, then the role of death and the dead is clearly of central importance. H. Sawyer has recently argued that in West African religion God is indeed the Great Ancestor.[4] On another level, since death is the ultimate misfortune, religious cults that offer some hope of dealing with man's calamities, with disease and with want, inevitably have to deal with death. Herein lies a basic contradiction; such cults have not only to ward off death but also to comfort the bereaved and the dying, since mortality is a state of being both avoidable in the shorter run and inevitable in the long. Christ is at once the earthly healer and the heavenly savior.

The complex of beliefs and practices surrounding death are of great significance to the sociologist and historian alike. In treating general aspects of the "world view," the historian is inevitably handicapped because what usually persists as documentary evidence of "belief" are the written elaborations of specialists. Indeed the very fact of reducing such beliefs to writing may well have some radical influence upon them. For those working in a living society, there is the questionnaire, which often has similar disadvantages, or, better still, the passive ear, an instrument of research whose utility is often greatly underrated. But apart from the literary reflections of priest, poet and philosopher, death leaves other material traces of which historians and sociologists have recently begun to make considerable use. In the first place we have the will, that is, testaments made in anticipation of death, which in earlier times were concerned not only with the disposition of property but also with the fate of the soul. Notable among achievements in this field has been the work of French historians of the "Annales" school, especially that of M. Vovelle. Following up the study of Daumard and Furet based on marriage contracts, a work that was central in the formation of a school of "l'histoire quantifiée," Vovelle examined a large number of wills not in a search for the manner of distributing property but in order to es-

---

[4]*God: Ancestor or Creator?* (London: Longmann, 1970).

tablish "l'histoire des mentalités," a history of the mind rather than ideas, since he was interested in the generality of individuals and hence the over-all distribution of will-making among the population at large was of crucial importance. In this regard he was fortunate in his choice of 18th century Provence, where even in the rural areas between 60 and 70 per cent of males and 40 to 50 per cent of females made written testaments, as compared with less than 20 per cent around Lyon.[5] Looking at the spiritual testaments that developed as part of the will after the Counter-Reformation, Vovelle attempts to assess the popular mind. The spiritual element has certain formulaic qualities about it, repeated in will after will over determined geographical areas. But the formulas are not fossilized; they change over time, and hence can be used, Vovelle argues, to reconstruct changing attitudes to death. This examination leads him to conclude that there was a profound change in the collective sensibility during the 18th century, the century of the Enlightenment, which he describes as "dechristianisation." As compared with the Baroque world which preceded it, men were less confident of their passage to the other world, and more concerned with the physical aspects of death. Such changing attitudes are linked with the changing position of women and with changing attitudes within the family.[6]

Similar kinds of study can be carried out on other of the material remains that the advent and actuality of death leave behind. The analysis of grave goods is central to reconstructions of prehistoric societies, where they throw light on technology, stratification and migration as well as indicating attitudes toward death. Apart from grave goods, there are the markers of graves, tombstones, which in literate societies offer a rich harvest of biographical and sometimes attitudinal material. Using the inscriptions on Roman tombstones K. Hopkins and earlier writers have made a useful contribution to social and demographic studies.[7] In many societies funerary artifacts also take a more artistic form, playing a major part in the history of art. The impetus is to preserve some material memorial of the dead, part of his physical being, then an object such as the stool he sat on, imbued with

---

[5] G. and M. Vovelle, "La Mort et l'au-delà en Provence d'après les autels des âmes du Purgatoire (XVe–XXe siècle)," *Annales E.S.C.,* 24 (1969), 1602–34 [repr. as *Cahier des Annales,* No. 29]; and M. Vovelle, *Piètè baroque et déchristianisation en Provence au XVIIIe siècle* (Paris: Plon, 1973). The same kind of variation is encountered with written marriage contracts, the figure of 50 per cent in Paris contrasting with the rare occurrence in Normandy. It should be added that the testators are often themselves illiterate; at the beginning of the century some 31–38 per cent of men sign their wills, only 15 per cent of women (Vovelle, 1969, p. 606), and there is little change by the time of the Revolution. Cf. A. Daumard and F. Furel, *Structur et relations sociales à Paris au XVIIIe siècle (Cahiers des Annales,* No. 18).

[6] Cf. Philippe Ariès, "L'apparition du sentiment moderne de la famille dans les testaments et les tombeaux." Communication to the conference on the History of the Family, Cambridge, 1969.

[7] K. Hopkins, "On the Probable Age Structure of the Roman Population," *Population Studies,* 20 (1966), 245–64.

his body dirt, and therefore his personality, and subsequently (with the development of plastic and graphic techniques) the shift to abstract or figurative artifacts representing the individual, of which the modern forms are perhaps a sculpture in a prominent place, an ancestral portrait in the hall, a tinted photograph on the mantlepiece.[8] At earlier stages, the physical memorial was both a place of communion as well as one of simple commemoration; it was a focus for propitiating the ancestors rather than for a mere cult of the dead.

The nature of the physical memorial varied from the ancestral tablets of traditional China to the stools of Ashanti, the clay pots of the Tallensi to the simple anthropomorphic shrines of the LoDagaa, and the completely naturalistic heads of bronze that played a part in the worship of royal ancestors in Ife and in Benin.[9] In Africa the religious significance of wood carving, bronze casting and sculpture hardly needs comment; much of this centers around the dead.

These material objects, significant in themselves for the study of religion and the history of art, have also been used as indices of social attitudes. The style of the bronze heads of Benin kings became increasingly decorated and florid, a change which Bradbury sees as going hand in hand with the greater centralization in the state, the greater isolation of the monarch. In Provence, G. and M. Vovelle have traced changes in the iconography of altarpieces of chapels for souls in purgatory between the 15th and 20th centuries, changes which they see as indicating shifts in the collective sensibility; for example, during the course of the 19th century, the souls in purgatory are not simply recipients of the prayers of the living, rather they are acting as mediators with the deity; there is a shift from service to serving.[10]

It is not only in the sphere of the graphic arts that funerals have had an influence on creative activity. Without wishing to espouse a theory of the

---

[8]See, for example, W. A. Douglass, *Death in Murelaga: Funerary Ritual in a Spanish Basque Village* (Seattle: Univ. of Washington Press, 1969), p. 140: "There is one Basque custom that does serve to preserve the memory of specific individuals. In the *sala,* a dining room furnished with the household's finest furniture and reserved for banquets on special occasions, the walls are covered with photographs of former and present household members. Over time a picture gallery of deceased members is established."

[9]On China see Emily M. Ahern, *The Cult of the Dead in a Chinese Village* (Stanford: Stanford Univ. Press, 1973); these shrines were tablets in the literal sense, on which were inscribed the names of the dead, not unlike the engravings on a war memorial or the fancy lettering of a roll of honour. On the Tallensi see Meyer Fortes, *Oedipus and Job in West African Religion* (Cambridge: Cambridge Univ. Press, 1959); Fortes, "Pietas in Ancestor Worship," *Journal of the Royal Anthropological Institute,* 91 (1961), 166–91; and Fortes, "Some Reflections on Ancestor Worship in Africa," in Fortes et al., *African Systems of Thought* (London: Oxford Univ. Press, 1965). On the LoDagaa see Goody, *Death, Property and the Ancestors.* And on Ife and Benin see R. E. Bradbury, *Benin Studies* (London: Oxford Univ. Press, 1973); and F. Willett, *African Art* (London: Thames and Hudson, 1971).

[10]G. and M. Vovelle (1969), p. 1625.

kind put forward by Ridgway for Greek drama, which he saw as owing its birth to funeral performances, there can be little doubt about the dramatic quality of those rites in many societies. This is particularly true in oral cultures where the funeral sums up, in a significant way, the past history as well as the social relations of the man who died. In other words the obituary is acted out, as indeed are many of his closest ties.[11] The result is a dramatic performance utilizing standardized incidents in the past life of the deceased or the methods of punishment to be meted out to those who had harmed him. For the funeral is often an inquest as well as an interment, a pointer to revenge against a supposed killer or to ways of warding off death in general.

We can look at the rituals and beliefs of death not only to get an idea of collective attitudes toward the other world, beliefs about spiritual beings and the fate of the soul, or indeed bereavement, that is, the individual's reaction to loss. We can also examine them to throw light upon the relations between members of the social group, whether living or dead. For behavior at funerals is often the occasion for revealing not only details of individual life histories, "family secrets" otherwise hidden, but also the generalized attitudes, both positive and negative, characteristic of the actors in the funeral drama, husband and wife, father and son, mother and daughter, brother and sister. Such attitudes are brought out with greatest clarity in matters dealing with the transmission of relatively exclusive rights, whether pertaining to material property or to less tangible possessions such as roles and offices. We can look at such transfers from two angles, firstly from the relational one, secondly from the wider standpoint of the community and the transmission of the basic means of production. For in pre-industrial societies, and often in industrial ones, inheritance has to do with control of "the commanding heights of the economy," being the major way of transferring land and small enterprises. The fact that such transfers are usually between kin helps to perpetuate certain forms of social differentiation and turn it into a "class" system.

On the relational level, interpersonal tensions are often revealed in the course of the funeral ceremonies both in generalized and in individual form. Expression is often given, again in the customary or personal form, to the kind of ambivalent attitudes toward the death of close relatives that is epitomized in the words spoken by Mark Anthony, when in the midst of his affair with Cleopatra, he hears of the death of his wife, Fulvia.

> There's a great spirit gone! Thus did I desire it:
> What our contempts do often hurl from us,
> We wish it ours again; the present pleasure,
> By revolution lowering, does become

[11]E.g., Goody (1962), p. 129.

The opposite of itself: she's good, being gone;
The hand could pluck her back that shov'd her on.

(Anthony and Cleopatra, I, ii, 123–28)

The incidence of these tensions, that is, the particular relationships within which they fall, will vary with the particular mode of transmission. Let us consider first the transfer of office. Where succession occurs at death, the funeral (or the death itself) may well be the occasion for the installation of a successor. Hereditary succession, involving the passage of office between kin, varies in several ways. For example, there is the extent of dynastic eligibility: narrow dynasties, such as characterized modern Europe, entailed the continual shedding of the more distant members; while mass dynasties of the Anglo-Saxon type (widespread in Africa) involved election or rotation between segments.[12] In the first case the inevitable tensions between the incumbent and his successor fall between close kin, while in the latter, such relationships are relatively free of potential conflict on this score. Systems of inheritance also differ in the laterality (i.e. whether siblings are eligible), in direction (patrilineal or matrilineal) and in the eligibility of women. Each of these variables, which are interconnected in various ways, shifts the balance of interfamilial tensions in critical ways, ways that are often given explicit expression in the funeral ceremonies, or in less formal behavior that surrounds the death, providing an insight into the innermost reaches of family cleavages and solidarities. Of this the reader of English detective fiction needs hardly to be reminded. Where would the investigators or indeed the plot get were one unable to ask the question, which of the interested parties stood to lose or gain by the death?

There are many problems in the analysis of societies that are related to variations in the mode of transmission. For example, where the family farm, the industrial enterprise or in Lear's case the kingdom, is passed on before the death of the holder, his situation is inevitably more precarious and very precise arrangements are often made for his continuing support. Does this early handing over also affect the attitude of the survivors to his death or indeed to death in general? Is this reflected in mortuary custom or funerary monument? Is the relatively small attention given to funerals in contemporary societies related to the earlier establishment of one's descendants, to the non-familial avenues for placement and opportunity, the state schemes for the maintenance of the old and the bureaucratic procedures for retirement?

Why is it that in the present day funerals are of much less significance than in earlier times and in other cultures, the main spheres of the work of the social historian and the social anthropologist? The reason is simple.

[12]Jack Goody, ed., *Succession to High Office* (Cambridge: Cambridge Univ. Press, 1968).

Today funerals have so much less work to do. There is the sense of personal loss to be dealt with. But bereavement is more personal and less a matter for joint participation, given that local ties are limited by frequent change of residence (mobility), by the diversity of work (division of labor, participation in different enterprises), and sometimes by the deliberate search for anonymous neighbors that marks many urban areas. The lack of *communitas,* of *gemeinschaft,* the growth of individualism, involves a certain withdrawal from each other's personal problems including their deaths and their dead, unless these occur within the context of national calamity. Aligned with this change is the shift of responsibility, even for one's own parents and children, onto the resources of the state rather than of the individual or even of the community. The individual's links run direct to the state, mediated by income tax officials and the appropriate ministry, rather than by kith or kin.

Hence only the bare bones of death are seen today in Western societies. With smaller households and low mortality, each individual experiences a close death very infrequently, if we understand close in both a spatial and social sense. In childhood, one is often kept away from the immediate facts of death, either by parents (if it is a sibling) or by relatives or friends, if it is a parent. Grief is suppressed rather than externalized.

As an adult, one is immediately concerned only with the death of spouses (usually husbands, because of differential marriage ages) and parents (usually the father first, followed by the mother); even the deaths of siblings, separated by space and by sentiment, take on little significance. Indeed they often assume less importance than the funerals of work colleagues and even of national leaders.

This has not always been so, nor is it necessarily so in contemporary society. There are important class differences, not simply related to mobility; and there are important cultural differences, even in the urban setting. It is more common in the United States than in England to see the kind of announcement that one finds so often in the *New York Times:* "The Alumni Association Academy Mt. Saint Vincent, Tuxedo Park, records with deep sorrow the untimely death of its beloved member and extends its deepest sympathy to the members of her family." Here the associations to which an individual belongs announce their loss, not simply by representation at the funeral but by public advertisement. In Israel, the epitome of the associational state, the newspapers are filled with large displays from the members of the same associations, while the bereavement of more important national figures receives attention from state corporations, office workers and private individuals who can afford to take the advertising space in newspapers. The extent of the consumption in funerals and their expense, a fact to which social reformers have often devoted attention, has always been an important aspect of domestic and societal economy.

The fact of death still provides the theme for much human contemplation and social action; it gives rise to an area of human behavior where the interests of both Marx and Freud are equally relevant, where the analysis of both economic and psychological variables is called for. It is the most critical, the most final, of crisis situations, which capitalizes culture and social organization for actor and observer alike.

Further References Useful in the Comparative Study of Death Customs and Cultural Organization

Ariès, P. "Attitudes devant la vie et devant la mort du XVIIe au XIXe siecle," *Population,* 4 (1949), 463–70.

Bloch, M. *Placing the Dead: Tombs, Ancestral Villages, and Kinship Organisation in Madagascar* (New York: Seminar Press, 1971).

Brain, J. "Ancestors as Elders in Africa: Further Thoughts," *Africa,* 43 (1973), 122–33.

Busia, K. A. "Treatment of the Sick and Funeral Rites in Akan Culture," in *The Challenge of Africa* (New York: Praeger, 1962).

Feret, M. et al. *Le mystère de la mort et sa célébration.* (Paris: Coll. Lex Orandi, 1956).

Gorer, G. *Death, Grief, and Mourning in Contemporary Britain* (London: Cresset Press, 1965).

Keesing, H. "Death, Property, and the Ancestors: A Reconsideration of Goody's Concepts," *Africa,* 40 (1970), 40–49.

Kopytoff, I. "Ancestors as Elders in Africa," *Africa,* 41 (1971), 129–42.

McKnight, J. D. "Extra-descent Group Ancestor Cults in African Societies," *Africa,* 37 (1967), 1–21.

Mandelbaum, D. G. "Social Uses of Funerary Rites," in H. Feifel, ed., *The Meaning of Death* (New York: McGraw-Hill, 1959).

Martelet, G. *Victoire sur la mort. Eléments d'anthropologie chrétienne* (Paris, 1962).

Morin, E. *L'Homme et la mort dans l'Histoire* (Paris, 1951).

Nketia, J. H. *Funeral Dirges of the Akan People* (Achimota, 1955).

Plath, D. W. "Where the Family of God Is the Family: The Role of the Dead in Japanese Households," *American Anthropologist,* 64 (1964), 300–17.

Sangree, W. H. "Youths as Elders and Infants as Ancestors; The Complementarity of Alternate Generations, Both Living and Dead, in Tiriki, Kenya, and Irigwe, Nigeria," *Africa,* 44 (1974), 65–70.

Tenenti, A. "La vie et la mort à travers l'art du 15e siecle," *Cahier des Annales E.S.C.* (Paris, 1952).

———. *Il senso della morte e l'amore de la vita nel Rinascimento* (Torino, 1957).

DEATH AND THE
PURITAN CHILD

DAVID E. STANNARD

FROM TIME TO TIME IN THE HISTORY OF MAN A NEW IDEA OR WAY OF LOOK-
ing at things bursts into view with such force that it virtually sets the terms
for all relevant subsequent discussion. The Copernican, Darwinian and
Freudian revolutions—perhaps, as Freud on occasion noted, the three most
destructive blows which human narcissism has had to endure—are among
the extreme examples of such intellectual explosions. Others have been of
considerably more limited influence: the concept of culture in anthropology
is one example, the frontier thesis as an explanatory device for American
history is another. At still another level is the seminal study of a particular
problem. An instance of this is the fact that throughout the past decade historians of family life have conducted their research in the shadow of Philippe Ariès' monumental study, *Centuries of Childhood,* a work that established much of the currently conventional wisdom on the subject of the
family in history.

One of Ariès' most original and influential findings was that childhood as
we know it today did not exist until the early modern period. "In medieval
society," he observed, ". . . as soon as the child could live without the
constant solicitude of his mother, his nanny or his cradle-rocker, he
belonged to adult society."[1] It was not until the 16th and 17th centuries, and
then only among the upper classes, that the modern idea of childhood as a
distinct phase of life began to emerge.

The picture Ariès sketched, drawing on such diverse sources as
portraiture, literature, games and dress, was predominantly one of French
culture and society; but it was clear that he felt his generalizations held true
for most of the Western world. Recent studies in colonial New England
have supported Ariès' assumption of the representativeness of his French

[1]Philippe Ariès, *Centuries of Childhood: A Social History of Family Life* (New York:
Random House, 1962), p. 128.

findings in extending his observations on medieval life to 17th and 18th century Massachusetts; but the support for this contention is unsteady, balanced as it is on much less substantive data than that on which Ariès' argument rests. The clothing of children as adults—only one strand of evidence in Ariès' historical tapestry—has been seized by some colonial historians and used as the principal basis for claiming that in 17th and 18th century Massachusetts there was little or no distinction between children and adults. "If clothes do not make the man," writes Michael Zuckerman, "they do mark social differentiations"; and, adds John Demos, "the fact that children were dressed like adults does seem to imply a whole attitude of mind."[2] The phenomenon that both writers accurately describe, the similarity of dress for children and adults, may well suggest social differentiations and/or imply a whole attitude of mind—but not necessarily the one claimed.

In the first place, to argue in isolation of other data that the *absence* of a distinctive mode of dress for children is a mark of their being viewed as miniature adults is historical presentism at its very best; one might argue with equal force—in isolation of other facts—that the absence of beards on men in a particular culture, or the presence of short hair as a fashion shared by men and women, is a mark of that culture's failure to fully distinguish between men and women. In all these cases there are alternative explanations, explanations that do not presuppose that special clothing for children, or beards for men, or different hair lengths for adults of different sexes, are universally natural and proper cultural traditions. As to the specific matter of dress, children in New England were treated much the same as children in England. Until age six or seven they generally wore long gowns that opened down the front; after that, they were clothed in a manner similar to that of their parents. Rather than this stage marking an abrupt transition from infancy to adulthood, as Alan Macfarlane has pointed out it more likely was merely a sign that children had then reached an age where sexual differentiation was in order.[3]

Second, and most important, the supporting evidence that Ariès brings to bear in making his case for the situation in medieval France generally does not exist for colonial New England; when it does, it makes clear the fact that there was no confusion or ambiguity in the mind of the adult Puritan as to the differences between his children and himself. Puritan journals, autobiographies and histories are filled with specific references to the differences between children and adults, a wealth of parental advice literature exists for

[2]Michael Zuckerman, *Peaceable Kingdoms: New England Towns in the Eighteenth Century* (New York: Random House, 1970), p. 73; John Demos, *A Little Commonwealth: Family Life in Plymouth Colony* (New York: Oxford Univ. Press, 1970), p. 139.

[3]Alan Macfarlane, *The Family Life of Ralph Josselin, A Seventeenth Century Clergyman* (Cambridge: Cambridge Univ. Press, 1970), pp. 90–91.

the 17th century that gives evidence of clear distinctions between adults and children well into their teens, and a large body of law was in effect from the earliest years of settlement that made definitive discriminations between acceptable behavior and appropriate punishment for children, post-adolescent youths and adults.[4]

The matter of children's literature is one case in point. Ariès has argued, both in *Centuries of Childhood* and elsewhere, that in France "books addressed to and reserved for children" did not appear until "the end of the 17th century, at the same time as the awareness of childhood." Recently Marc Soriano has supported Ariès' contention by showing that prior to the stories of Perrault in the 1690s, French literature and folk tales were directed "almost entirely" at an adult audience, though of course children were exposed to them as well.[5] The situation was quite different in both old and New England in the 17th century, as William Sloane showed almost twenty years ago. Limiting himself to a definition of a child's book as "a book written *only* for children"—a limitation which excludes books which subsequently became children's fare and "works which are the tools of formal instruction"—Sloane compiled an annotated bibliography of 261 children's books published in England and America between 1557 and 1710.[6] It is true that most of the books listed would not meet Zuckerman's definition of a child's book as one which provides "a sequestered simplicity commensurate with a child's capacities," but that is not because children were viewed as synonymous with adults; rather, it is because 17th century New Englanders had a different view from that held by Zuckerman or other 20th century parents of the nature and capacities of children.[7]

The differentness of that view is crucial to this essay, and it will be developed at some length. But first it must be recognized that there were indeed children at home and in the streets of Puritan New England, and that this was a fact recognized—and never questioned—by their parents, ministers and other adults in the community. In many ways those children were seen and treated as different from children of today. In many ways they *were* different: to analyze, as this essay will, the Puritan child's actual and

[4]For a convenient collection of some of this material see Robert H. Bremner, ed., *Children and Youth in America* (Cambridge, Mass.: Harvard Univ. Press, 1970), 1:27–122.

[5]Philippe Ariès, "At the Point of Origin," in Peter Brooks, ed., *The Child's Part* (Boston: Beacon Press, 1972), p. 15; Marc Soriano, "From Tales of Warning to Formulettes: The Oral Tradition in French Children's Literature," ibid., pp. 24–25.

[6]William Sloane, *Children's Books in England & America in the Seventeenth Century* (New York: Columbia Univ. Press, 1955).

[7]Zuckerman, p. 77. It should be acknowledged that some of Ariès' contentions have been challenged within the French historical setting. On the matter of the presence or absence of an adolescent stage, for example, see the important essay by Natalie Z. Davis, "The Reasons of Misrule: Youth Groups and Charivaris in Sixteenth Century France," *Past and Present*, 50 (Feb. 1971); an extension of Davis' argument to 17th century London is Steven R. Smith, "The London Apprentice as Seventeenth-Century Adolescent," *Past and Present*, 61 (Nov. 1973).

anticipated confrontation with death is but one of many ways in which the extent of that difference can be seen. But it is too much of a leap, and there is no real evidence to support the contention that in 17th century New England, as in 15th and 16th century France, there was little or no distinction between children and adults.

Probably at no time in modern history have parents in the West agreed on the matter of the correct and proper approach to child-rearing. Certainly this is true of our own time, but it was equally so in the age of the Puritan.

"A child is a man in a small letter," wrote John Earle in 1628,

> yet the best copy of *Adam* before hee tasted of *Eve* or the Apple. . . . Hee is natures fresh picture newly drawne in Oyle, which time and much handling dimmes and defaces. His soule is yet a white paper unscribled with observations of the world, wherewith at length it becomes a blurr'd Notebooke. He is purely happy, because he knowes no evill, nor hath made meanes by sinne, to be acquainted with misery. . . . Nature and his Parents alike dandle him, and tice him on with a bait of Sugar, to a draught of Worme-wood. . . . His father hath writ him as his owne little story, wherein hee reads those dayes of his life that hee cannot remember; and sighes to see what innocence he ha's outliv'd.[8]

In view of this attitude among certain Englishmen of the 17th century—an attitude that, it appears, became prevalent in colonial Maryland and Virginia—it should come as no surprise to read in the report of a visiting Frenchman at the end of the century that "In England they show an extraordinary complacency toward young children, always flattering, always caressing, always applauding whatever they do. At least that is how it seems to us French, who correct our children as soon as they are capable of reason." This judgment was echoed a few years later by an Englishman reflecting on the customs of his people: "In the *Education* of *Children*," wrote Guy Miege in 1707, "the indulgence of Mothers is excessive among the *English;* which proves often fatal to their children, and contributes much to the Corruption of the Age. If these be Heirs to great Honours and Estates, they swell with the Thoughts of it, and at last grow unmanageable." Had Miege been writing a bit later in the century he might have sought evidence for his assertion in the life of Charles James Fox who, at age five, had been accidentally deprived of the privilege of watching the blowing up of a garden wall; at his insistence his father had the wall rebuilt and blown up again so that the boy might witness it. On another occasion,

---

[8]*Micro-cosmographie or, A Piece of the World Discovered in Essays and Characters* (London, 1628), p. 5.

when the young Charles announced his intention of destroying a watch, his father's reply was: "Well, if you must, I suppose you must."[9]

But neither John Earle in 1628, nor Charles Fox in 1754 were Puritans; and neither Henri Misson in 1698, nor Guy Miege in 1707 were commenting on Puritan attitudes toward children. Had they been, their reports would have read very differently.

In 1628, the same year that John Earle was rhapsodizing on the innocence and purity of children, and on parental accommodation to them, Puritan John Robinson wrote:

> And surely there is in all children, though not alike, a stubbornness, and stoutness of mind arising from natural pride, which must, in the first place, be broken and beaten down. . . . This fruit of natural corruption and root of actual rebellion both against God and man must be destroyed, and no manner of way nourished, except we will plant a nursery of contempt of all good persons and things, and of obstinacy therein. . . . For the beating, and keeping down of this stubbornness parents must provide carefully for two things: first that children's wills and willfulness be restrained and repressed. . . . The second help is an inuring of them from the first, to such a meanness in all things, as may rather pluck them down, than lift them up.[10]

In place of Earle's child, seen as "yet the best copy of Adam before hee tasted of Eve or the Apple," the Puritan child was riddled with sin and corruption, a depraved being polluted with the stain of Adam's sin. If there was any chance of an individual child's salvation, it was not a very good chance—and in any case, the knowledge of who was to be chosen for salvation and who was not to be chosen was not a matter for earthly minds. "Because a small and contemptible number are hidden in a huge multitude," Calvin had written, "and a few grains of wheat are covered by a pile of chaff, we must leave to God alone the knowledge of his church, whose foundation is his secret election."[11] The quest for salvation was at the core of everything the devout Puritan thought and did; it was the primary source of the intense drive that carried him across thousands of miles of treacherous ocean in order to found a Holy Commonwealth in the midst of a

[9]Henri Misson, *Mémoires et Observations Faites par un Voyageur en Angleterre* (Paris, 1698), p. 128; Guy Miege, *The Present State of Great Britain* (London, 1707), p. 222; John Drinkwater, *Charles James Fox* (London: Ernest Benn, 1928), pp. 14–15. On the leniency of parental discipline in some families in the American colonial South see Edmund S. Morgan, *Virginians at Home* (Charlottesville: Univ. Press of Virginia, 1952), pp. 7–8, where an English traveler is quoted as saying of Maryland and Virginia: "The Youth of these more indulgent Settlements, partake pretty much of the *Petit Maitre* Kind, and are pamper'd much more in Softness and Ease than their Neighbors more Northward."

[10]*New Essays: Or, Observations Divine and Moral,* in Robert Ashton, ed., *The Works of John Robinson* (Boston: Doctrinal Tract and Book Soc., 1851), 1:246–48.

[11]John Calvin, *Institutes of the Christian Religion,* ed. John T. McNeill (Philadelphia: Westminster Press, 1960), 2:1013.

wilderness; it was his reason for being. And yet, despite his conviction of God's purposeful presence in everything he did or encountered, from Indian wars to ailing livestock, full confidence in his own or anyone else's salvation was rendered impossible by the inscrutability of his God. He was driven to strive for salvation at the same time that he was told his fate was both predetermined and undetectable.

To be sure, Puritans believed there were signs or "marks," indications of God's will, that laymen and ministers alike could struggle to detect in their persons and in those of members of the congregation. But these signs were subject to interpretation and even feigning, and could never be regarded as more than *suggestions* of sainthood. Further, only very rarely was an apparent childhood conversion accepted as real by a congregation. Thus, Jonathan Edwards devoted a great deal of attention to youthful conversions during the stormy emotionalism of the Great Awakening, but only after first noting: "It has heretofore been looked on as a strange thing, when any have seemed to be savingly wrought upon, and remarkably changed in their childhood." And even James Janeway, whose *A Token For Children: Being an Exact Assessment of the Conversion, Holy and Exemplary Lives, and Joyful Deaths of Several Young Children,* was one of the best-read books of 17th and 18th century Puritans, admitted in a later edition that one of his examples of early spiritual development—that of a child who supposedly began showing signs of salvation between the ages of two and three— seemed to many "scarce credible, and they did fear [it] might somewhat prejudice the authority of the rest."[12]

But if conversion was unlikely at an early age, it was at least possible. Given the alternative, then, of apathetic acceptance of their children as depraved and damnable creatures, it is hardly surprising that Puritan parents urged on their offspring a religious precocity that some historians have interpreted as tantamount to premature adulthood. "You can't begin with them *Too soon,*" Cotton Mather wrote in 1689,

> They are no sooner *wean'd* but they are to be *taught.* . . . Are they *Young?* Yet the *Devil* has been with them already. . . . They go astray as soon as they are born. They no sooner *step* than they *stray,* they no sooner *lisp* than they *ly.* Satan gets them to be proud, profane, reviling and revengeful, as *young* as they are. And I pray, why should you not be afore-hand with *him?*[13]

Puritan children, even "the very best" of whom had a "Corrupt Nature in them, and . . . an Evil Figment in their Heart," were thus driven at the

<hr>

[12]Jonathan Edwards, *A Faithful Narrative of the Surprising Work of God,* in *The Works of Jonathan Edwards,* ed. C. C. Goen (New Haven: Yale Univ. Press, 1972), 4:158; James Janeway, *A Token for Children* [1679] (Boston: Caleb Bingham, 1802), p. 59.

[13]*Small Offers Towards the Service of the Tabernacle in this Wilderness* (Boston, 1689), p. 59.

earliest age possible both to recognize their depravity and to pray for their salvation. In the event that children proved intractable in this regard the first parental response was to be "what saies the Wise man, *A Rod for the fools back*"; but generally more effective—and more insidious—was the advice "to watch when some *Affliction* or some *Amazement* is come upon them: then God opens their ear to Discipline."[14] If Puritan parents carried out these designs with fervor it was of course out of love and concern for their children. But at least some of the motivation may well have had guilt at its source; as Mather and others were frequently careful to point out: "Your Children are Born Children of Wrath. Tis *through you,* that there is derived unto them the sin which Exposes them to infinite Wrath."[15]

We should not, however, pass too quickly over the matter of the Puritan parent's genuine love for his children. Even a casual reading of the most noted Puritan journals and autobiographies—those of Thomas Shepard, Samuel Sewall, Cotton Mather—reveals a deep-seated parental affection for children as the most common, normal and expected attitude. The relationship between parents and children was often compared with that between God and the Children of God. "That God is often angry with [his children]," Samuel Willard wrote in 1684, "afflicts them, and withdraws the light of his countenance from them, and puts them to grief, is not because he loves them not, but because it is that which their present condition requires; they are but Children, and childish, and foolish, and if they were not sometimes chastened, they would grow wanton, and careless of duty."[16] Indeed, in the same work in which Cotton Mather referred to children as "proud, profane, reviling and revengeful," he warned parents that *"They must give an account of the souls that belong unto their Families. . . .* Behold, thou hast *Lambs* in the *Fold,* Little ones in thy House; God will strain for it, —if wild beasts, and Lusts carry any of them away from the *Service* of God through any neglect of thine thou shalt smart for it in the fiery prison of God's terrible Indignation."[17]

Children, then, were on the one hand deeply loved, "Lambs in the Fold"; as Willard noted: "If others in a Family suffer want, and be pincht with difficulties, yet the Children shall certainly be taken care for, as long as there is anything to be had: they are hard times indeed when Children are denied that which is needful for them."[18] On the other hand they were depraved and polluted; as Benjamin Wadsworth wrote: "Their Hearts naturally, are a meer nest, root, fountain of Sin, and wickedness."[19] Even

---

[14]Cotton Mather, *The Young Mans Preservative* (Boston, 1701), p. 4; *Small Offers,* p. 62.
[15]*Cares About the Nurseries* (Boston, 1702), p. 32.
[16]*The Child's Portion* (Boston, 1684), p. 31.
[17]*Small Offers,* pp. 18–19.
[18]Willard, p. 16.
[19]"The Nature of Early Piety as it Respects God," in *A Course of Sermons on Early Piety* (Boston, 1721), p. 10.

most innocent infants, dying before they had barely a chance to breathe, could at best be expected to be given, in Michael Wigglesworth's phrase, "the easiest room in Hell."[20]

If the state of a child's spiritual health was an extremely worrisome and uncomfortable matter for the Puritan parent, the state of his physical health was not less so. In recent years historians of colonial New England have convincingly shown that the colonists of certain New England towns in the 17th and early 18th centuries lived longer and healthier lives than did many of their countrymen in England. This finding and the many others by these new demographic historians are important to our understanding of life in early New England; but in acknowledging the relative advantages of life in some New England communities compared with parts of England and Europe in the 17th century, we should be careful to avoid blinding ourselves to the fact that death was to the colonist, as it was to the Englishman and Frenchman, an ever-present menace—and a menace that struck with a particular vengeance at the children of the community.

Philip J. Greven's study of colonial Andover, Massachusetts is noteworthy for both the skill of the author's analysis and the stability and healthiness of the families whose lives he studied. As Greven explicitly points out, compared with Boston and other New England communities, Andover's mortality rate was exceptionally low, though it did climb steadily in the 18th century. It is worth dwelling briefly on the differences between Boston and Andover, because the power and sophistication of Greven's work can tend to suggest an implicit, and erroneous, picture of Andover as a representative New England town. It may or may not be representative of a certain type of Puritan community—a sufficient number of collateral studies have not yet been done to determine this—but demographically it was vastly different from Boston, the hub of the Holy Commonwealth. Mortality rates in Andover during the early 18th century, when those rates were on the increase, fluctuated within a normal annual range of about half those in Boston during the same period—somewhere between fifteen and twenty per thousand in Andover, somewhere between thirty-five and forty per thousand in Boston. Epidemic years are excluded from these calculations in both cases, but it should be noted that Andover's worst epidemic lifted the death rate to seventy-one per thousand, while Boston's worst epidemic during the same period pushed the death rate well over one hundred per thousand—or more than 10 per cent of the resident population.[21] In the 17th century, the smallpox epidemic of 1677–78, joined by the normal death

[20]*The Day of Doom* (London, 1687), stanza 181.

[21]Philip J. Greven Jr., *Four Generations: Population, Land, and Family in Colonial Andover, Massachusetts* (Ithaca: Cornell Univ. Press, 1970). For Greven's brief specific comparison of Andover and Boston, see pp. 196–97, note 14; detailed information on Boston can be found in

rate, probably killed off more than one-fifth of Boston's entire population. "Boston burying-places never filled so fast," wrote a young Cotton Mather:

> It is easy to tell the time when we did not use to have the bells tolling for burials on a Sabbath morning by sunrise; to have 7 buried on a Sabbath day night, after Meeting. To have coffins crossing each other as they have been carried in the street. . . . To attempt a Bill of Mortality, and number the very spires of grass in a Burying Place seem to have a parity of difficulty and in accomplishment.[22]

Indeed, if Andover fares well in comparison with mortality figures for English and European towns, Boston does not: it was not at all uncommon for the death rate in Boston to hover near or even exceed that for English towns like Clayworth that have been cited for their exceptionally high mortality rates.[23]

One of the problems with all these figures, however, is the almost inevitable underestimation of infant mortality; as Greven and other demographic analysts freely acknowledge, most infant deaths were unrecorded and their number can now only be guessed at. One such guess, a highly informed one, has been made by Kenneth A. Lockridge. In a study of Dedham, Massachusetts in the 17th and early 18th centuries, Lockridge found that an upward adjustment of 1/9 on the town's birth rate would most likely take account of unrecorded infant deaths.[24] If the same adjustment is made on the birth rate of colonial Andover a fairly accurate comparison of childhood birth and mortality rates can be made.

Although Greven traces a trend throughout the generations examined showing a steady drop in fertility and life expectancy rates as Andover became more urbanized, if we view the period as a whole the town remains a

John B. Blake, *Public Health in the Town of Boston, 1630–1822* (Cambridge, Mass.: Harvard Univ. Press, 1959), Appendix II; an excellent recent study is E. S. Dethlefsen, "Life and Death in Colonial New England," Diss. Harvard University 1972.

[22]Cotton Mather to John Cotton, Nov. 1678, in Massachusetts Historical Society *Collections*, series 4, 8 (1868), 383–84; contemporary estimates of the toll of the epidemic were made by John Foster and Increase Mather in Thomas Thatcher, *A Brief Rule to Guide the Common People* (Boston, 1678). See Blake, p. 20; for the population of Boston at the time and an estimate of the death toll of the disease, see Carl Bridenbaugh, *Cities in the Wilderness: Urban Life in America, 1625–1742* (New York: Capricorn Books, 1964 [orig. pub. 1936]), pp. 6,87.

[23]Peter Laslett, *The World We Have Lost: England Before the Industrial Age* (New York: Scribner's, 1965), pp. 146–47.

[24]"The Population of Dedham, Massachusetts, 1636–1736," *Economic History Review*, 19 (1966), 329. Cf. John Demos' estimate that in Plymouth Colony a 10 per cent infant mortality rate, though seemingly "surprisingly low," is a reasonable figure. Demos, pp. 131–32. Seventeenth century attitudes to early infant death are reflected in sources other than the formal records: on the first page of his *Journal* Thomas Shepard enumerated the birth dates, and in one case the death date, of his five sons—but Shepard had seven sons, the two not mentioned having died in infancy. See Michael McGiffert, ed., *God's Plot: The Autobiography and Journal of Thomas Shepard* (Amherst, Mass.: Univ. of Massachusetts Press, 1972), pp. 81, 33, 69.

good example of one of the healthier communities in New England. Using the Lockridge adjustment to include unrecorded infant deaths, the average number of children born per family in Andover throughout the century under discussion was 8.8. Of those, an average of 5.9 survived to adulthood. In other words, approximately three of the close to nine children born to the average family would die before reaching their twenty-first birthday. But, as Greven notes, the most vulnerable period in life was that "beyond infancy but prior to adolescence—the age group which appears to have been most susceptible, among other things, to the throat distemper prevalent in the mid-1730's." Again applying the infant mortality adjustment to Greven's figures, the rate of survival to age ten for all children born between 1640 and 1759 was approximately 74 per cent—with a generational high of 83 per cent and a low of 63 per cent, this latter figure of course indicating that at one point fewer than two out of three infants lived to see their tenth birthday. During the period as a whole, more than one child in four failed to survive the first decade of life in a community with an average birth rate per family of 8.8.[25]

Thus a young couple embarking on a marriage did so with the knowledge and expectation that in all probability *two or three* of the children they might have would die before the age of ten. In certain cases, of course, the number was more than two; Greven discusses instances when parents lost six of eleven children in rapid succession, including four in a single month, and four of eight children in less than a year—and this in a town remarkable for the relative health and longevity of its residents. In Boston the rate was much higher and even the most prominent and well cared for residents of that city were constantly reminded of the fragility of life in childhood. Thomas Shepard, for instance, had seven sons, three of whom died in infancy; the other four outlived their father, but he died at 43—having in that short time outlived two wives. As Joseph E. Illick has recently pointed out, Samuel Sewall and Cotton Mather each fathered fourteen children: "One of Sewall's was stillborn, several died as infants, several more as young adults. Seven Mather babies died shortly after delivery, one died at two years and six survived to adulthood, five of whom died in their twenties. Only two Sewall children outlived their father, while Samuel Mather was the only child to survive Cotton."[26]

It is important for us to recognize that conditions for living in colonial New England were sometimes superior to those in 17th century England and Europe. But it is equally important for us not to lose sight of the fact

[25]Greven, pp. 188–203.
[26]"Parent-Child Relations in Seventeenth-Century England and America," in Lloyd de Mause, ed., *The History of Childhood* (New York: Psychohistory Press, 1974). I am grateful to Professor Illick for allowing me to examine his manuscript prior to publication.

that the Puritan settlements were places where "winter was to be feared," as Kenneth Lockridge has written, where "harvests were a gamble that kept men's minds aware of Providence, plague arose and subsided out of all human control and infants died in numbers that would shock us today."[27]

It has often been noted by writers on the Puritan family that the prescribed and common personal relationship between parents and children was one of restraint and even aloofness, mixed with, as we have seen, an intense parental effort to impose discipline and encourage spiritual precocity. Parents were reminded to avoid becoming "too fond of your children and too familiar with them" and to be on their guard against "not keeping constantly your due distance."[28] Edmund S. Morgan has shown how this "due distance" worked in both directions, as when Benjamin Colman's daughter Jane wrote to her father requesting forgiveness for the "flow of affections" evident in some of her recent letters. Colman responded by urging her to be "careful against this Error, even when you say your Thoughts of Reverence and Esteem to your Father, or to a Spouse, if ever you should live to have one," and commended her for having "done well to correct yourself for some of your Excursions of this kind toward me."[29] Morgan has also seen the common practice of "putting children out," both to early apprenticeship and simply extended stays with other families, often against the child's will, as linked to the maintenance of the necessary distance between parent and child; "these economically unnecessary removals of children from home," he writes, probably resulted from the fact that "Puritan parents did not trust themselves with their own children, that they were afraid of spoiling them by too great affection."[30]

Morgan's suggested explanation for this practice seems logical and convincing, but there may have been an additional, deeper source for both this practice and the entire Puritan attitude toward severely restrained displays of fondness between parents and children. For children, despite the natural hold they had on their parents' affection, were a source of great emotional discomfort for them as well. In the first place, there was a very real possibility, if not a probability, that parental affection would be rewarded by the death of a child before it even reached puberty; the "due distance" kept by Puritan parents from their children might, at least in part, have been an instinctive response to this possibility, a means of insulating themselves to some extent against the shock that the death of a child might bring. This, of course, would be potentially true of any society with a relatively high rate of

[27] Lockridge, p. 343.
[28] Thomas Cobbett, *A Fruitfull and Usefull Discourse* . . . (London, 1656), p. 96.
[29] *The Puritan Family* (New York: Harper & Row, 1966), p. 107.
[30] Ibid., p. 77; cf. Demos, p. 74.

childhood mortality. But to the Puritan the child was more than a loved one extremely vulnerable to the ravages of the environment; he was also a loved one polluted with sin and natural depravity. In this, of course, he was no different from any other members of the family or community, including those Visible Saints viewed as the most likely candidates for salvation: Original Sin touched everyone, and all were considered polluted and not worthy of excessive affection. What is important here, however, is not that this dictum touched everyone, but that in the process it touched those most emotionally susceptible to its pernicious effects—the children of the zealous and devoted Puritan.

The Puritans of New England held as doctrine the belief that they were involved in a binding contract or "covenant" with God. This belief was complex and multifaceted, but one aspect of it viewed the entire community as having contracted a "social covenant" with God by which they promised strict obedience to his laws. Failure to obey on the part of any individual within the community could result in God's wrath being vented on the entire community. Thus, whenever signs of God's anger appeared, might they be comets or earthquakes or the deaths of eminent men, Puritans searched for the source of the divine displeasure and fearfully awaited future expressions of it. When the younger Thomas Shepard died in 1677, the Reverend Urian Oakes wrote in lamentation:

> What! must we with our God, and Glory part?
> Lord is thy Treaty with New England come
> Thus to an end? And is War in thy Heart?
> That this Ambassadour is called home.
> So Earthly Gods (Kings) when they War intend
> Call home their Ministers, and Treaties end.[31]

The depraved and ungodly child was, it is true, naturally repellent in his sinfulness; but more than that, the activity that might easily grow out of that sinfulness posed a very real danger to the well-being of the community. In response, understandably enough, the Puritan parent strove mightily to effect conversion or at the least to maintain a strict behavior code, but at the same time—when these effects were combined with the love he felt for his child, the tenuous hold the child had on life, the natural repulsiveness of sin—he may well have been driven to find ways of creating emotional distance between his offspring and himself.[32]

---

[31]*An Elegie Upon the Death of the Reverend Mr. Thomas Shepard* (Boston, 1677), p. 7; seeing portentous meaning in the deaths of eminent men was particularly common during the latter half of the 17th century as Puritans saw about them real and imagined signs of waning piety. For other examples see, for instance, James Fitch, *Peace the End of the Perfect and Upright* (Boston, 1673), p. 9; and Samuel Willard, *A Sermon Preached Upon Ezekiel* (Boston, 1679), p. 12.

[32]There is a large body of psychological and anthropological literature on related phenomena and it has been helpful in formulating some of the ideas in this section. On the effects of

But if separation was emotionally beneficial to the Puritan parent, it may have had precisely the opposite effect on the Puritan child. John Demos has recently speculated on the "profound loss" experienced by many Puritan children in the second and third years of life because of the fact that they were probably weaned at the start of the second year and very often witnessed the arrival of a younger brother or sister at the start of the third year.[33] This in itself, it might be argued, does not make Puritan children unique: the spacing of children at two-year intervals is common among many of the world's cultures, and weaning at twelve months is hardly an exceptional custom. But added to these practices was the conscious effort of Puritan parents to separate themselves from an excessively intimate relationship with their children. If this normal practice of separation was not enough, Cotton Mather was probably echoing a fairly common sentiment in viewing as "the sorest Punishment in the Family" the banishment of the child from the parents' presence.[34] Separation, however, can be both real and imagined, can be both present and anticipated. And, of course, the ultimate separation is death. This was a fact of which the Puritan parent was well aware and which the Puritan child, from the earliest age possible, was never allowed to forget.

May of 1678 was a month of great apprehension in Boston. The smallpox plague referred to earlier had entered the city some months before and had begun its relentless slaying of the population. By May hundreds had died and the governments of the colony and the town were hurriedly passing legislation aimed at holding down the spread of the deadly infection—people were directed not to hang out bedding or clothes in their yards or near roadways, and those who had been touched by the disease and survived were forbidden contact with others for specified periods of time.[35] The worst was yet to come: by the time it was over it was as though, proportionate to the population, an epidemic were to kill over a million and a half people in New York City during the next eighteen months. The city girded for it.

Only two years earlier New England had endured the devastation of King Philip's War, in which—not counting the enormous numbers of Indian

---

pollution fear see Mary Douglas, *Purity and Danger: An Analysis of Concepts of Pollution and Taboo* (London: Routledge & Kegan Paul, 1966); on the psychological problem of "approach-avoidance conflict," see, among many relevant monographs, W. N. Schoenfeld, "An Experimental Approach to Anxiety, Escape, and Avoidance Behavior," in P. H. Hoch and J. Zubin, eds., *Anxiety* (New York: Grune & Stratton, 1950), pp. 70–99; and Murray Sidman, "Avoidance Behavior," in W. K. Honig, ed., *Operant Behavior* (New York: Appleton-Century-Crofts, 1966), pp. 448–98.

[33]Demos, p. 136.

[34]"Diary," in Massachusetts Historical Society *Collections*, series 7, 7:535.

[35]Boston Record Commissioners, *Report*, VII, 119. Cited in Blake, p. 19; see also Bridenbaugh, p. 87.

dead—greater casualties were inflicted in proportion to the population than in any other war in subsequent American history.[36] Death was everywhere in 1678 when, on May 5, Increase Mather addressed his Boston congregation and prayed "for a Spirit of Converting Grace to be poured out upon the Children and *Rising Generation* in *New England*."[37] A decade later Increase's son Cotton would write, as I have noted earlier, that a particularly effective means of disciplining children was "to watch when some *Affliction* or *Amazement* is come upon them: then God opens their ear to Discipline." On May 5, 1678, the then teen-aged young man probably witnessed a particularly effective demonstration of this principle as it was directed toward an entire congregation.

Some years earlier—at first against Increase Mather's will, then later with his support—the churches of New England had succumbed to the need for what its detractors later called the "Half-Way Covenant," in which as yet unconverted adult children of church members were acknowledged as church members (with the right to have their own children baptized) but not as full communicants. Bound up with this change in the notion of Puritan exclusivity was the growing belief that, in his covenant with his holy children, God had promised to "be thy God, and the God of thy seed after thee."[38] In his sermon of May 1678, Mather alluded to this belief very early: "Now God hath seen good to cast the line of Election so, as that it doth (though not wholly, and only, yet) for the most part, run through the loins of godly Parents." It is well to remember here that before any comforts could be gained from this doctrine the Puritan parent had also to face the impossibility of ever being truly assured of his own election. But that is not the reason Mather cluttered his sentence with such awkward qualifications—"though not wholly, and only, yet . . . for the most part." God remained inscrutable, and it was heresy to think otherwise; but also: "Men should not think with themselves (as some do) if their children do belong to God, then he will convert them, whether they pray for him or no, but should therefore be stirred up to the more fervency in cries to Heaven, for the blessing promised. *I* (saith the Lord) *will give a new heart to you, and to your Children,* yet you must pray for it."[39]

When he turned to address the youth of the congregation Mather mentioned explicitly the "affliction and amazement" that was at hand:

Young men and young Women, O be in earnest for Converting Grace, before it be too late. It is high time for you to look about you, deceive not yourselves with false

[36]See Douglas Edward Leach, *Flintlock and Tomahawk: New England in King Philip's War* (New York: W. W. Norton, 1958), p. 243.

[37]*Pray for the Rising Generation* (Boston, 1678).

[38]John Cotton, *The Covenant of Gods Free Grace* (London, 1645), p. 19.

[39]Increase Mather, *Pray for the Rising Generation,* p. 12.

Conversions (as many young men do to their eternal ruine) or with gifts instead of Grace. . . . Death waits for you. There is now a Mortal and Contagious Disease in many Houses; the Sword of the Lord is drawn, and young men fall down apace slain under it; do you not see the Arrows of Death come flying over your heads? Why then, Awake, Awake, and turn to God in Jesus Christ whilst it is called today, and know for certain that if you dy in your sins, you will be the most miserable of any poor Creatures in the bottom of Hell.[40]

But Mather's most determined and terrifying words were reserved for the youngest and most vulnerable members of the congregation, those of less "discretion and understanding" than the other youths addressed. It was with them that the specter of parental and ministerial separation and betrayal was merged with the promise of death and damnation. "Beg as for your lives that the God of your Fathers would pour his Spirit upon you," he exhorted these littlest of children,

Go into secret corners and plead it with God. . . . If you dy and be not first new Creatures, better you had never been born: you will be left without excuse before the Lord, terrible witnesses shall rise up against you at the last day. Your godly Parents will testifie against you before the Son of God at that day: And the Ministers of Christ will also be called in as witnesses against you for your condemnation, if you dy in your sins. As for many of you, I have treated with you privately and personally, I have told you, and I do tell you, and make solemn Protestation before the Lord, that if you dy in a Christless, graceless eatate, I will most certainly profess unto Jesus Christ at the day of Judgement, Lord, these are the Children, whom I spake often unto thy Name, publickly and privately, and I told them, that if they did not make themselves a new heart, and make sure of an interest in Christ, they should become damned creatures for evermore; and yet they would not repent and believe the Gospel.[41]

If there is one thing on which modern psychologists have agreed concerning the fear of death in young children it is that such fear is generally rooted in the anticipation of separation from their parents. Time and again experimental studies have shown that, as one writer puts it, "the most persistent of fears associated with death is that of separation—and the one which is most likely to be basic, independent of cultural, religious, or social background." "In children," this writer adds, "dread of separation seems to be basic."[42]

[40]Ibid., p. 22.
[41]Ibid.
[42]Marjorie Editha Mitchell, *The Child's Attitude To Death* (London: Barrie & Rockliff, 1966), p. 100; cf. Sylvia Anthony, *The Discovery of Death in Childhood and After* (London: Allen Lane, 1971), esp. chap. 8; Roslyn P. Ross, "Separation Fear and the Fear of Death in Children," Diss. New York University 1966; Eugenia H. Waechter, "Death Anxiety in Children With Fatal Illness," Diss. Stanford University 1968; and the now almost classic studies of J. Bowlby, esp. "Separation Anxiety," *International Journal of Psychoanalysis and*

There are, certainly, ways that children seem to have of defending against separation anxiety resulting from anticipation of death. One of these—one that has inspired poets down through the ages—is the expectation of reunion in death, a defense that makes separation a temporary matter.[43] But this was a defense denied the Puritan child. As if addressing this question directly, Increase Mather in 1711 remarked on

> What a dismal thing it will be when a Child shall see his Father at the right Hand of Christ in the day of Judgment, but himself at His left Hand: And when his Father shall joyn with Christ in passing a Sentence of Eternal Death upon him, saying, Amen O Lord, thou art Righteous in thus *Judging:* And when after the Judgment, children shall see their Father going with Christ to Heaven, but themselves going away into Everlasting Punishment![44]

As Edmund S. Morgan has pointed out, this verbal "picture of parent and child at the Day of Judgment . . . was a favorite with many Puritan ministers, for it made the utmost of filial affection."[45] It was probably not of much comfort to the Puritan child to hear that, if he was to be separated from his parents, he would at least still have the companionship of certain playmates—given the circumstances. For, as Jonathan Edwards put it in one of his sermons specifically addressed to young children: "How dreadful it will be to be all together in misery. Then you won't play together any more but will be damned together, will cry out with weeping and wailing and gnashing of teeth together."[46]

Another common defense against childhood fear of separation and death that is mentioned in the psychological literature is supplied by parental interjection that only old people die, not children.[47] Puritan children met precisely the opposite advice. The young "may bear and behave themselves as if imagining their hot blood, lusty bodies, activity, beauty, would last alwayes, and their youthful pleasures never be at an end," acknowledged Samuel Wakeman at a young man's funeral in 1673; "but," he warned, "*Childhood and Youth are vanity:* Death may not wait till they be gray-headed; or however, the earliest Morning hastens apace to Noon, and then to Night." From the moment they were old enough to pay attention children were repeatedly instructed regarding the precariousness of their

---

Psychiatry, Vols. 41 and 42 (1961), and "Childhood Mourning and Its Implications for Psychiatry," *American Journal of Psychiatry,* Vol. 118 (1961).

[43]Anthony (see note 42), p. 151.

[44]*An Earnest Exhortation to the Children of New England to Exalt the God of their Fathers* (Boston, 1711), p. 35.

[45]Morgan, pp. 178–79.

[46]Jonathan Edwards, unpublished sermon in Edwards' manuscripts in Yale University Library. Quoted in Sanford Fleming, *Children and Puritanism* (New Haven: Yale Univ. Press, 1933), p. 100.

[47]Anthony, p. 153.

existence. The sermons they listened to, the parents who corrected them, the teachers who instructed them, and eventually the books they read, all focused with a particular intensity on the possibility and even the likelihood of their imminent death. Further, those who died young, it was often noted, died suddenly—"Death is oftentimes as near the young man's back as it is to the old man's face," wrote Wakeman—and matter-of-fact repetitions of this ever-present threat joined with burning pictures of Judgment Day to hammer the theme home. "I know you will die in a little time," the esteemed Jonathan Edwards calmly told a group of children, "some sooner than others. 'Tis not likely you will all live to grow up."[48] The fact that Edwards was only speaking the very obvious truth did not help matters any.

Nor did the literalness with which Puritan children must have taken the descriptions of depravity, sin, imminent death, judgment and hell offer anything in the way of relief. At least since the early writings of Piaget psychologists have been familiar with the various stages of the child's sense of causal reality, one central and persistent component of which is termed "realism." Realism, as one writer puts it, "refers to the fact that initially all things are equally real and real in the same sense and on the same plane: pictures, words, people, things, energies, dreams, feelings—all are equally solid or insubstantial and all mingle in a common sphere of experience. . . . Realism does not imply fatalism or passive resignation, but simply a failure [on the part of the young child] to doubt the reality of whatever comes into awareness."[49] The children observed in the psychological experiments that gave rise to the identification of these stages of reality awareness were the children of 20th century parents, children living in, if not a secular universe, at least one in which a fundamentalist view of divine creation and judgment is largely absent. Puritan children, however, lived in a world in which their parents—indeed, the greatest scientific minds of the time: Bacon, Boyle, Newton—were certain of the reality of witches and subterranean demons. In 1674, surprised at Spinoza's skepticism regarding spiritual entities, a correspondent of the freethinking philosopher doubtless spoke for most men of his time, the famed "Age of Reason," when he replied: "No one of moderns denies specters."[50]

It has long been known that one component of death in the Middle Ages

---

[48]Samuel Wakeman, *A Young Man's Legacy* (Boston, 1673), pp. 6, 41; Edwards quoted in Fleming, p. 100.

[49]Joseph Church, *Language and the Discovery of Reality* (New York: Random House, 1961), pp. 15–16. For full discussion of this and other stages see Jean Piaget, *The Construction of Reality in the Child* (New York: Basic Books, 1954), and *The Child's Conception of Physical Causality* (Totawa, N.J.: Littlefield, Adams, 1966), esp. pp. 237–58.

[50]On the belief of 17th century scientists in the reality of the invisible world, see Lynn Thorndike, *A History of Magic and Experimental Science* (New York: Columbia Univ. Press, 1958), Vols. 7 and 8. The reference quoted is from 8:570.

was concern over the fate of the body of the deceased, and worry that a fully disintegrated corpse or one that had been destroyed in war might be unable to be present at the Judgment.[51] It is less well known, or less often acknowledged, that a similar literalism retained a hold on the Puritan mind into the 18th century. Thus in 1692 a highly respected New England minister could effectively deal with questions concerning the Last Judgment in the following manner:

> Where will there be room for such a Vast Multitude as Adam, with all his Children? The whole surface of the earth could not hold them all? Ridiculous exception! Allow that this World should Last no less than *Ten-Thousand* Years, which it *will not*; Allow that there are at once alive a *Thousand Millions* of men, which there *are not;* Allow all these to march off every *Fifty years,* with a New Generation rising up in their stead; and allow each of these Individuals a place *Five Foot* Square to stand upon. I think these are Fair Allowances. I would now pray the Objector, if he have any skill at *Arithmetick,* to Compute, Whether a Spot of Ground, much less than *England,* which contains perhaps about Thirty Millions of Acres, but about a *Thousandth Part* of the Terraqueous Glob, and about the *Three Hundred thirty third* part of the Habitable Earth, would not hold them all.[52]

In a world in which the presence of early death was everywhere, and in which the most sophisticated and well regarded adults expressed such a literal sense of spiritual reality, it is hardly surprising that children would respond with a deadly serious mien to reminders of "how filthy, guilty, odious, abominable they are both by nature and practice," to descriptions of parental desertion at the day of Judgment and subsequent condemnation to the terrors of hell where "the Worm dyeth not . . . [and] the Fire is not quenched," and to the exhortations of respected teachers to "Remember Death; think much of death; think how it will be on a death bed."[53] In such a world it is far from surprising that a girl of seven should react "with many tears"—and her father with tears of sympathy—to a reading of Isaiah 24, in which she would have encountered:

> Therefore hath the curse devoured the earth, and they that dwell therein are desolate: therefore the inhabitants of the earth are burned, and few men left. . . . Fear, and the pit, and the snare, are upon thee, O inhabitant of the earth. And it shall come to pass, that he who fleeth from the noise of the fear shall fall into the

[51]On this, with special reference to the catechistic treatment of such matters in the medieval text *La Lumiere as lais,* see C. V. Langlois, *La Vie en France au Moyen Age* (Paris: Librairie Hachette, 1928), 4:111–19.

[52]Samuel Lee, *The Great Day of Judgment* (Boston, 1692), pp. 19–20.

[53]Benjamin Wadsworth, "The Nature of Early Piety," p. 15; Solomon Stoddard, *The Efficacy of the Fear of Hell to Restrain Men From Sin* (Boston, 1713), p. 24; Joseph Green, *The Commonplace Book of Joseph Green* (1696), ed., Samuel Eliot Morison, Colonial Society of Massachusetts *Publications,* 34 (1943), 204.

pit; and he that cometh up out of the midst of the pit shall be taken in the snare: for the windows from on high are open, and the foundations of the earth do shake.

Nor, in such a world, should we consider it unusual that later in her youth this same girl would again and again "burst out into an amazing cry . . . [because] she was afraid she should goe to Hell," would "read out of Mr. Cotton Mather—why hath Satan filled thy heart, which increas'd her Fear," and would eventually be unable to read the Bible without weeping, fearing as she did "that she was a Reprobat, Loved not God's people as she should."[54]

The case of young Elizabeth Sewall is by no means unique. Puritan diaries and sermons are filled with references to similar childhood responses to the terrors of separation, mortality and damnation. As with so many other things Puritan, these fears seem to have reached a crescendo with the emotional outpourings of the Great Awakening in the 1740s.[55] But the fears were always present, following children into adulthood and combining there with the disquieting complexities of Puritan theology and Christian tradition to produce a culture permeated by fear and confusion in the face of death.

The Christian tradition that the Puritans had inherited counseled peace and comfort in one's dying hour. Elaborate procedures for coping with the fear of death had been devised throughout long centuries of experience. Extreme unction, the viaticum, indulgences, requiem masses, the prayers of family and friends—all these served the Catholic as a cushion against an excessively fearful reaction in the face of death. The relative optimism that grew out of this tradition was passed on, in different form, to much of Protestantism during the Renaissance and Reformation. Thus, Renaissance poetry on the theme of death, Edelgard Dubruck observes,

> . . . stressed immortality and the afterlife. The word "death" was often avoided and replaced by euphemisms . . . [and] depiction of the realistic aspects of death was carefully suppressed. . . . In the early sixteenth century, poets dwelt upon fame and immortality rather than death, and in the Reformation writings death had at least lost its sting, and both Lutherans and Calvinists insisted that death was at long last vanquished with the help of Christ.[56]

Although the Puritans inherited, and tried to live with, the *prescription* that a peaceful death was a good death, the deterministic pessimism of the faith was contradictory to Christian tradition and caused exceptional dis-

[54]Samuel Sewall, "Diary" in Massachusetts Historical Society *Collections,* series 5, V, 308, 419–20, 422–23, 437. See also the terrified reaction of Sewall's young son Sam to the death of a companion and his father's reminding him of the "need to prepare for Death," ibid., pp. 308–9.

[55]See the numerous references to violent childhood reactions to death in *The Christian History,* I and II (Boston, 1743–44); cited in Fleming.

[56]Edelgard Dubruck, *The Theme of Death in French Poetry of the Middle Ages and the Renaissance* (The Hague: Mouton, 1964), pp. 152, 154.

comfort as the devout Puritan awaited the end of his life.[57] To the adult Puritan the contemplation of death frequently "would make the flesh tremble."[58] To the Puritan child it could do no less.

Puritan New England, in this respect at least, seems a far cry from England in the same period, at least if Peter Laslett is correct when he writes that people there were "inured to bereavement and the shortness of life."[59] But in recognizing this, we should also be wary of finding in Puritan attitudes and behavior too much grist for our psychological mills. The fear of death, to many Freudians, is "closely interwoven with castration fear," a fear which "is so closely united with death fear that it has often been described as its origin." It is, writes psychoanalyst J. D. Howard, "purely . . . a secondary substitutive phenomenon of the castration fear which grew out of an inadequately resolved Oedipal conflict."[60] Turning to Freud himself, a more sophisticated interpreter with some knowledge of Puritanism might seize on the similarity between the Puritan requirement for uncertainty and his preoccupations with death, and Freud's treatment of uncertainty and obsessional neurosis.[61] But interpretations of this type are hopelessly bogged down by the arrogance and myopia of the historical present.[62]

The world of the Puritan—child and adult—was a rational world, in many ways, perhaps, more rational than our own. It is true that it was a world of witches and demons, and of a just and terrible God who made his presence known in the slightest act of nature. But this was the given reality about which most of the decisions and actions of the age, throughout the entire Western world, revolved. When the Puritan parent urged on his children what we would consider a painfully early awareness of sin and death, it was because the well-being of the child and the community *required* such an early recognition of these matters. It merits little to note that the

[57]For an extended treatment of this matter, see David E. Stannard, "Death and Dying in Puritan New England," *American Historical Review*, 78 (Dec. 1973), 1305–30.

[58]James Fitch, *Peace the End of the Perfect and Upright* (Boston, 1673), p. 6.

[59]Laslett, p. 96.

[60]J. D. Howard, "Fear of Death," *Journal of the Indiana State Medical Association* (1962), quoted in Hattie R. Rosenthal, "The Fear of Death as an Indispensable Factor in Psychotherapy," in Hendrik M. Ruitenbeek, ed., *Death: Interpretations* (New York: Delta Books, 1969), p. 171; the previous quotation is from Mary Chadwick, "Notes Upon the Fear of Death," in Ruitenbeek, p. 75.

[61]Sigmund Freud, "Notes Upon a Case of Obsessional Neurosis," Part II, *The Standard Edition of the Complete Psychological Works of Sigmund Freud*, James Strachey, ed. (London: Hogarth Press, 1957), 10:229–37.

[62]A particularly egregious example of this, with specific bearing on the subject at hand, is the apparent raison d'être of a new journal, *History of Childhood Quarterly*, as the interminable psychoanalytic explication of the theme that: "The history of childhood is a nightmare from which we have only recently begun to awaken." It is the insistent and quite serious claim of the founder and editor of this journal that prior to the 18th century there did not exist in Western history a single "good mother."

Puritans (and Bacon and Boyle and Newton) were mistaken in their beliefs in hobgoblins; the fact is they were real to men of the 17th century, as real as Ra and his heavenly vessels were to the ancient Egyptians, and at least as real as the unconscious is to devout followers of Freud; and the responses to that reality were as honest and as rational, in the context of the times, as are the responses to reality of any parent today.

If children were frightened, even terrified, by the prospects of life and death conjured up by their parents and ministers, that too was a natural and rational response. As more than one Puritan writer suggested, to fail to be frightened was a sure sign that one was either spiritually lost, or stupid, or both.[63] Death brought with it, to all but a very few, the prospect of the most hideous and excruciating fate imaginable. One necessary though by itself insufficient sign of membership in that select company of saints was the taking to heart of the warning to "beware of indulging yourselves in a stupid secure frame."[64] Thus, wrote Samuel Willard with remarkably cool detachment and insight,

> Here we see the reason why the People of God are so often doubtful, disquiet, discontent, and afraid to dy (I put things together). The ground of all this is because they do not as yet see clearly what they shall be: It would be a matter of just wonderment to see the Children of God so easily and often shaken, so disturbed and perplexed in hours of Temptation, were it not from the consideration that at present they know so little of themselves or their happiness: Sometimes their sonship itself doth not appear to them, but they are in the dark, at a loss about the evidencing of it to the satisfaction of their own minds, and from hence it is that many doubtings arise, and their souls are disquieted.[65]

Willard knew first hand of what he spoke. He was often the one chosen to try to calm the fears of those who found the prospect of death too much to bear; Judge Sewall in fact called him in to help with young Elizabeth's disconsolate weeping. It may be, despite their experience, that ministers and parents like Willard were unaware of all the components that went into the making of the Puritan child's fear of death. It was, as we have seen, a complex problem touching on a variety of matters which Puritan children and adults alike had to face every day of their lives. But they did at least know that when a young Betty or Sam Sewall broke down in tears over the prospects of death and damnation, the children—and they were children, not miniature adults—were most often acting normally, out of their own experience in the world, and in response to their parents' solemn, reasoned warnings.

[63]See, for example, Leonard Hoar, *The Sting of Death* (Boston, 1680), pp. 11–12.
[64]Ibid.
[65]Willard, *The Child's Portion*, p. 67.

DEATH IN THE POPULAR MIND
OF PRE-CIVIL WAR AMERICA

LEWIS O. SAUM

"AND WHEN MEN DIE, WE DO NOT MENTION THEM." WITH THOSE WORDS
Emerson concluded his gloomy forecast for a society suffering a "decaying
church and a wasting unbelief."[1] In time, cultural commentators saw something resembling Emerson's contention. Over a century later the Spanish
scholar Julián Marías wrote of the United States that death assumes here
"the air of an undesirable alien and has therefore made no progress towards
citizenship."[2] Neither of the two philosophers, Emerson or Marías, spoke
quite accurately. Marías allowed a faulty inference. Death had once had full
citizenship, but had suffered exile, probably with the rise of naturalistic and
materialistic moods emergent in the late 19th century. Emerson in 1838
played Jeremiah with overmuch intensity. As forecast, his observation had
accuracy; but as description, it fell very wide of the mark. In fact his was a
society saturated with concern with death, and fastidious to a fault in obser-
vances pertaining to it. Carl Bode in *The Anatomy of American Popular
Culture, 1840–1860* concluded with "A Trio for Columbia," three themes
about which American culture of that era might be focused. Two of the
three, Love and Success, involved aspiration and possibility. The third,
Death, had certainty and universality.

Interestingly, however, Bode showed some impatience in his handling of
the appreciation of death evidenced in poetry, plays and novels. Aspects of
that theme seemed to impress him as fulsome and, perhaps, emotionally ex-
ploitative. Bode's readers have difficulty forgetting that, after Little Mary

[1] *The Complete Works of Ralph Waldo Emerson,* Concord Edition (Boston: Houghton
Mifflin, 1903), I, 143.
[2] Michael Aaron Rockland, ed., *America in the Fifties and Sixties: Julián Marías on the
United States,* trans. Blanche De Puy and Harold C. Raley (University Park: Pennsylvania
State Univ. Press, 1972), p. 41.

Morgan of *Ten Nights in a Bar-Room* fell at the strike of a hurled whiskey glass, author Timothy Shay Arthur devoted "most of the next sixty pages to her lingering, pathetic demise." Nor can one readily disassociate the fact that Mrs. Sigourney was "a classical example of an extremely popular bad poet" from the fact that "her favorite single subject" was death.[3] Kenneth S. Lynn more abruptly showed a later age's misgiving about the presentation of death in pre-Civil War culture. In an essay praising the artistry of *Uncle Tom's Cabin,* Lynn spoke of Harriet Beecher Stowe's characters as "shockingly believable." But, he allowed, Stowe did employ some "factitious" dramatic situations, most notably the death of Augustine St. Clare. To Lynn, it was an exercise in "saccharine phoniness," one that "strikes us today as hackneyed from beginning to end."[4] It would not do justice to Bode and Lynn to suggest that their artistic and cultural criticisms illustrate what Geoffrey Gorer called "an unremarked shift in prudery" in the 20th century—from sex to death. But there seems to be little hazard in suggesting, as Gorer did, that theatrical, poetical and literary mileage gotten from deathly dramatics derived from the fact that such situations were among the relatively few "that an author could be fairly sure would have been shared by the vast majority of his readers."[5]

The following essay seeks to get at certain perceptions and moods of the comparatively unelevated by what seems to me the sensible, if not always inspiring method of reading the diaries, the letters and the commonplace jottings of people in unprepossessing circumstances. Possibly this will circumvent the inferential leaps inherent in efforts to derive a portrayal of humble sentiments from expressions directed at them or written about them by those in positions of intellectual, literary, journalistic, political or some other form of attainment. Simply, the essay attempts to convey what ordinary people themselves said about death, and, in part, it attempts to relate those attitudes and beliefs to the depictions rendered by better minds both at the time and later.

At the end of his diary Connecticut cook and sailor William Sprague inscribed a toast:

> Here is to the world that goes
> round on wheels
> Death is a thing that all
> man feels
> If death was a thing that
> the rich could buy

[3](Berkeley, Calif.: Univ. of California Press, 1960), pp. 122, 193–94.
[4]"Editor's Introduction," *Uncle Tom's Cabin or, Life Among the Lowly* (Cambridge, Mass.: Harvard Univ. Press, 1962), p. xi.
[5]"The Pornography of Death," *Encounter,* 5 (Oct. 1955), 50–51.

The rich would live and
the poor would die[6]

Death was indeed that thing "that all man feels"; and it behooved all men to give that fact sober consideration. A great many assiduously fulfilled their obligation, giving almost ceaseless advice to self and others to keep death firmly in mind. Here we encounter a persuasion and an appetite that would seem by later standards a blend of the gargantuan and the pathological. Thus a New Yorker's diary page titled "Needful Counsel" had, centered at the left, the injunctive opening, "let your." To the right of that came a vertical series of subjects—"Conduct," "Diet" and "Sleep," among others—followed, in turn, by the single verb "be." At the right came an appropriately arranged vertical series of compound predicates, thus giving, for example, "let your Diet be temperate, wholesome sober." Appropriately, this diagrammatic didacticism concluded with: "let your Reflection be of death and future state."[7] In Alabama, schoolboy Isaac Barr filled entire pages of his penmanship book with reminders, most of which have a more solemn tone than the following: "School expires Isaac on the 8th day of May 1852." Whatever his exact age, young Isaac had an ample number of years to contemplate sobering ultimates, and thus, far outnumbering the notices of the end of school, came reminders of the end of life. "Death takes the young as well as the old"; "Remember this life is not long"; or simply "Remember you must die."[8]

The risk of idle supererogation or even impertinence looms large in any effort to explain the superabundant musings and dotings on death. Accepting the hazard, one must note first that death was an ever present fact of life. As a normally unreflective Maine farmer cited the conventional wisdom, " 'in life we are in the midst of death.' "[9] Few cultural commentaries on that era fail to remark the intimacy most people had with death. Their's was an immediate, not a derivative or vicarious, awareness. Thus, in the context of melancholy poetry Carl Bode reminded his readers of the "somber story" told by mortality statistics.[10] In this case, Bode mentioned figures from New York City. But the condition was general, not particular; and, as Perry Miller remarked about Concord, "the supreme fact was death."[11] Others, however, have shown puzzlement bordering on im-

---

[6] William Y. Sprague Diary, after the entry of Sept. 17, 1859 (Connecticut State Library).

[7] Hiram Peck Diary, undated miscellany at beginning (New-York Historical Society). (This item is catalogued as the Henry Peck Diary, but it was kept by Henry's brother Hiram.)

[8] Isaac S. Barr Penmanship Book, Mrs. I. S. Barr Mss. (Mss. Div., Alabama Dept. of Archives and History).

[9] Seth H. Willard Diary, Apr. 4, 1859 (Maine Historical Society).

[10] P. 192.

[11] *Consciousness in Concord; the text of Thoreau's hitherto "lost journal," 1840–1841, together with notes and a commentary by Perry Miller* (Boston: Houghton Mifflin, 1958), p. 75.

patience when treating the popular inclination to dwell on death at the expense of what a later age would deem more important. One editor of humble writings, though he took satisfaction from the "few references to political and social events" that appeared in his material, had to admit that, of such, there were "not as many as one might hope for." That illness and death should receive so much attention he guardedly ascribed to "the uncertainty of individual life."[12] In that conclusion he was right at least in part.

When upstate New York common schoolteacher Sophronia Beebe opened a letter to an old friend, she did so in this way: "The grim messenger has been at work all over the land calling for his thousands. The lovely child has been taken from its sports; the youth has been taken from its circle of loved ones; the teacher from his arduous duties, the lawyer from the bar, the doctor from his office, the statesman from the senate chamber . . . ."[13] This doleful overture left matters in the comparatively abstract, as perhaps befit the lady's calling. Far more commonly, the immediacy took on almost awesome proportions. Farm woman Annis Pierce sent what consolation she could to a daughter who had lost an infant child. Mother Pierce expressed herself awkwardly, but not with the callousness one might infer from the following: "I wast not any disappointed when we heard of the death of little Emma I was very sure that I would hear of the death of some one of those dear little ones. . . ."[14] Routinely people specified what proportion their living offspring bore to the total. If Little Eva and Little Mary Morgan were accorded so much time and attention in dying, it probably had much to do with the fact that mortality among children was staggering.

> My brothers [and] sister kind & dear
> How soon youve passed away
> Your friendly faces now I hear
> Are mowldren in the clay

This Indiana youngster can well be forgiven his or her contribution, "On the death of my 2 brothers & sister," to the melancholy poetry of the period.[15]

The immediacy reflected in mortality rates conjoined in deathly impact with the lack or incipient condition of professional or institutional services for handling the dying and the dead. Ineluctable realities brought people to

---

[12]Robert W. Lovett, "Augustus Roundy's Cincinnati Sojourn," *Historical and Philosophical Society of Ohio Bulletin,* 19 (Oct. 1961), 260–61.

[13]Sophronia C. Beebe to Jennie Akehurst, Feb. 4, 1858, Akehurst-Lines Collection (Div. of Special Collections, University of Georgia Libraries).

[14]Annis Pierce to Caleb and Emily Carr, Nov. 6, 1856, Caleb M. Carr Letters (Collection of Regional History, Cornell University).

[15]"On the Death of my 2 brothers & sister," Feb. 1851, Harris Family Papers (Indiana Historical Society).

most direct contact with fundamentals. In February of 1846 Brigham Nims
of New Hampshire recorded what may have been his first full participation
in handling the dying and the dead, and he did so in a straightforward way
that suggests the routineness of the function. On the night of the 10th he
"watched with Seth Towns he was very wild the fore part of the night more
calm toward morning." Nims visited Seth again on the 11th, and, when
word came that all was over, he returned to prepare the deceased for burial:
"I went and helped Lay him out, and shaved him the first person that I tried
to shave."[16] Late in 1834 a young Maryland store clerk did such duty at the
end of September, again in the middle of November, and again on the last
day of the year. In one case it was a friend, in another it was the daughter of
a friend, and the third was a cousin. In the case of the dying friend, he sat by
the deathbed for several nights consecutively. The end came at 11:40 at
night. "I then shaved & washed him," the clerk wrote, "& Marker assisted
me in dressing him (*he died hard*)."[17]

In turn, the familiarity with death may have been intensified by urges that
were, on the one hand reportorial, and, on the other, therapeutic. In the
former regard, letters of the period partake so heavily of the deathly aura in
part because communications had not kept pace with population mobility.
People at far remove and in infrequent contact concentrated on fundamentals, among which the death list came foremost. Letters often had,
given the circumstances of the time, a quality that brought this reflection
from a Carolina woman: "I dread mail days . . . the sight of a letter makes
me so nervous."[18]

It did not always suffice to tell who had died. The manner of their going
received a good deal of attention, and not just in terms of the spiritual
considerations to be treated later. Time and again, descriptive comments on
death incorporated so much physiological detail as to suggest a purposive
eye to medical or therapeutic concerns. Humble people probably communi-
cated and pooled empirical data because there was not a ready resort to
trusted and respected experts. Little in the shape of an institutional shield
stood between the lay person and the untidy details of disease and dying.
Left often to their own needs and devices, common folk recorded and
conveyed, not gratuitous morbidity, but the information of pathology. Her
daughter "little Lydia," an Ohio woman wrote in an account of the child's
death, "did not swell as much as some." This is only an earnest of the

[16]Brigham Nims Diary, Feb. 11 and 12, 1846, Brigham Nims Family Papers (New Hampshire Historical Society).

[17]Archibald B. Knode Diary, Sept. 30, Nov. 15, and Dec. 31, 1834, Archibald B. Knode
Papers, Diaries and Account Books (Indiana Historical Society).

[18](Mrs. Oswald) to William Garland, Sept. 30, 1839, William Harris Garland Papers
(Southern Historical Collection, University of North Carolina).

graphic description of the course of Lydia's trials: measles in January, then the whooping cough, then smallpox and on to this May day on which she died and on which her mother wrote.[19] On his way west to work as foreman of a carpenter crew on the Illinois Central construction, Charles Rich wrote from Bangor, Maine to his wife back on the farm at Milo. At the very outset of this long and particularly revealing correspondence, the 45-year-old husband wrote of death. One Gilman, a man who had started with Rich on the way to the West, had fallen ill almost at the outset and died in a tavern at Waterville. Charles stood not on delicacy in addressing his 26-year-old wife, Albina, nor did he spare her the details. The deceased carpenter had been constipated for several days, Rich noted, and the pills and the oil had worked no relief. At the tavern, when Gilman had become incapacitated, some others "took hold and helped" Rich administer enemas. Lobelia and thoroughwort in two or three such applications yielded a half-pint "of what appeared more like sheep manure only in larger rolls and very black." The pathological particulars changed when a doctor arrived with the predictable calomel. Shortly, the dead carpenter was on his way back to Milo.[20]

Gilman would build no more houses, Albina mused as she wrote late in the night after the funeral. At the service itself "while looking at his dead bodie," she had entertained other questions and other associations: "I thought who heard his last words, who laid him out, it was my own *dear husband*." With that dead body before her, she felt "as if I wanted to see you and ask many questions."[21] To ask and receive the details of a person's death was standard. Here it appears that Albina had in mind some spiritual concerns. Her husband had probably given satisfactory account of the temporal, physical and medical aspects of Gilman's demise. It would be fair to assume that Charles Rich had not burdened his wife with idle unsavory details, but that, out of some positive, informative urge, he had sought to share his knowledge of a particular path from disease to death. In more than the ultimate sense, death was inescapable. People knew it by its existential proximity as well as by its actuarial prevalence.

If there was a powerful intimacy with death, a spiritual fascination with death—the outlines of which will be discussed shortly—there was as well a seeming insouciance, a capacity to register without questioning. At one level that capacity represented no more than an extension of the resignation to

[19]Julia Adams to Hannah Watrous, May 2, 1848, Phinehas Adams Papers (Huntington Library). By permission.
[20]Charles Rich to Albina Rich, Dec. 5, 1853, Rich Family Papers (Maine Historical Society).
[21]Albina Rich to Charles Rich, Dec. 7, 1853, Rich Family Papers.

Providence of the time. At another level it may have been little more than being inured, inevitably, to the sorts of situations described by the Maryland store clerk and so many others. "Not simply as a matter of rhetoric," Fred Somkin wrote, "but in frightening actuality, Americans seemed strangely able to accept the possibility of violent death on a mass scale." That most indiscriminate killer, the steamboat, appeared as no more than the "most recent embodiment of the elemental power."[22] Mark Twain provided an illustration that Somkin might well have used. Writing of antebellum America, and assuring us in footnote that he was not fictionalizing, Mark Twain told in *The Gilded Age* of the race between the *Boreas* and the *Amaranth*. There was pride, "hurrah," juvenile swagger, a "nigger roosting on the safety-valve," and "then there was a booming roar." When the horror and the screams of the dying subsided, 39 were injured, 22 were dead and 96 were missing. The head engineer of the *Amaranth* took off his ring, peeling steam-eaten flesh with it, and handed it and his eternal curse to the man who had been in command at the time. But the court of enquiry returned "the inevitable American verdict which has been so familiar to our ears all the days of our lives—'NOBODY TO BLAME.' "[23]

Mark Twain did more than indulge an intense and mordant irony. On his way from St. Louis to Glasgow, Missouri, in 1842 New Englander Walter B. Foster's boat, the *Satan,* tied up for the night at the mouth of the Missouri. As the *Satan* pulled away in the morning, another boat near by, the *Edna of the Platte,* exploded. Writing a few days later in Glasgow, Foster took some care to describe the ghastly scenes that unfolded as the *Satan* went to assist. For explicit horror, his account far exceeds the *Amaranth* episode in *The Gilded Age.* The "screams and groans, curses and prayers" that "resounded from all sides" established the general aura. Foster then pressed on into the particulars of the pathology of disaster. Some begged "in piteous accents" to be killed forthwith; others lay perfectly still and quiet; those who had inhaled steam screeched hideously; a "respectable looking" man with a demolished hand and various scald wounds graciously accepted a glass of wine; a German woman scalded over most of her body pleaded with Foster to remove the skin of her arm and hand that now hung from her nails like a rolled-off glove. He did. Foster's was an eye to clinical detail, an eye that observed the quick as well as the dying. Some of the sound aided as they could; some shrank in horror; some suffered such shock as to be rendered "incapable of attending to anything"; and some "drank, smoked, and laughed." Some did worse. Around the body of a German killed and denuded by the blast and the steam hung a

---

[22] *Unquiet Eagle: Memory and Desire in the Idea of American Freedom 1815–1860* (Ithaca, N. Y.: Cornell Univ. Press, 1967), pp. 40–41.
[23] *The Gilded Age: A Tale of To-Day* (New York: Harper & Bros., 1915), I: 44–54.

"belt of sovereigns." "An Irishman standing by pocketed it." Almost at the end of his account, Foster found it "strange" that anyone "could be so depraved!" "But enough," he concluded, not bothering to ask how or why it was that the *Edna of the Platte* had taken so many to such a dreadful end.[24]

It has been common to see ambition as much of the causal context for the seeming heedlessness of American society. Fred Somkin's previously quoted observation about the American ability to accept violent death came, for example, in a chapter titled "Prosperity the Riddle." And one finds intimations of that theme in humble writing. As did so many others, A. P. Moss of Texas related in an 1853 letter "some quite melancholly" news, an account of the ravages of the flux in his area. But then, "laying aside mortality," he wrote that Smith County was prospering. It was "live with enterprise," and "Railroads is all the go."[25] Here, of course, we are edging into Colonel Beriah Sellers' neighborhood. But, however inviting, the idea of progress and its various concomitants do not fit very well with common views of that era. If people showed a seeming indifference or a stoic equanimity, it probably stemmed far more from enforced intimacy with death and, in turn, from what they would have considered a Christian, providential resignation.

The tentative mood reigned supreme. After a New Hampshire mountain tour young Josiah Chaney gave a typical expression of it. He thought it probable that he would some day travel more, but he added the necessary qualifier—if he lived.[26] Walter Foster, before going up the Mississippi to the scene of the *Edna* explosion, had a birthday while at New Orleans. In the diary entry of the preceding day he announced it this way: "Tomorrow I'm twenty-three if I live. . . ."[27] That grimly remindful reservation—if life is spared—resonated around pre-Civil War America. It went to the self, where perhaps it was most needed; but with palsying frequency it went to others, to the old who least required reminding, to the sound and the active who might forget, and to the very young who might not understand.

Christian doctrine joined with hard fact to emphasize the emotional desirability of approaching life with a tentative, almost interrogative mien. When "hannah marthy" of Indiana drowned for venturing onto a shaky footbridge over a freshet-swollen stream, Mary Jane Crane gave poetic statement of the proper reaction to the fate of this "blooming youth":

[24] Walter B. Foster Journal, July 24, 1842 (Missouri Historical Society).
[25] A. P. Moss to Dear Emily, Sept. 18, 1853, Smith Collection (Six Vault, Ga. Dept. of Archives and History).
[26] Josiah B. Chaney Diary, Sept. 17, 1845, Josiah B. Chaney Papers (Minnesota Historical Society).
[27] Walter B. Foster Journal, Jan, 16, 1842.

> But there is something says bestill
> Tis God's most righteous holy will[28]

From such an attitude could come that "great comfort" enjoyed by
Melville's Turkish "Fatalists," a type that suddenly merged for him into almost everyone.[29] Melville probably saw Emerson as one of those "amiable
philosophers of either the 'Compensation' or 'Optimist' school."[30] But in
"Fate" Emerson brought together in mood the Turk, the Arab, the Hindoo
and "our Calvinists"—our Calvinists "in the last generation."[31] For seeing
the *persisting* similarity, Melville, it seems to me, came nearer the truth.
Emerson saw American fatalists in the past but not in the present; had he
looked more closely he might well have shared Melville's conviction that
they were all about him.

Less than eloquent testimony of the trembling quality of hope can be seen
in the census files of the period. Very frequently the family list that ran from
husband and wife through the children in order of age would end with
"anonymous," "not named" or "unnamed." Infants so designated often
had attained several months, sometimes over a year of age. In keeping with
this practice J. S. Brown of Phillips, Maine, concluded a letter-listing of the
names and ages of his seven children with one who was "a year old has no
name yet."[32] Upstate New York farmer Francis Squires made frequent
diary references to a son born in July of 1852. But only after weathering a
severe illness in March 1853, did "bub" assume full identity in his father's
writings. In an entry that probably marked the naming, Squires wrote:
"*Clarence Augustine Pierce Squires* weighs 20 lbs."[33]

On the occasion of the birth of a daughter, Josiah Crosby of Westernville,
New York, received a letter conveying congratulations and the hope that
the child would be a great blessing. "But dont," came the ritual warning,
"set too mutch by it."[34] George and Fidelia Baldwin of the same state in-
dulged in the happiness that came with their healthy new baby; "but how
long we shal be allowed to keep him is inknown to us." This same letter
referred to a previous child they had lost, and that fact as well as the general
mood probably accounts for their use of a fairly common designation for

---

[28] Untitled poem apparently written by Mary Jane Crane, Feb. 9, 1841, Joel Crane and
Eunice Fitch Family Correspondence (Indiana Historical Society).

[29] *White Jacket or the World in a Man-of-War,* chap. 31.

[30] *Pierre or, The Ambiguities,* Book 20, Pt. 1.

[31] *The Complete Works of Ralph Waldo Emerson,* Centenary Ed. (Boston: Riverside Press,
1904), 6: 5.

[32] J. S. Brown to Ebenezer Brown, Sept. 20 and Oct. 9, 1850, Ebenezer Brown Papers (New
Hampshire Historical Society).

[33] Francis W. Squires Diaries, Mar. 1853 (Collection of Regional History, Cornell
University).

[34] Simeon Ives to Josiah Crosby, Sept. 8, 1847, Lyman Stuart *Collector.* Stampless Covers
(Collection of Regional History, Cornell University).

the new arrival—the "little stranger."[35] However high the hopes, caution dominated as the admonitory byword. A letter from Carrolton, Alabama, to a grieving brother and sister had the comparative sophistication and the crushing personal experience that allowed fuller explicit expression of the dilemma of loving indifference. In their bereavement the couple must, this writer urged, turn to their remaining children for comfort.

> But do not O do not I beseech you lean too much on this fond hope lest in a moment you least suspect it shall be torn away *forever* . . . O how heart-rending it is for us to be told that we must call off our affections from these dear second selves and yet if we do not in some degree turn our affections away from them we sharpen the Arrow that is to pierce our vitals.[36]

In the full despondence that ensued—"the heart whithers and joy sickens & dies and existance becomes a troubled dream"—this Alabaman went beyond that quiet resignation counseled and sought by most. But a situation incorporating "little strangers" and involving the self-preservative need to "in some degree turn our affections away from them" tells much about childhood, life and death in pre-Civil War America.

Philosophy has been referred to as the learning to die, and insofar as humble Americans philosophized they did indeed learn to die. Countering the assertive optimism of the Emersonian position, Melville bespoke that older resigned mood. *Pierre* becomes an almost angry rejection of the specious felicity of the Transcendental war on circumstances. Pierre Glendinning's insurgency leads only to "conclusive proof that he has no power over his condition." Involuted into the "author-hero, Vivia," Pierre comes to "deep-down, unutterable mournfulness": " 'Away, ye chattering apes of a sophomorean Spinoza and Plato, who once didst all but delude me that night was day, and pain only a tickle.' " Here, young Pierre "is fitting himself for the highest life, by thinning his blood and collapsing his heart. He is learning how to live, by rehearsing the part of death."[37] The common man arrived at that position somewhat more readily for having no " 'chattering apes' " to circumvent.

The American drift to comfortable worldliness had not run its course by the pre-Civil War period. Cyclone Covey has given us a brief and imaginative account of the move away from a world-view centered on "a symbolic pilgrimage through the wilderness of this world to an ultimate

---

[35] George and Fidelia Baldwin to Lawrence Parker, Oct. 2, 1847, Barbour-Parker Family Letters (Collection of Regional History, Cornell University).

[36] R. Owen to brother and sister, April 22, 1836, Julia Bryce Lovelace Letters (Manuscripts Division, Alabama Department of Archives and History).

[37] *Pierre*, Book 22, Pts. 3 and 4.

home-town in the next." At the outset of our history the mood appeared in the Augustinian equation: "Destination: Death." By the end of a century in the new world the Pilgrim found himself in "Vanity Fair," and, a moment later, "The Big Switch" had been completed. With this 18th century "revolution to modernity," Covey wrote, "death has been the subject to be most avoided of most considered."[38] The conspiracy of silence settled in, and Abraham Lincolm's deathly melancholia assumes the guise of atavistic epilogue. Covey's trenchant work notwithstanding, the move to "modernity" probably came far more slowly than such an overview indicates. What he called "The Psychology of Bereavement" took expression in ever-lessening eloquence and intensity; but the humble writings of mid-19th century bear powerful resemblance in thrust to the elevated statements of three centuries before.

When Francis Squires' wife died in March 1860 the minister chose Romans 13:12 to elucidate the meaning for the survivors: "The night is far spent, the day is at hand: let us therefore cast off the works of darkness, and let us put on the armour of light." "I am very lonesome today," the forty-year-old widower wrote, "& feel that the world is not our home."[39] Most directly, death partook of warning. As a dying man in Sterling, Massachusetts, stated it to the wife who conveyed his words to others, "Tell them that my being about to be cut off in the midst of my years may prove a warning to my dear friends to be ready."[40] The bridegroom cometh, the lamps must be kept trimmed. With a litany's regularity the metaphor of Matthew 25 informed the mood of the period. The fullness of God's purpose was, of course, never clear; but patently the death of a loved one alerted the survivors, and, in turn, it prepared them by weaning them from worldly attachments. When Lawrence Parker's baby died (and his wife was soon to follow), relatives did what they could to explain: "You have now one less object to attach you to the earth, and one more to draw you towards heaven. Undoubtedly this was God's design in taking the *Dear Babe*."[41] To be sure, the "Pilgrim" was indeed in "Vanity Fair," and "the ties of nature are strong."[42] But people resisted the allurements and did what they could to keep the ties loose. Lincoln's poetic statement differs in quality but not in essence from the bereaved sense of his humbler counterparts:

---

[38] *The American Pilgrimage: The Roots of American History, Religion and Culture* (New York: Collier Books, 1961), p. 105.

[39] Francis W. Squires Diaries, Mar. 9, 1860.

[40] Lucy Holcomb to Nahum Holcomb, May 10, 1837, Holcomb Family Letters (Connecticut State Library).

[41] Fidelia and George Baldwin to Lawrence Parker, Nov. 2, 1845, Barbour-Parker Family Letters.

[42] John Barber to Lawrence Parker, Nov. 2, 1845, Barbour-Parker Family Letters.

O memory! thou mid-way world
'Twixt Earth and Paradise,
Where things decayed, and loved ones lost
In dreamy shadows rise. . . .
Till every sound appears a knell,
And every spot a grave.[43]

"And every spot a grave" involved less poetic license than one might suppose. In the writing of the unelevated, that could be illustrated by the superabundant reflections on some "interesting" spot, by courtship walks through graveyards, by school compositions treating weeping willows bending to caress the mounded turf. For the sophisticated, such things had extensions or parallels in the graveyard poetry that abounded in the periodicals, in the blend of the sanitary and the aesthetic in the rural cemetery movement, and perhaps even in what Mario Praz called "The Romantic Agony." But participation in the ritual of death centered more directly on the deathbed than on the grave. Indeed, to an almost unnerving degree, the imagination, emotion and memory of humble America hovered about that sacrosanct place. Small wonder that dramatic and literary creators gravitated to it, or that, when the muse moved the pen of a lesser sort, it might seek to express the poetic perception of "the Death Bed of my friend."[44] Geoffrey Gorer knew well whereof he spoke in emphasizing its genuine rather than contrived or spurious significance.

Postulates and conditions must have varied widely; still, a discernible generic format emerges from the descriptions of and reflections about that hallowed setting. The imperious finality allowed no neat programming, but within death's small sanctions and flexibilities efforts and hopes went to assure certain preparations and meet certain prescriptions. First and most simply there was the solicitude, the emotional comfort and reassurance that the loved ones could give the departing. In turn, for the gathered circle there was the hope of receiving inspiration—the reciprocal reassurance—by witnessing a calm clear-eyed death. Finally, and inseparable from the former, there was the guarded hope for the soul of the deceased that derived from a demonstration of Christian fortitude and resignation. Death could be a powerful lesson and reassurance for the living, and, as well, a spiritual earnest or a final outward sign of an inward grace evidenced by the departing.

A preliminary though important ingredient of the setting for final transformations involved the gathering of family and most intimate friends. In the general mode of expression of the time this desideratum appeared as

---

[43] Quoted in Covey, *The American Pilgrimage,* p. 107.
[44] Obadiah Ethelbert Baker Journal, Mar. 12, 1860, Obadiah Ethelbert Baker Collection (Huntington Library). By permission.

"among friends," the word here designating more intense connections than the indiscriminate host it would later come to cover. Humble folk gave negative description of the gathering of the friends by noting the terror and the spiritual and emotional loss incurred by an unattended death in the wilderness. "On the death of Ephraim Beeson who died in Iowa teritory of the Chills and Fever in the fall of 1843" gave emphasis to the painful disparity between proper and improper setting:

> But if no parents near him stand
> To raise the drooping head
> If no kind sister lend a hand
> To smooth the sufferers bed
>
> Oh then let pitty more and more
> Tears of affection shed
> For him who on the strangers shore
> Now sleeps among the dead[45]

Surely, an unappreciated dimension of the fear of westering centers on this matter. The blurring of its significance in the passing of time probably involves the transmutation of death from profound consecration to what William James called "nothing but"[46]—in this case nothing but statistic and biological process. At the end of his trek, Forty-Niner E. D. Perkins perceived the "grim monster" now grown "doubly" ominous; "the grave has more terrors than I ever before felt."[47]

Whether the "grim monster" came to one who was in solitude or "among friends," it was deemed essential that death's presence be recognized. An East Texas woman gave the concern a characteristic statement in asking about the death of her sister, especially if the departed "wose in her senses . . . and if she read enny thing about ding [dying]."[48] Indeed, a part of the function of those gathered about the afflicted seems to have been to assure that matters were faced squarely. Visiting a sick friend or relative who had been married only three weeks, Minerva Bacon of Ogdensburg, New York found her "pale as death." Minerva evidently shuffled delicacy into a position of low priority in conversing with this woman who had but a week to live: "I told her thene she was worse of than she had a ware of."[49] When a friend was dying there were considerations far greater than tact. Just who generally performed Minerva's function is difficult to ascertain; but evi-

[45] Henry Beeson Flanner Family Correspondence (Indiana Historical Society).

[46] "The Present Dilemma in Philosophy," in *Pragmatism: A New Name for Some Old Ways of Thinking* (New York: Longman, Green, 1922), p. 16.

[47] Elisha D. Perkins Diary, Jan. 8, 1850, HM 1547 (Huntington Library). By permission.

[48] Mary and James Cole to brother (John Jones), Sept. 1, 1852, Morgan D. Jones letters (Mss. Div., Ala. Dept. of Archives and History).

[49] Minerva Bacon to Lydia Barnhart, June 27, 1841, Lyman Stuart *Collector*.

dently someone did. Time and again it would be marked as a source of satisfaction that the dying person was "sensible" of the situation. Indeed,
someone unwilling or unable to recognize his condition, as was a man in
Pawlet, Vermont, might be described as "very stupid."[50]

With the circle gathered, and with all alerted to the imminent issue, it was
in turn important that all be resigned to the working of Providence. The
sober, explicit statement of submission to God's will by the dying became
central. It was a thing much hoped for, though of course not always forthcoming. In the fictive ideal, Harriet Beecher Stowe and Timothy Shay
Arthur gave paradigmatic illustrations in Little Eva and Little Mary
Morgan. And Parson Weems' Washington, one might contend, endeared
himself quite as much to the two succeeding generations for his deathbed
patience and submission as for his inability to tell a lie. Melville, whose
philosophical meanderings often put him on the track of death and the pos-
ture appropriate thereto, concluded a disquisition on the subject in this way:
"To expire mild-eyed in one's bed transcends the death of Epaminondas."[51]

"To expire mild-eyed" had a beatific quality the presence or absence of
which almost always received mention. Mrs. Andrew Adams, herself
bearing the privations of Minnesota pioneering, took great satisfaction
from knowing that a dead neighbor had departed conscious and resigned:
"Am rejoiced to know these facts."[52] With the more intense emotional in-
volvement of a family relation, A. J. Hayter of Saline County, Missouri
wrote to his mother to get the details of the death of "dear old pappy."
"Mother i should have liked to have node whither he was resined to gow
Joseph could not tell me exackly whither or not you must tell A to rite to
me and let me now all about that gives me eas if he was perfectly resined to
gow mother in that triing ower if he was prepared to gow what sweet
thoughts to himself and all of his children."[53] The style was characteristically faulty; the sentiment was characteristically central.

Evidently there were deviations in the path from time to eternity. Not all
died to expectations. But the passing of a fellow mortal always had instructive quality. If all went well it could be a privilege to behold the death. At
one level this could involve a celebration of man in humanist terms—the
witnessing of a person's calmly and rationally putting the things of the
world into order, and unflinchingly accepting the bodily change. Mark
Twain, in emphasizing the "privilege" it was to Laura to attend her dying

[50]L. Clark to Mrs. Ann Bromley, June 18, 1850, Lyman Stuart *Collector.*
[51]*Mardi: and a Voyage Thither,* Chap. 9.
[52]Mrs. Andrew W. Adams Diary, Apr. 12, 1856, Andrew W. Adams and Family Papers
(Minnesota Historical Society).
[53]A. J. Hayter to Sa. A. G. Hayter, June 14, 1855, Coleman-Hayter Letters, 1840–1900
(Western Historical Manuscript Collection, University of Missouri, Columbia).

father, left things, by and large, in that realm. Indeed Si Hawkins expired with dimming eye and halting tongue still on the chimerical Tennessee land grant.[54]

Mark Twain did not seek to be ironically macabre in presenting Laura's deathwatch as a "privilege." Frequently the term itself, and nearly always the sentiment appear in humble writings of the time. Not to be able to attend at the deathbed was almost routinely set down as a striking deprivation. Six years after leaving Nicholville, New York, a Wisconsin couple wrote back to express grief at the death of a mother. The sense of loss involved more than the death itself: "if I could have had the privilege of being with her in her sickness & have felt her loss, it would have been a great satisfaction. . . ."[55] Apparently, normal relations had to degenerate to outright sourness before any contrary mood received expression. A rare instance appears in the diary kept by the wife of a small Virginia slaveowner. Driven to her emotional and physical limits by sickness and death among her children, and suffering the endless vexation of directing four or five slave women, Pauline Stratton found it not within her resources to react properly when her mother-in-law took to the deathbed. Relations between the two had long been bad, and now, when Pauline made soup for the apparently dying woman, her effort and thoughtfulness brought only complaint. Much given to self-recrimination, Pauline assumed yet another emotional burden by becoming "so hardhearted that I felt. . . . I did not want to see her die. . . ."[56] Much rancor must have been needed to make her willing to forego that "privilege." Positive and fully enunciated expression of the theme came from a New England woman Lizzie Robbins while she ministered endlessly to her dying husband. Though the expiring man was a "great sufferer," Lizzie felt the toll, and now she slipped into a reference to her "task." The correction and clarification came immediately: " 'task,' *indeed it is not*"; it is "not only my duty but my great privilege."[57]

The acme of privilege came in witnessing a "triumphant" death. In the abstract one encounters the contention that "holy dying" represented the logical finality of "holy living." Moved by a Northeast Pennsylvania revival to contemplate general matters, visitor Horatio Chandler of New Hampshire put it this way: "The last act, on earth, of our gratitude to our deer

[54] *The Gilded Age,* 1:109–11.

[55] Elizabeth and James Olin to Alfonso R. Peck, July 28, 1850, Peck Family Papers (Collection of Regional History, Cornell University).

[56] Pauline H. Stratton Diary, Jan. 12, 1855 (Western Historical Manuscripts Collection, University of Missouri, Columbia).

[57] Lizzie Robbins to Julia Pelton, Sept. 8, 1858, Oliver Pelton Correspondence (Connecticut State Library).

Redeemer, to set the example of *holy dying,* as well as *holy living;* surely in proportion do we glorify God; & do a real blessing to those around us. May we be prepared to say with the martyrs,—'Welcome death.' "[58] This restatement of Jeremy Taylor's *Holy Living and Dying* seems an unimpeachable expression of Christian mood; but people employed it in comprehensive rather than specific or existential context. "Holy" dying adumbrated more than unpretentious folk were wont to hazard. What was "holy" in the abstract became "triumphant" or "happy" in the concrete.

Of course there were many gradations between a "very stupid" death and one that was "triumphant." And it is well to recognize that, in letters particularly and in diaries to a lesser degree, motivation toward prevarication or omission occasionally obtained. But humble people probably had full preparation for accepting the fact that, in death as in life, high hopes came reluctantly to realization. Writing back to Connecticut in regard to a grandmother's death, an Ohio man noted the "pleasing evidence of her interest in the L. Jesus Christ. This is all we could have expected & nearly all we could have wished. We should indeed have been glad if her departure had been of the more extatic and triumphant cast. . . ."[59]

That "extatic and triumphant cast" came as the final intensification of the knowing acquiescence in God's will. Grief, fatigue, pain and spiritual awe supplied the context for ecstasy, that last emotional balm acting in double sense as transportation—the easing of the living past a profoundly unnerving moment, and the easing of the departing from time to eternity.

Late in 1838 John and Rachel Ricketts of Franklin County, Indiana, conveyed to a brother the details of the mother's death. With the letter went a lock of her hair, "some of the grave clothese," and the uging to "till all the purtikler about the death of our Old Mother." Surely, in this case, the "purtikler" were worth relating: "I feel gratified to inform you that she left the wourld in the triumfs of faith, in her dying moments Jesse and myself Sung a Cupple of favorite hyms and She Slapt her hands and shouted give glory to god and retained her senses while she had breath which gave us all a great deel of Satisfaction to See her happy. Such a great witness that she went happy out of the wourld."[60] "Happy" pertained particularly to things religious. It indicated spiritual transportation, in this case the salving ecstasy that allowed at least the Pyrrhic victory over death itself. For simple people accomplishments and victories came infrequently, and probably were prized the more when they did. Everyone, not just movers and shakers,

[58] Horatio N. Chandler Account Book, Jan. 15, 1841 (New Hampshire Historical Society). This item is both diary and account book.

[59] C. S. Boardman to Homer Boardman, Oct. 9, 1839, Lyman Stuart Papers.

[60] John and Rachel Ricketts to brother, Dec. 23, 1838 (Kentucky Historical Society).

was provided the chance for a final, illimitable conquest. "And to yield the ghost proudly," Melville mused, "and march out of your fortress with all the honors of war is not a thing of sinew and bone."[61] The weakest and lowest could do that. They could draw the fangs of the "grim monster" it-self, the witnessing of which "triumphant" spectacle was a "privilege" indeed.

Happiness and triumph involved foremost the intimation of a Christian hereafter. And it can hardly be doubted that this was the most compelling source of interest in the deathbed. Surely the scene of dying came under close scrutiny for earnests of felicitous immortality. However, undeniable as that may be, a striking thing about the deathly reflections is the almost total absence of explicit references to otherworldly rewards or even to the assurance that, whatever they were, a particular person would enjoy them. To be sure, people died "happy" in a prospect, or in the "triumph" of the faith, or with the consolation of a Christian hope. But these people, like Gray's paradigm, possessed only "trembling hope." However fraught with otherworldly implications and intimations, deathbed writings resolutely maintained a general, vague and allusive quality where the most profound matter was concerned. Even when a striking portent occurred, common people retained a caution in delving and construing. For example, when a Missouri man had been laid out in a back room, a dove lit in an open win-dowsill near where his body lay. That bird betokened things ultimate. "Pore John," a sister wrote, "could not talk to nun of us if he could he would have told us he was agowing home whare christians are at rest." But this letter stopped well short of heavenly visions; indeed it has an abrupt shift to im-mediacy and reality. Whatever "pore John's" immortal destiny, "that dove came to console us." In a world where "i have nothing to write to you but greaf and trouble" no more could be asked of the delicate harbinger on the windowsill. People with intense awareness of "the trouble in this world for humane beaings to gow through"[62] left eternal projections and certainties to those purporting to have greater discernment.

When 24-year-old Halbert Stryker of Brownstown, Indiana, lay mo-ments from eternity he informed his parents that "he was goeing to Jesus and Exhorted us all to try to meet him in haven." A burst of illumination allowed the dying man to say that the path "from Earth to Haven looked clear to him."[63] Characteristically, the path, not the destination became manifest. Heavenly imagery entered humble writings almost not at all.

[61]*Mardi: and a Voyage Thither,* chap. 9.
[62]Sarah Hayter and Elizabeth Coleman to C. J. Hayter, Oct. 9, 1844, Coleman-Hayter Letters, 1840–1900.
[63]Aaron and Eliza Stryker to David Ireland, Sept. 7, 1859, James Ireland Family Correspondence (Indiana Historical Society).

Instead, the imagery regarding death and departure had a more prosaic, more immediate, less contestable and less sublime quality. It centered far more on what was to be escaped than on what was to be realized. Whatever "trembling hope" of heaven may have informed their deepest longings, these people spoke more often of death as a release from whatever had plagued them. Of course that human circumstance to which they sought an end took a myriad of forms. In 1848 the Thompsons of Mt. Meigs, Alabama, seem to have fallen on evil days. John killed his uncle Solomon; and Nancy, having been "to frindly" with someone, appeared to be in a "family way." In the midst of such unfoldings, Mary, another member of the family, took mortally ill and professed to be quite ready to go. "All she wanted," a neighbor wrote of her death, "was ease." With "the Devil . . . turned loose amongst the Thompsons," Mary may have felt the quite ample attraction of unadorned withdrawal.[64] In another letter which, like so many, gave generous reason for the sufficiency of the limited vision, an Indiana man told simply of a newly married person who had been "cald to try the realities of a better world."[65]

Only in an occasional instance regarding children did such people conjure any specific, rapturous images of the condition beyond the gates. Perhaps mankind has ever been quicker to conceive a heaven for children. In the spring of 1852 Charles Riddick of Yalobusha County, Mississippi, received the particulars regarding the death of a woman named Ginnie. Twelve months earlier she had lost a child, and now, following the birth of another, she took to her deathbed. The stricken woman was not, she averred, "affread" to die; and near the end she told of hearing children singing, among them her departed little Willie. Ginnie's husband, hoping perhaps to keep her to earth, suggested that she heard children in the yard; but the dying woman perceived what was beyond her spouse. A tear in the letter prevents exact rendering; but evidently Ginnie, with a "sweet smile" on her countenance, gently demurred.[66] As is the case here, about the only specific glimmering of the hereafter involved children, singing children. When Annis Pierce of New York State attempted the previously mentioned comforting of her daughter Emily, she did awkward rhapsody on the departed child's now singing "the song of Moses and the Saints."[67] Typically, about Ginnie who had divined something of the condition of a child who had preceded her,

[64]Elizabeth Baskin to Miss N. J. Baskin, May 21, 1848, William Davis Boaz Papers (Manuscripts Division, Alabama Dept. of Archives and History).

[65]Clark Sanderson to nephew, July 22, 1854, James Ireland Family Correspondence (Indiana Historical Society).

[66]R. E. Riddick to Charles C. Riddick, Mar. 18, 1852, Charles C. Riddick Papers (Southern Historical Collection, University of North Carolina).

[67]Annis Pierce to Caleb and Emily Carr, Nov. 6, 1856, Caleb M. Carr Letters.

the glass now darkened. It was enough for the describer of her death to express the ritual trust that she was now beyond the cares and vexations with which mortality had burdened her. Or, as a Pennsylvania woman put it, there was the hope of a "wresting place . . . whare the wicked shall for ever ceace to trouble us."[68]

Thus, in a general, endlessly stated sentiment, death represented escape from the world's sadness, an end to the "pilgrimage" through spiritual and bodily hostility. In particular application of that, and in metaphor unexcelled in frequency, it meant the passage to that realm "where parting is no more." Years earlier Keziah Herrick and her sister Eunice parted on Lake Seneca's shores. Since then Keziah had neither seen nor heard from her westering sister. Now in 1854 any hope for reunion yet remaining centered on "fairer climes than these where the fears of parting will no more trouble us."[69] Therein resided the fullest tenable hope, the anticipation of an end to earthly separation and, as an Ogdensburg, New York man put it, the place "where monster(death) will part us no more."[70] This involved a qualified, even a negative vision. But for people whose quotient of delight had had severe limitations, it seems to have been heaven enough. The headier divinations of limitless bliss and glory stayed in the condition of unused abstraction, perhaps humbly to be accepted should Providence see fit to bestow.

[68] Ann Woods to Aaron Nevius, Oct. 30, 1843, Orrin F. Smith and Family Papers 1829-1932 (Minnesota Historical Society).

[69] Keziah Herrick to Mary J. Bass, Feb. 10, 1854, Joel Crane and Eunice Fitch Family Correspondence.

[70] Morgan Eastman to Lydia Barnhart, July 25, 1841, Lyman Stuart *Collector.*

HEAVEN OUR HOME: CONSOLATION LITERATURE IN THE NORTHERN UNITED STATES, 1830–1880

ANN DOUGLAS

LYDIA HUNTLEY SIGOURNEY, THE ONCE FAMOUS "SWEET SINGER OF Hartford," in one of her more striking obituary poems, "Twas But a Babe," rhetorically upbraided an unspecified urban male passerby, apparently absorbed in his commercial profit mongering and indifferent to a sad funeral procession wending its way behind a little coffin to the local grave-yard. "Poise Ye, in the rigid scales/ Of calculation, the fond bosom's wealth?" she inquired bitterly. Sigourney's implicit point is that the private rituals of mourning should outweigh the public demands of business, that the claims of home and church. should count for more than the imperatives of the marketplace. Her indignant tone suggests, however, her awareness that, in plain fact, most middle-class competitive American men did not share her priorities. Yet Mrs. Sigourney was hardly alone in her persistent effort to focus the attention of her society on its minors and its outsiders, the innocent children, pure maidens, holy women and sanctified men whose deaths could be seen as exemplars and warnings to a culture which in key ways ignored them.[1] Openly fictionalized and avowedly factual accounts of deathbed scenes and celestial communications crowded the bookstalls in the decades before and after the Civil War. This consolation literature, an important phenomenon in 19th century American culture,[2] incessantly

[1]Mrs. Sigourney's poem has been reprinted in Gail Parker's anthology *The Oven Birds: American Women on Womanhood 1820–1920* (New York: Doubleday, 1972), pp. 59, 60.

[2]I am defining "consolation literature" to include not simply actual mourners' manuals, but also prayer manuals, poetry, hymns, fiction and biographies whose purpose is clearly consola-tory; whose authors, in other words, are writing to reach and comfort those suffering bereave-ment or loss. I have read hundreds of examples of this genre and will cite the most interesting

stressed the importance of dying and the dead: it encouraged elaborate funerary practices, conspicuous methods of burial and commemoration, and microscopic viewings of a much inflated afterlife.

The causes of this literary, and in some part actual, magnification of mourning in America between 1830 and 1880 are complex and elusive. The historian's first instinct is to turn to demography and to consider the possibility of an unusually high death rate in this period. There was of course the Civil War which took a million lives as its toll: massive, even national need for consolation and curiosity about the destination of the departed seem inevitable. Elizabeth Stuart Phelps claimed that she wrote her best-selling novel, *The Gates Ajar* (1868), a fictionalized mourning manual, touched by the grief of the thousands who had lost beloved sons and husbands in the war.[3] Yet the shock imparted by the Civil War merely dramatized and accelerated a trend already well under way. Phelps' own father had felt for years that only his "conception of heaven as a place . . . not unlike this world," an idea key to the appeal of *Gates Ajar,* made living tolerable to him.[4] Furthermore, writers both in England and America had anticipated Elizabeth Phelps' preoccupation with death and the afterlife;[5] and *Gates Ajar* was even more successful in England, which had had no Civil War, than in America.

Again, many cultural historians have assumed or implied that 19th century American children died of more or less natural causes in staggering numbers. In this view, the copious consolation literature, so largely concerned with deceased children, was a sentimental but viable way to cope with a widespread and valid sense of loss and deprivation. Recently, however, scholars have begun to speculate that the mortality rate of the period was not so high as once supposed.[6] Although final results are not in, it is at least uncertain that the death rate for infants had increased from the 18th to the 19th century in the northern United States; it may well have decreased. The outpouring of mourners' manuals needs further explanation. The answer may well lie in contemporary perceptions or misperceptions of demographic data, perceptions shaped by economic and social fac-

---

in the course of this article. Let me state here my awareness of the limitations of trying to get at a cultural phenomenon through its literary expression: of course the expression becomes conventionalized, even formulaic, and begins to conform to readers' literary expectations rather than to their fluctuating "real-life" needs.

[3] *Chapters From A Life* (Boston, 1897), p. 97.

[4] Elizabeth Stuart Phelps, *Austin Phelps: A Memoir* (New York: Scribner, 1891), p. 18.

[5] The most interesting and popular English examples are by William Branks, *Heaven Our Home* (Boston, 1864) and *Life in Heaven* (Boston, 1865). The former went through 60 editions in England. For American examples, see note 54.

[6] I am relying for information here on the unpublished computer-based research of Maris Vinovskis, History Dept., Univ. of Wisconsin.

tors. Northern middle-class families by mid-century were beginning to "plan" their families; women hoped to have three or four children, rather than keep three or four. In a period of increasing prosperity and incipient scientific investigation, expectations were perhaps raised beyond the level of available medical competence.

The historian can approach the problem from a different and non-demographic angle, however. For it is clear that, whatever the actual facts or readings of them may have been, certain groups were particularly active in promoting funerary ritual and literature in the North between 1830 and 1880. Liberal clergymen and devout women were the principal authors of the mourners' manuals, lachrymose verse, obituary fiction and necrophiliac biographies popular at the time, and the characteristic features of such works make the clearest sense when placed in a context of clerical and feminine anxieties and ambitions.

It has long been accepted that, during the course of the 19th century, ministers in the more traditional denominations in the Northern states were struggling with limited success against their diminishing status and weakening authority.[7] In the opinion of many historians, clergymen compelled by disestablishment to turn from a state-supported to a voluntary system magnified and capitalized on the tactics of moral suasion which were their logical means of survival and self-promotion. In this reading, the so-called "Protestant crusades" of the period, for example, were the outgrowth of a clerical and conservative alliance to redefine and regain power. Relatively little attention has been paid, however, to the more covert aspects of the liberal ministry's attempt to exploit the inevitable weakness of its position as a new kind of strength. One can interpret the well recognized softening of Protestant theology especially among Unitarians and Congregationalists at this time as in part a reflection and a rationalization of the less authoritative and less commanding role its clerical formulators were forced to assume among their contemporaries. On a broader front, the non-evangelical sects promoted, if not altogether consciously, the sentimentalization of Northern culture as a way to make the "Christian" values—passivity, meekness, gentleness, reverence for the past and for the weak—consigned to them by a busily industrializing and expanding nation dominant at least in theory and in literature.

[7]Among Northern Protestant non-evangelical sects, I have focused particularly on the Congregationalists and Unitarians: their ministers seem to have been more vulnerable to loss of status than the clergy of the Episcopal or Presbyterian denominations, the other major non-evangelical groups. The Episcopalians had a complex ritual to sustain their identity; the Presbyterians, a powerful and semi-hierarchical system of church organization. The Unitarians, and the Congregationalists from whom they derived, had neither, although they were at various times attracted to both. The evangelical sects, most importantly the Baptists and Methodists, of course had the techniques of full-blown revivalism, sometimes allowed but always controversial in the non-evangelical sects, at their disposal.

Liberal ministers propagated their changed theology not only in person but, often more effectively, in print. They edited religious and secular periodicals; they published sermons, tracts, poetry, even fiction. There is no better way of measuring the radical shift in the relationship between the minister and his culture in the period from the Great Awakening to the Civil War than to note how many prominent ministers over its course turned to *belles lettres* as a means of self-expression and communication. At the turn of the 19th century, Nathaniel Emmons, a stern follower of the great New Light theologian Samuel Hopkins, returned a novel by Sir Walter Scott lent him by a friend with protestations of genuine horror.[8] Yet a scant 50 years later, not simply notorious lightweights like Henry Ward Beecher, but sedate and serious Unitarians like the Ware brothers and more or less orthodox professors of theology like Austin Phelps and Bela Edwards, were making secular literature a concern and even an occupation. Literature, with its aptness in substituting feeling for dogma,[9] was an indispensable tool for a group of men who came increasingly to see their avenue to influence in their ability to soothe rather than to discipline and who perforce wanted to persuade the public that emotional nurture was its greatest need.

Part of the problem facing the non-evangelical clergyman settled in the Northeast at mid-century was that his audience was feminine. The members of his church were more and more likely, in his opinion, to be women.[10] Benevolent organizations concerned with temperance, purity, education, pacifism, missions and other religious causes came to play a bigger and bigger part in parish life; and these were largely supported by feminine interest. The very reading public the non-evangelical clergymen wished to reach was principally middle-class, female and by definition attracted to the sentimental fare turned out briskly by successful women writers. To enlist and attain masculine authority, the liberal minister had to assimilate feminine demands and tactics. As a result, he suffered the taint of feminiza-

---

[8]It was characteristic of Emmons to boast, "I never thought of any style; I wrote as I thought"; see Edwards A. Park, *Memoir of Nathaniel Emmons* (Boston, 1861), 1: 296.

[9]The most important ministerial discussions of this process in the period are Horace Bushnell, "Preliminary Dissertation on the Nature of Language as Related to Thought," from *God in Christ* (Hartford, Conn., 1849), repr. in *Horace Bushnell*, ed. H. Shelton Smith (New York: 1965), pp. 69–105; and Edwards A. Park, *The Theology of the Intellect and of the Feelings* (Andover, Mass., 1850). For a discussion of the meaning of Bushnell's theory for contemporary American literature, see Charles Fiedelson Jr., *Symbolism and American Literature* (Chicago: Univ. of Chicago Press, c. 1953), pp. 152–56, 311–15.

[10]There are no reliable figures for sex breakdown of Protestant congregations as yet. My own impression from the few figures I have gathered is that the ratio did not shift dramatically in the 19th century, but that the ministers registered the more active presence of the women. They genuinely believed such a shift in sex proportion had occurred. For a dramatic statement, see Howard Allen Bridgeman, "Have We a Religion for Men?" *Andover Review*, 13 (1890), 388–96.

tion,[11] but he also learned much from the skillful methods of subversion and exploitation which his more prominent middle-class feminine peers had developed in a complicated attempt to improve without overtly revolutionizing their own position.

Liberal clergymen and literate women shared several common preoccupations. With incipient urbanization and the transfer of many industries from the home to the factory during the first half of the 19th century, middle-class New England women were losing their status as productive units in their economy.[12] Not surprisingly, their most articulate members were interested, like the liberal ministers, in exploring the possibilities of "influence," in asserting rather than proving themselves as indispensable to their culture's less material and less apparent needs.[13] Literature was their natural vehicle also. Furthermore, while of course barred from the official ministry, writing women, whether their matter was fiction, tracts, biographies or manuals, were impelled by contemporary opinion toward a religious tone and message as consonant with their special feminine nature.[14] Paradoxically, clerical views of women's role pushed women onto clerical terrain as colleagues and competitors.[15] Both groups used the same setting to display their virtues: ladies and ministers tended to meet in theory if not in practice in the home; both, at least in part, identified themselves in

[11]I base this remark on a study of approximately a hundred ministerial biographies and of the changing terminology used to describe non-evangelical clergymen in William Sprague's monumental compilation of contemporary accounts of American ministers over two and a half centuries, *Annals of the American Pulpit*, 9 vols. (New York: Carter, 1857–69). Adjectives connotating "feminine" are increasingly used (in praise) of 19th century non-evangelical clergymen.

[12]For the most perceptive contemporary statement about this process, see Horace Bushnell, "The Age of Homespun," in *Litchfield County Centennial Celebration* (Hartford, 1851). For more recent studies, see Alice Clark, *Working Life of Women in the Seventeenth Century* (New York: Harcourt, 1920); Gerda Lerner, "The Lady and the Mill Girl: Changes in the Status of Women in the Age of Jackson," *Mid-continent American Studies Journal*, 10 (1969), 7, 8; Mary Ryan, "American Society and the Cult of Domesticity, 1830–1860," Diss. University of California at Santa Barbara 1971; and Kathryn Kish Sklar, *Catharine Beecher: A Study in American Domesticity* (New Haven: Yale Univ. Press, 1973).

[13]For the doctrine of "influence," the single most valuable source is *The Ladies' Magazine*, 1828–36, edited by Sarah J. Hale who was to edit *Godey's Lady's Book*. See also Glenda Gates Riley, "The Subtle Subversion: Changes in the Traditionalist Image of the American Woman," *Historian*, 32 (1969–70), 210–27.

[14]For several classic statements of the clerical position, see "The Pastoral Letter" of 1837 provoked by early feminist activity, included in Aileen Kraditor, ed., *Up From the Pedestal: Selected Writings in the History of American Feminism* (Chicago: Quadrangle, 1968), pp. 50–52; and Horace Bushnell, *Woman's Suffrage: The Reform Against Nature* (New York: Scribner, 1869).

[15]Many ministers expressed their often uneasy awareness that women writers were competing successfully with pulpit utterance. See in particular William Ellery Channing's view that "woman, if she may not speak in the church, may speak in the printing room, and her touching expositions of religion . . . sometimes make their way to the heart more surely than the minister's homilies," *Works* (Boston: J. Munroe, 1843), 2: 280.

parental roles. Women were assigned to familial and hearthside duty by popular mythology heavily backed by Christian precept;[16] non-evangelical clergymen were more and more consigned to a pastoral rather than an ecclesiastical part, to the private rather than the public sphere. It is no accident that a large percentage of the domestic and etiquette manuals poured out in such profusion in the first half of the century came from the hands of ministers. Nor is it accidental that ministerial biography was an art increasingly taken over in the same period by women, and by women who concentrated on the personal lives of their subjects.[17] Neither group had the strength or consequently the inclination to repudiate the domestic arena as unworthy of their talents. Their largely unconscious strategy was to exalt home tasks and values and to depict a nation in crying want of domestication.[18] Officially at least they accepted the home as their world, but they were understandably very concerned to define this world and even the next, as a home.

One of the family dramas which ministers and women picked as a favorite was that of death; and here we return to the consolation literature in whose production and shaping both groups were so influential. Tellingly, death in this literature was scaled to almost exclusively domestic proportions. Where an earlier author like Jeremy Taylor, who wrote the perennially popular *Holy Dying* (1651), intended his work for the Christian seeking general devotional and doctrinal instruction, the authors of the 19th century American death manuals directed their books toward the actually and recently bereaved parent, husband or wife seeking reassurance. Private, particular grief, in other words, was their declared starting point and *raison d'être*. Moreover, such writers usually chose to commemorate the lives, last words and funeral rites of women and clergymen like themselves, seldom participators in the competitive world, and of small children who perforce had never left the nest. Finally, their attention was increasingly drawn, and in novel ways, to the world to which the dead gained admission. Unlike previous religious thinkers in America and abroad, they were not concerned exclusively or even predominantly with the kind of life a believer must pursue on earth to attain heaven. They focused rather on the accessibility of the ce-

[16]See Ryan, "American Society and the Cult of Domesticity"; Barbara Welter, "The Cult of True Womanhood 1820–1860," *American Quarterly,* 18 (1966), 151–74; Ann Douglas Wood, "The 'Scribbling Women' and Fanny Fern: Why Women Wrote," *American Quarterly,* 23 (1971), 3–24.

[17]The most interesting of these are *The Life and Letters of Horace Bushnell* (New York, c. 1880) by his daughter Mary Bushnell Cheney; the *Memoir* of Charles Follen in his *Works* (Boston: Munroe, 1842), vol. 1 by his wife Eliza Follen; *Life and Character of the Reverend Sylvester Judd* (Boston: Crosby, 1854) by his cousin Arethusa Hall; and *Austin Phelps: A Memoir* (New York, 1891) by his daughter Elizabeth Stuart Phelps.

[18]See Sklar, *Catharine Beecher,* passim; Ann Douglas Wood, "The War Within a War: Women Nurses in the Union Army," *Civil War History,* 18 (1972), 197–212.

lestial kingdom to earthly intelligence and the similarities between the two worlds which made communication possible. They depicted and emphasized heaven as a continuation and a glorification of the domestic sphere. The celestial regions and their occupants were to pay, in other words, an intricate compliment to themselves.

To suggest that problems of professional class or sexual status played a part in the creation and character of an important literary phenomenon of 19th century America is not, I hope, to suggest a conspiracy view of history in any pejorative sense. The authors of the consolation literature were intent on claiming death as their peculiar property, one conferring on them a special professional mission and prerogative: necessarily they wished to inflate and complicate its importance. To say this is to imply that they were rightly insecure about their position, that they sought to gain indirect and compensatory social control, and even that they and their readers were in part debased by their effort; it is not to imply that they were insincere, ill-intentioned or simple-minded. It must be remembered how these people saw themselves, and with what good reason: they were in the main genuine and sincere Christians reinterpreting their faith as best they could in terms of the needs of their culture. Sentimental as much of their output is in modern eyes, it indisputably served a valid function for those who read it as well as for those who produced it. Historians, inevitably finding various groups clearly motivated by forms of self-interest, occasionally tend to act as if they have detected hypocrites or villains, forgetful perhaps that self-interest, like class and status, is as pervasive and as complex as identity itself.[19]

Elizabeth Prentiss, daughter of one minister and married to another, was herself a successful leader of various prayer and Bible classes. A popular religious author, she produced her best-seller in *Stepping Heavenward* (1869), a classic of 19th century consolation literature. She once gave an interesting and revealing definition of the function of "a pastor's wife": "to feel the *right* to sympathize with those who mourn, to fly to them at once, and join them in their prayers and tears." She goes on: "It would be pleasant to spend one's whole time among sufferers, and to keep testifying to them what Christ can and will become to them, if they will only let him."[20] One can not help suspecting that Christ's was not the only power apparent at such moments. To up-play the psychological and spiritual crisis of a be-

---

[19]For a somewhat different viewpoint on this issue, see Henri Lefebvre, *Everyday Life in the Modern World,* trans. Sacha Rabinovitch (New York, 1971), pp. 41–42.

[20]George L. Prentiss, *The Life and Letters of Elizabeth Prentiss* (New York: Randolf, 1882), p. 295. E. Prentiss' father was the famous evangelist preacher Edward Payson of Portland, Me.

reaved parent was both to spotlight the mother, confined in any case to a world of domestic joys and sorrows, and to summon the minister—or his wife, increasingly a hearthside authority. Furthermore, the mourner was susceptible to feminine and ministerial authority. At least temporarily, he turned his attention from the competitive world where such authority had little force to the spiritual sphere where it was presumably most relevant and trustworthy.

The ordeal of the Christian survivor forced to realize that he has "idolized" a loved one taken from him by a chastening God was a traditional one in New England religious writing. The 17th and 18th centuries, however, had no real cult of mourning literature. The griever was seen as culpable, if human. His condition was hardly considered one of particular fascination in the same way, for example, that the state of a sinner on the eve of "conviction" might be. Thomas Shepard, a prominent 17th century divine, devoted only an eloquent page and a half to the loss of his adored wife, and he concluded his account with a characteristic stroke of partial self-condemnation: "Thus god hath visited & scourged me for my sins & sought to weene me from this woorld, but I have ever found it a difficult thing to profit even but a little by the sorest & sharpest afflictions."[21]

In sharp contrast, the bereaved 19th century authors of tributes like *The Empty Crib: The Memorial of Little Georgie* (1873) and *Agnes and the Key of Her Little Coffin* (1837), frankly assumed, and apparently got, the engrossed attention of significant portions of their society in their emotional and moral welfare. The Reverend Theodore Cuyler, the prominent New York clergyman who wrote *The Empty Crib,* received thousands of more than sympathetic letters from kindred mourners. Cuyler added some of these epistles in later editions of *The Empty Crib.* I will quote from one to give the flavor of all:

> My dear Sir,—If it ever falls in your way to visit Allegheny Cemetery, you will see there "a flower" on *three* "little graves." "*Anna,* aged 7 yrs; *Sadie,* aged 5 yrs; *Lillie,* aged 3 yrs;" all died within six days, and all of scarlet fever! ["Georgie" died of scarlet fever also.] It sometimes may reconcile us to our own affliction to hear of one still greater elsewhere; and this is the reason why I, a perfect stranger, venture to trespass upon you in your sore bereavement, and to tell you of my heartfelt sympathy.[22]

The Reverend Nehemiah Adams, a New England minister, wrote a fascinatingly unabashed account of the protracted and all-absorbing grief he and his

---

[21]Perry Miller and Thomas H. Johnson, eds., *The Puritans* (New York: Harper & Row, c. 1963), 2: 475.

[22]Cuyler, *The Empty Crib* (New York, 1873), pp. 81–82. Cuyler produced two other very popular mourning manuals, *Beulah Land: or Words of Cheer for Christian Pilgrims* (New York, c. 1896), and *God's Light on Dark Clouds* (New York, c. 1882).

wife experienced over the death of their daughter, Agnes. By Adams' confession, the couple spent large portions of time at Agnes' grave and with other similarly afflicted parents talking about the merits of the departed and the possibilities of heavenly reunions.

There is no escaping the sense that grief is not being used here as discipline, in the way Shepard used it, but as therapeutic self-indulgence. Mourning is still intended clearly to foster spiritual development, but a curious kind of exhibitionism seems to be doing the work formerly expected of the rituals of self-scrutiny. Here as everywhere in the consolation literature we find a slight but crucial transformation of that essential Christian precept, "the last shall be first." The losers shall be the winners, if not of the world's goods and positions, at least of its concern. The mourner figure even if neither a minister or a mother is, through the experience of powerlessness grieving entails, a possible stand-in for them. As such, the attention he is so lavishly granted by his authors compensates him for more losses perhaps than he has consciously suffered.

This is not to imply that the deceased always take second place to their survivors in these annals of grief. Indeed, it is usually the dying or dead child who is the most conspicuous exemplar of the new turn to the old prophecy, "the last shall be first." "Agnes" and "Georgie" were supposedly guides to their adult supervisors in ways that must have been both suggestive and flattering to their maternal and ministerial biographers, many of whom knew well what it was like to be treated, even to function, as children in a world of unheeding adults. Furthermore, these small saints usually chose their mother or their minister as their model. Little James, an early deceased son of the Universalist minister Sylvester Cobb, was memorialized by his mother Eunice Hale Cobb in 1852. According to her account, he was a clergyman in embryo. As a very young child, he disliked "to mingle with the boys [at school], so as to hear their profane and vulgar language." He advised "respect of the aged" and once rebuked a man who referred to his father as "the old gentleman." He loved the Bible, took communion at age seven, and was wont to argue with fellow passengers on boats and trains against the use of tobacco. But if he emulated his ministerial father, he adored his mother. During his last sickness, he expressed his wish to her that "we could die with our arms around each other's neck."[23] Only she, he implied, was worthy to approach the confines of the heavenly kingdom with him. The dying infant was made supremely to flatter his feminine and clerical biographers: he shared their weakness while he dignified and extended their authority.

The death scene had too much crucial psychological and sociological

[23]*Memoir of James Arthur Cobb* (Boston, 1852), pp. 24, 30, 111.

potential for the minister and his feminine counterpart to be left to children, however, even to children who operated in a sense as their proxies. Many of the "memorials" of the day devoted to the lives of pious women and clergymen were consolation literature in very thin disguise. They revealed as much of the art of the mortician or the gravestone cutter as the craft of the biographer. From their opening pages, the reader is repeatedly reminded that their subjects are going to die, perhaps young, and certainly well. No example is more striking than the biography of the Reverend William Peabody written shortly after his death in 1849 by his brother Oliver.

Peabody was a fervent Christian, an opponent of "controversial divinity,"[24] a defender of the Sabbath and a pioneer in the cemetery and Sabbath School movements. A literary man of real if minor talent who contributed to the *Christian Examiner,* the *North American Review* and *The Token,* he published rather gentle pieces on autumn and death. His best poem began with characteristic melancholy: "Behold the western evening light!/ It melts in deepening gloom;/ So calmly Christians sink away/ Descending to the tomb."[25] He was a clear candidate for a special sentimentalized kind of martyrdom, and his biography is an exercise in necrophilia. From the start, his brother depicts him as one too good to live, the kind of pale, serious, sickly, pious little child that wise old women were always clucking prophetically over in the domestic novels of the day. He survived to marry an extremely devout woman whose resolve to give "all the powers of . . . [her] soul to a private intercourse with God" had an immense impact on her husband. When she died at an early age in 1843, he told himself that she had been called first so that he might learn through sorrow to be more worthy of her. Cherishing his grief, he liked to sit by moonlight near her grave. His links with this life were further attenuated when his eldest daughter died suddenly only four months after his wife.

At this point in the Peabody biography an extraordinary thing happens. A new and anonymous writer explains, "the pen fell from the hands" of Oliver Peabody just, symbolically, as he approached his brother's moving deathbed scene. Oliver, a consumptive, originally a lawyer but unsuited to enforced contact with a quarreling and litigious world, became a minister in his last few years. He apparently felt in writing his brother's story "as if he were carving the letters on his own gravestone." The second biographer survives his task, describes William's saintly and gentle death and includes a memoir of Oliver for good measure.

The special quality of a biography like this is in the rather sepulchral

[24]*Sermons by the Late William B. O. Peabody with a Memoir by His Brother* (Boston, 1849), p. xxv.
[25]Rufus Wilmot Griswold, ed., *The Poets and Poetry of America* (New York: Miller, 1872), p. 266.

sense it gives the reader that she is listening to a posthumous voice. During William Peabody's last months, he seemed to his loving congregation to be increasingly "standing on the confines of the eternal world, as one ready to be offered; permitted just before entering its gate to point out to those he loved, with the failing accents of a dying voice, the way to reach its blessedness."[26] Death is anticipated and lingered over precisely because it lends significance, even authority, to its victim. Once again, the "last" is "first"; paradoxically, the dead live.

Young women were especially popular subjects, both in biography and fiction, for the necrophiliac drama.[27] Mary Clemmer Ames' account of the poetical Cary sisters, Phoebe and Alice, or George Prentiss' tribute to his wife Elizabeth, are as thoroughly morbid by modern standards as the Peabody memorial. And one remembers little Eva's doomed fragility and her generous deathbed disposal of locks of hair in Mrs. Stowe's *Uncle Tom's Cabin*. Mrs. Sigourney of Hartford, however, was the undisputed mistress of feminine mourning literature. Any corpse was fair game for her verse; she ranged so far afield as to commemorate the long-deceased Venerable Bede; she came so close to home as to fantasize her own demise. In fascinating ways, she played daringly on the enticing boundaries between life and death where the Peabody brothers apparently lingered. Mrs. Sigourney's last recorded words were the benignly all-inclusive ones, "I love everybody." This is surely a commonplace if over effusive deathbed platitude, but one feels a little shiver when one remembers that a few decades before, Mrs. Sigourney had published a sentimentalized biographical sketch entitled *Margaret and Henrietta: Two Lovely Sisters* (1832). According to her account, Margaret had died with the same phrase on her lips. Could Mrs. Sigourney have mentally noted the appeal of such a last line, stored it up, and finally reenacted a deathbed scene which she had in part invented?[28]

Long before she uttered her last words, Mrs. Sigourney was prone to plagiarize from the dead. Before her marriage in her late twenties she had been a distinguished schoolteacher in Hartford. At the first reunion she held for her former pupils she spoke of, and for, the girls who had already passed away. Moreover, although presumably in her usual plump and ruddy good health, she urged her listeners to go on meeting annually even if "the voice that now addresses you should be silent, the lip that has uttered prayers for your welfare should be sealed in the dust of death." In 1823 she told her

---

[26]*Sermons,* pp. xlvii, xc, lxxiv.

[27]Striking evidence of this sexual preference is seen in R. C. Waterston's *Thoughts on Moral and Spiritual Culture* (Boston: Crosby and Nichols, 1842). He opens his book with a description of a child being born: it is a boy. He closes with an account of dying children: they are all girls.

[28]Mrs. L. H. Sigourney, *Letter of Life* (New York: Appleton, 1867), p. 408.

hearers that since they last met, she had been sick "(at least in thought) on the confines of the abode of spirits," and had brought back solemn words of wisdom.[29] Mrs. Sigourney had become her own medium.

The Fox sisters did not begin their table rappings in upstate New York until 1848, but Mrs. Sigourney had in several senses anticipated them.[30] She was straining for the authority conferred on the Peabodys, the power granted by the privilege of extraterrestrial communication. Several of the little saints whose early deaths drew so many sympathetic tears showed extrasensory abilities similar to Mrs. Sigourney's. It was not just a matter of the conventional little finger pointing upward, the smile on the once rosy lips, the last gasped "Mother" or "Jesus." A dying child like James Cobb enjoyed extended communications with the spirit world: he watched angels dancing in anticipation of his speedy arrival, saw various deceased members of his own family and relayed their messages back to the living. He was quite literally a medium, and after his death he continued to appear to his relatives. Death, province of minister and mother, instead of marking the end of power, had become its source. Spiritualism in its most generalized and most specific sense, was a manifestation of a complex retransfer of force from the living to the dead, from the apparently strong to the apparently weak.

It was absolutely essential to this process that the deceased not truly die. The planned and picturesque new "rural cemeteries," promoted and rapturously described by the same groups who produced the consolation literature of the period, were dedicated to the idea that the living, and the dead, still "cared." Paths with pastoral names, gentle rills, green slopes and newly popular graveside flowers[31] were all meant to flatter the guaranteed but enduring docility of the deceased. Developing funeral customs reflected the same carefully fostered illusions.[32] Elaborate and highly differentiated metal caskets replaced wooden ones in the early 19th century, although many protested their use. The metal casket, unlike its predecessor, insured that neither it nor its contents would disintegrate or return to the earth for a

[29]"A Record of My School," unpublished MS in Sigourney Collection, Connecticut Historical Society.

[30]I am basing my interpretation of Spiritualism on work in progress by R. Lawrence Moore of Cornell University, "The Profession of the Medium and Nineteenth Century American Women" (unpublished paper).

[31]On flowers, see Jessica Mitford, *The American Way of Death* (New York: Simon & Schuster, 1963), pp. 198–99. The new graveyards were modeled on the ideas of the "picturesque" propagated by architect Andrew Jackson Downing. See Neil Harris, *The Artist in American Society: The Formative Years 1790–1860* (New York, 1966), pp. 208–15; George B. Tatum, "The Beautiful and the Picturesque," *American Quarterly*, 3 (1951), 36–51.

[32]The publications of the directors of the funeral homes which appeared in the decades after the Civil War provided an unconscious parody of the earlier consolation literature. See Mitford, *American Way of Death*, p. 222.

frighteningly long time.[33] Such changes were pushed and applauded by the authors of mourners' manuals. Nehemiah Adams began his account of *Agnes and the Key of Her Little Coffin* by explaining that there had been a great improvement in the design of children's coffins. They no longer had "broken lines and angles. . . . They look like other things, and not like that which looks like nothing else, a coffin." He added maladroitly, "You would be willing to have such a shape for the depositing of any household article." There was apparently a soft lining and a nameplate inside the box, and a "lock and key" had replaced the old "remorseless screws and screw-drivers."[34]

The sensibility of the consolation literature manifested itself in the new cemeteries in other ways as well. The simple and severe tombstones of 17th century America with their stark reminders of death, a cross or a death's-head or an hourglass, gave way in the late 18th century to new anthropomorphic designs. Actual if crude portraits of the deceased appeared, willow trees and allegorical pictures of the resurrection were all in evidence by 1800.[35] By the 1840s statues of what one popular graveyard guidebook calls "weeping female figures"[36] marked various family plots in Mt. Auburn: Mrs. Sigourney had been immortalized and mass-produced in marble. Euphuistic sepulchral inscriptions like "asleep in Jesus," a favorite for children's graves, poetically stressed the continuing presence of the deceased.[37] This was the spirit and the language of the consolation literature. The Reverend Mr. Cuyler, passing an afternoon at New York's Greenwood cemetery near the grave of his son "little Georgie," bid his son a by-no-means-final adieu in a similar mode: "The air was as silent as the un-numbered sleepers around me; and turning toward the sacred spot where my precious dead was lying, I bade him, as of old, '*Goodnight!*'" Greenwood was to him "simply a vast and exquisitely beautiful dormitory."[38]

Cuyler's choice of terminology is important here. It was typical of the authors of consolatory literature to refer to the rural cemeteries, of which Greenwood was one of the most famous, in domestic terms. Their origina-tors and supporters had designed them to fulfill the same kind of sanctuary function the home was traditionally supposed to serve. To begin with, the new rural cemeteries were, in accordance with their name and in contrast to

[33]Ibid., pp. 196–97.

[34]Nehemiah D. D. Adams, *Agnes and the Key of Her Little Coffin By Her Father* (Boston: Whipple, 1857), p. 15.

[35]Harriette Merrifield Forbes, *Gravestones of Early New England and the Men Who Made Them 1653–1800* (Boston: Houghton Mifflin, 1927), pp. 63–67.

[36]Moses King, *Mt. Auburn Cemetery* (Cambridge: the author, 1839), pp. 46–48.

[37]Theodore Cuyler explained that no phrase was as popular for tombstone inscriptions as "Asleep in Jesus"; see *Light on Dark Rivers*, p. 164.

[38]Cuyler, *The Empty Crib*, pp. 158, 173.

the old intramural churchyards they replaced, located on town outskirts, away from urban bustle and noise. Furthermore, their quiet atmosphere was guaranteed and policed. Those responsible for the creation of Mt. Auburn in 1831, for example, laid down careful regulations about the planning and use of its grounds: the trustees of the spot had the right to remove "offensive and improper" monuments; no "vehicles" were allowed but those owned by "proprietors" (owners of plots); no one was allowed within the gates on Sundays and holidays except proprietors.[39] The "influence" of the rural cemetery was to be pre-industrial, uncrowded, privitized. One commentator on "The Law of Burial and the Sentiment of Death" for the *Christian Examiner* in 1836 expressed his belief that the new graveyards could foster "the sentiment of retrospection and reverence" and draw their visitors from "the busy competition" and "hurried . . . ambitious spirit" of the day.[40] The home, in the words of a popular domestic manual by a Rev. Mr. Phillips, was the "heart's moral oasis"; like the cemetery, it was a "refuge" for the "bereaved and disappointed."[41] In several very important senses, Cuyler, in saying that little Georgie is but asleep in a "dormitory," is implying that his son, such an exemplar of domestic virtue, has never left home at all.

Books on spiritualism and the afterlife with titles like *Watching Spirits, Voices from the Silent Land, Angel Whispers* and *Our Children in Heaven* convey the clear impression that death widens rather than limits the ministerial and maternal sphere of influence. These sainted dead hovering around their old haunts, whether women, ministers or pious children eternally firm in the virtues inculcated by their mothers and their pastors, are so many witnesses, even spies, for the church and the home. There seems some kind of compensation process at work here: declare converts among the deceased if you cannot make them among the living. To bring heaven closer to earth was not only to underscore sacerdotal and domestic authority by creating a kingdom to which ministers and women alone had the keys: it was to endow them at once with legions of invincible allies. No wonder that the creators and purveyors of consolation literature increasingly felt, with William Holcombe, the need of "some great spiritual telescope to bring [the dead] . . . near to us in all their beautiful reality," the need of "a clear, consistent, philosophical authorized revelation of the life after death."[42]

[39]See *The Picturesque Pocket Companion and Visitor's Guide Through Mt. Auburn* (Boston, 1839), pp. 3 ff.

[40]*Christian Examiner,* 61 (1836), 338–39.

[41]The Rev. Samuel Phillips, *The Christian Home* (Springfield, Mass., 1860), p. 15.

[42]William Holcombe, *Our Children in Heaven* (Philadelphia: Lippincott, 1870), p. 24. The other books mentioned in this paragraph are Daniel C. Eddy, *Angel Whispers; or, The Echo of Spirit Voices* (New York: Dayton and Wentworth, 1855); Mrs. Ellet, *Watching Spirits* (New

Consolation literature of all forms between 1830 and 1880 became ever more preoccupied not just with the last scenes and earthly resting places of the dead but with their celestial destination and doings. This was a great period in American hymnology: countless Americans sang hymns at home and in church, and serious theologians began to rank the importance of hymns with that of sermons, a view which previous religious thinkers would have deemed highly heretical.[43] The most popular hymns of the day were written by liberal clergymen and devout women authors; they were essentially consolatory rather than monitory, and their favorite theme was increasingly what Fanny Crosby, the blind poetess, eulogized as the "home beyond the skies."[44] Prayer manuals, another important part of the contemporary consolation literature, emphasized more and more the availability of the other world to the earnest supplicant. Austin Phelps, who published *The Still Hour: or Communion With God* in 1860, explained with the curious literalism characteristic of such manuals, "an astronomer does not turn his telescope to the skies with a more reasonable hope of penetrating those distant heavens than I have of reaching the mind of God by lifting up my heart at the Throne of Grace."[45]

Phelps' analogy suggests the pseudoscientific spirit of assurance which the writers of consolation literature brought to the subject of heaven. Somewhat as we might follow on television the lunar expeditions of our modern astronauts, mid-19th century Americans mourning their dead were encouraged to follow their journey to heaven in minutest detail; to inquire what they ate for breakfast (if they did), who they met, how they lived. The consolatory books on the afterlife increasingly promised them that such facts were part of available knowledge. Heaven, as they depicted it, was not only similar to home but as readily accessible. In the 1880s, Elizabeth Stuart Phelps, carrying her father's metaphor to its logical extreme, produced two novels, *Beyond the Gates* and *Between the Gates*, which set forth the eating habits, occupations, lifestyles, methods of child care and courtship current in heaven. She even described with some care an oration

---

York: Scribner, 1851); Mrs. H. Dwight Williams, *Voices from the Silent Land; or Leaves of Consolation for the Afflicted* (Boston, 1853).

[43]For the development of American hymnology and its context, see Louis F. Benson, *The English Hymn: Its Development and Use in Worship* (Philadelphia: Doran 1915), and *The Hymnology of the Christian Church* (Richmond, Va., 1927); Henry Wilder Foote, *Three Centuries of American Hymnology* (Cambridge: Harvard University Press, 1940); Edward S. Ninde, *The Story of the American Hymn* (New York: Abingdon, 1921); H. W. Stephenson, *Unitarian Hymn Writers* (London, 1931). For the new serious evaluation of hymns, see Austin Phelps, Edwards A. Park and Daniel L. Furber, *Hymns and Choirs* (Andover, Mass.: W. F. Draper, 1860).

[44]Quoted in Ninde, *Story of the American Hymn*, p. 247.

[45]*The Still Hour* (Boston, 1860), 43. Elizabeth Prentiss felt the same confidence; see George Prentiss, *Life and Letters of Elizabeth Prentiss*, p. 60.

Beethoven had just composed for a celestial audience. The only inquiry she could not answer was the natural one "touching the means" by which her deceased narrator, a male physician, was "enabled to give this record to the living earth." That is the only "secret" which, as she says in the last line of *Between the Gates,* she decides to let "remain such."[46]

The debate over the afterlife, to which the consolation literature made such an interesting contribution, had a complex history in American and European thought. Medieval Christians had shown an intense interest in the next world, an interest which created a special popular and long-enduring literary genre, the monastic vision. Yet built within this tradition was the notion that heaven itself was finally forbidden to human eyes. During and after the Reformation, Christian thinkers and believers showed an increasing preoccupation with the doctrine of the millennium, itself once ruled as heretical by St. Augustine.[47] Millennial speculation was particularly intense in America: many could not help associating the birth of this new nation with more general and religious possibilities of regeneration.

Before the Civil War, American Christians tended to be millenarians, although they split into two deeply opposed camps: premillenarians, usually members of the less educated and more evangelical sects, who believed that Christ would himself come to earth suddenly, even unexpectedly, at the start of the millennium to supervise its unfolding; postmillenarians who held that Christ would not appear until the end of the thousand-year period, leaving men to guess and execute his wishes in a more gradual and less dramatic fashion. The former group habitually, and accurately, accused the latter of an Arminian reliance on mortal powers, and even a glorification of them. Significantly, postmillennial views had won an easy victory in the North by the Civil War, a victory for gradualism so complete that the millennium itself largely ceased, at least in non-evangelical circles, to be an issue at all. Yet the differences between pre- and postmillenarians were not as great as they seemed. Both groups had increasingly confused the millennial period with the heavenly afterlife, and in doing so had sacrificed the Augustinian and Puritan stress on the importance of the Last Judgment and the commanding role an autocratic and even alien deity played in it.[48] Furthermore, both groups increasingly shared a conviction that this earth,

---

[46]*Between the Gates* (Boston, 1887), p. 223.

[47]For general discussion of the developing ideas of heaven and the millennium see James P. Martin, *The Last Judgment in Protestant Theology from Orthodoxy to Ritschl* (Grand Rapids, Mich.: Eerdmans, c. 1963); Ulrich Simon, *Heaven in the Christian Tradition* (New York, 1958); Ernest Lee Tuveson, *Millennium and Utopia: A Study in the Background of the Idea of Progress* (Berkeley: Univ. of California Press, 1949).

[48]See Martin, pp. xiii, 17–70; H. Richard Niebuhr, *The Kingdom of God in America,* passim; and Simon, pp. 20–37.

purified and transfigured, would be the locus of the millennium.[49] Since millennial and heavenly lives were no longer clearly separated, by implication this meant that this world and the next were more and more closely, if unintentionally, assimilated to one another.

Consequently, the millennial debate became part of a larger discussion over the nature of heaven: kingdom or home? American ministers of the 17th and 18th centuries had given relatively little attention to the subject. When they spoke of the next life, it was hardly in terms to attract the carnal heart. Nathaniel Emmons with his usual habit of calling a spade a spade had remarked in one of his grimmer sermons: "The truth is there is nothing which God requires men to do in this life in order to go to heaven that is harder to be done, than to be willing to be in heaven."[50] Emmons attributed this aversion to men precisely because he looked upon the next world as the Lord's possession, a landscape foreign to mortal eyes, a scene ineffably emblematic of the divine will.

There were men and women to uphold at least a portion of this view in the Northern United States at mid-century, but they were in the clear minority. Especially among non-evangelical groups, the out-and-out supporters of a domestic heaven were dominant: Andrew Peabody, F. W. P. Greenwood, the Wares, Charles Follen, William E. Channing and Austin Phelps, to name just a few, believed that heavenly life satisfied the human heart as presently constituted, that it offered homes restored, families regathered and friends reunited. They would have agreed with Henry Harbaugh, a Lutheran at Mercersberg Seminary who wrote a series of learned but widely read books on heaven in the late 1840s and early 1850s in the belief that

> The piety of the times has too little of heaven in it. We venture to say that the religion of the present day is too much the fruit of the impulsive, and not sufficiently of the attractive. . . . It seeks too much to woo heaven, and yields too little to being wooed by it. . . . It lacks the meek, the quiet, the serene, the childlike, and the patriarchal. Its faith lies too much in self-will.[51]

To establish the key importance of the domestic heaven is to grant final victory to the passive rather than to the aggressive virtues. Although Harbaugh is too close to the orthodox tradition not to stress "the beatific vision" and "Heavenly worship," the main message of his volumes is that

---

[49]For examples of premillennial books devoted to this thesis, see Henry F. Hill, *The Saint's Inheritance; or the World to Come* (New York, 1853); John Lillie, *The Perpetuity of the Earth; a Discourse Preached Before the Premillennial Advent Association* (New York, 1842); Anna Silliman, *The World's Jubilee* (New York, 1836).

[50]*The Works of Nathaniel Emmons*, ed. Jacob Ide (Boston, 1842), 1: 187.

[51]*Heaven; or An Earnest and Scriptural Inquiry Into the Abode of the Sainted Dead* (Philadelphia, 1853), 3: 17.

heaven is "our Father's home, with . . . familiar homelike scenes, . . . not the cold ivory hall of a strange king."[52]

Speculation about such "homelike scenes" became common in the less learned consolation literature of the period.[53] In the later 1850s a few daring souls began to write novels about heaven.[54] Given the tradition of the novel, to write a novel about anything was in a sense to domesticate it, to bring it from the pale of the church congregation to the family circle. No one was better aware of this than Elizabeth Stuart Phelps who took heaven as her fictional specialty to the delight of hundreds of thousands of Americans and the scorn of Mark Twain.[55] Phelps' best-seller *Gates Ajar* was published in 1868; two other books on the same subject followed it in the 1880s but she was able to claim, rightly, that her views were still what they had been in 1868 when she was only 24.

Phelps was the descendant, not just of Austin Phelps and Moses Stuart, but of ten generations of Congregational ministers and deacons.[56] She would have been a minister undoubtedly if such a path had been open to her.[57] While her two brothers played at mock-sermons, she turned to literary preaching. Self-consciously plain, reform-minded, over-earnest, nearly an invalid from neuralgia and insomnia, she did not marry until 44, and the world laughed, for her husband Herbert Ward was seventeen years her junior, an aspiring writer clearly more drawn to her literary success than her personal charms. The marriage was not happy. In *Gates Ajar,* Phelps quotes from a Scottish divine who speculated that "Heaven may be a place for those who failed on earth."[58] Phelps was hardly a failure—her books sold well throughout her long life—but she had missed not just love, but fulfillment. Always a sentimental, often a sloppy writer, seldom

---

[52]Ibid., pp. 181, 292 ff., 21–22.

[53]Of course the big influence here was Emanuel Swedenborg, *Concerning Heaven and Its Wonders and Concerning Hell: From Things Heard and Seen* (Boston: Carter, 1844). For an example from consolation literature, see Thomas Baldwin Thayer, *Over the River, or, Pleasant Walks Into the Valleys of Shadows and Beyond: A Book of Consolation for the Sick, the Dying, and the Bereaved* (Boston, 1862).

[54]The most interesting is George Wood's *Future Life* (New York: Derby and Jackson, 1858), which he published to little effect, then, capitalizing on Elizabeth Stuart Phelps' best-selling *Gates Ajar,* republished as *The Gates Wide Open: or Scenes in Another World* (Boston, 1869).

[55]See "Extract from Captain Stormfield's Visit to Heaven," in *The Complete Works of Mark Twain* (New York, c. 1922), 8: 223–78.

[56]See Mary Angela Bennett, *Elizabeth Stuart Phelps* (Philadelphia: Univ. of Pennsylvania Press, 1939), p. 2. For more recent interpretations of Phelps, see Christine Stansell, "Elizabeth Stuart Phelps: A Study in Female Rebellion," *Massachusetts Review,* 13 (1972), 239–56; Ann Douglas Wood, " 'The Fashionable Diseases,' Women's Complaints and Their Treatment in Nineteenth-Century America," *Journal of Interdisciplinary History,* 4 (1973), 25–52.

[57]See Elizabeth Stuart Phelps, "A Woman's Pulpit," *Atlantic Monthly,* 26 (1870), 11–22.

[58]Elizabeth Stuart Phelps, *Gates Ajar,* ed. Helen Sootin Smith (Cambridge: Harvard Univ. Press (Belknap), 1964), p. 108.

likeable, her talents sapped by her need of self-justification, she received little real personal or critical esteem. She came increasingly if comprehensibly
to see herself as a vehicle of suffering. In 1889 she wrote in a clear mood of
self-revelation of the point when pain ceases in any real sense to be
profitable: "there comes a limit . . . beyond which the best that Fate could
offer could not atone for the worst she has inflicted." Believing that God has
chosen to impose on his creatures "the final test of love [:] . . . trust under
apparent desertion," Phelps also stressed with a certain bitter animus that
he has pledged them all the redress in his power. If earth is an orphanage,
heaven surely must be home in every sense of the word.[59]

No one was more committed to the denial of death as a separate state
than Phelps. In 1885 she published an extraordinary volume entitled *Songs
of the Silent World,* filled with poems written by supposedly dead people to
their living and grieving relatives assuring them of their continued existence.
One such spirit addresses a mourning spouse:

> I lean above you as before,
>   Faithful, my arms enfold,
> Oh, could you know that life is numb,
>   Nor think that death is cold!

A trusting survivor expresses Phelps' credo in the best poem in the book:

> There *is* no vacant chair. The loving meet—
>   A group unbroken—smitten, who knows how?
> One sitteth silent only, in his usual seat;
>   We gave him once that freedom. Why not now? . . .
>
> Death is a mood of life. It is no whim
>   By which life's Giver mocks a broken heart.
> Death is life's reticence. Still audible to Him,
>   The hushed voice, happy, speaketh on, apart.[60]

Gates Ajar is posited on this hopeful, literal-minded assurance, and it
constitutes the apotheosis of the consolation literature of the day. It is self-
indulgent, domestic, "feminine." An admirer explained that the book
offered "a woman's gentle word—a sweet fireside word"[61] to the grieving.
The book appropriately focuses on the implicit conflict among the would-be
consolers of Mary, a New England girl in her mid-twenties who has lost her
adored brother in the Civil War.

On the one hand, there is Dr. Bland, the local Calvinist minister, who
preaches of a cold and abstract heaven as "'an eternal state'" where the

---

[59]*The Struggle for Immortality* (Boston, 1889), pp. 55, 61.
[60]*Songs of the Silent World* (Boston, 1885), pp. 11, 12, 17.
[61]Elizabeth T. Spring, "Elizabeth Stuart Phelps," *Our Famous Women* (Hartford, Conn.,
1885), p. 567.

regenerate "'shall study the character of God.'"[62] On the other, is Mary's
aunt Winifred who believes in a thoroughly concrete and domestic heaven
where dead soldiers will chat with President Lincoln and culturally starved
young girls will have pianos to play. After long talks with her aunt in the
local graveyard, Mary is reconciled to the loss of her brother precisely because she realizes that she has not lost him at all: she comes to believe he is
always watching her, waiting for her. Winifred teaches her own little girl
Faith to talk confidingly to her dead father and to expect that God will give
her everything she wants, even her favorite cookies, in heaven. Heaven in
Aunt Winifred's view is a consolation prize. It only takes a domestic
tragedy to bring Dr. Bland, following the rest of the town, into her camp.
When his wife burns to death he craves comfort, and only her creed can supply it. Personal need has become the invincible criterion of truth.

It is the confidently detailed information about celestial life which makes
this book and its successors such extraordinary documents of American religious and cultural history. Aunt Winifred predicts with assurance that her
hair will no longer be grey "in heaven," that heaven will look (at least to her)
like Kansas, the state she loves best. Given the depth of her knowledge of
the next world, it is hardly surprising that she finds it a more interesting, a
more *real* place than her present habitation. When she learns she is to die of
breast cancer, she has no regrets. Yet she, like her author, is hardly weaned
from the world in the way John Bunyan's pilgrim Christian finally is. Her
egocentricity has been transferred, not conquered. Her will to power has
been consecrated, not suppressed.

All the logic of *Gates Ajar,* as of the consolation literature of which it is
the culmination, suggests to the reader: you are going to end up, if you are
well-behaved and lucky, in a domestic realm of children, women and ministers (i.e. angels), so why not begin to believe in them now? Phelps has at her
disposal a bid for power which, if ignored, could become a threat of revenge.
This is not to condemn her or her followers. It is to realize that they had an
immense interest in visualizing the afterlife as one scaled to their domestic
and pastoral proportions, as a place where they would dominate rather than
be dominated. It is to understand that it was crucial to the rationalization
and exploitation of their status that they inflate the significance of death, di-
late heavenly time and compress earthly calendars, stake out a property in
territory where claims were by definition untestable. In doing so, they of
course confused reality with fantasy, they subordinated life to literature:
Phelps' account was ludicrously detailed precisely to show it was authentic.
By an inevitable instinct, she blew up that anticipated moment whose
meaning she could legislate: she was compelled to the celestial close-up.

[62]*Gates Ajar,* pp. 48, 49.

THE CEMETERY AS CULTURAL INSTITUTION: THE ESTABLISHMENT OF MOUNT AUBURN AND THE "RURAL CEMETERY" MOVEMENT

STANLEY FRENCH

IN HER ACCOUNT OF HER TOUR OF THE UNITED STATES IN THE LATE 1840s Lady Emmeline Wortley wrote that the first time she went to Cambridge, Massachusetts, she visited the family of President Edward Everett of Harvard College, and that for her first sight-seeing excursion in the area the Everetts took her on a carriage ride through nearby Mount Auburn Cemetery. After an enthusiastic description of the cemetery she mentioned that next "we went to see a little of the colleges."[1] For most Americans today this ordering of events is a curious inversion of priorities, if they would consider conducting a visitor through the local cemetery at all. Yet the statement reflects the prominence given to Mount Auburn at the time. From its beginnings in 1831 Mount Auburn ranked as one of the major points of interest in the Boston area. It was proudly displayed to foreign and native visitors in the decades before the Civil War when Americans were still self-consciously trying to disprove Sydney Smith's famous taunt in the *Edinburgh Review* that America was a cultural wasteland.[2]

---

[1]*Travels in the United States, etc. during 1849–1850* (New York: Harper & Bros., 1851), pp. 47–48.

[2]Review of "Adam Seybert, Statistical Annals of the United States of America," *Edinburgh Review,* 33 (Jan. 1820), 69–80, 79–80.

Only two years after Mount Auburn's establishment the English actress Fanny Kemble reported that it was already "one of the lions" of the area, and that "for its beauty Mount Auburn might seem a pleasure garden instead of a place of graves."[3] About the same time a Swedish visitor was so enchanted with Mount Auburn that he declared, "a glance at this beautiful cemetery almost excites a wish to die."[4] Lady Amelia Murray after her visit to Mount Auburn thought that "in feeling and taste it is really perfect. No crowding up in disgusting heaps like our own graveyards." She hoped that Mount Auburn would soon be copied in the vicinity of London.[5] The Boston entrepreneur Amos Lawrence bought a large family plot to which "he continually resorted," and he purchased adjacent plots for his living friends and for re-interring dead friends.[6] Forty-five years after its founding James Russell Lowell sardonically commented that the people of Boston seemed to have only two ideas of hospitality: a boring dinner party followed by a ride in Mount Auburn—"Your memory of the dinner is expected to reconcile you to the prospect of the graveyard."[7] These are but a sampling of comments about Mount Auburn from the middle decades of the 19th century. Clearly, the cemetery was a significant institution.

The creation of Mount Auburn marked a change in prevailing attitudes about death and burial. It was a new type of burial place designed not only to be a decent place of interment, but to serve as a cultural institution as well. Because of its influence the traditional generic terms "graveyard" and "burial-ground" were replaced by the word "cemetery." And the example of Mount Auburn became the prototype of the "rural cemetery" which was extensively duplicated throughout the country. The term "garden cemetery" would be a less misleading and more apt description, but since "rural cemetery" was the common term at the time it will be used in this paper.

Since the beginnings of settlement in New England the standard places of burial had been amid the living—in the middle of towns, in churchyards or in churches, a practice which in England dated back to the 8th century.[8] In New England town commons were also frequently employed as graveyards. It is obvious from the dearth of comments about early

[3] *The Journal of Frances Anne Butler, Better Known as Fanny Kemble* (1835; rpt. New York: B. Blom, 1970), pp. 175–76. Entry for Apr. 15, 1833.

[4] Carl David Arfwedson, *The United States and Canada in 1832, . . .* (1834; rpt. New York: Johnson Reprint, 1969), I, 211, 213.

[5] Amelia M. Murray, *Letters from the United States, Cuba and Canada* (New York: Putnam, 1856), p. 16.

[6] William R. Lawrence, ed., *Extracts from the Diary and Correspondence of the Late Amos Lawrence* (Boston: Gould & Lincoln, 1855), pp. 175–76.

[7] Quoted in Martin Duberman, *James Russell Lowell* (Boston: Beacon, 1966), p. 192.

[8] R. A. Smith, *Smith's Illustrated Guide to and through Laurel Hill Cemetery* (Philadelphia: Hazard, 1852), p. 13.

New England graveyards, from the nature of the comments that do exist and from the grim symbolism of the period's monuments, that graveyards were treated simply as unattractive necessities to be avoided as much as possible by the living. This attitude continued from the beginnings of settlement into the early years of the 19th century.[9]

The Rev. William Bentley, the voluminous diarist of Salem, Massachusetts, perhaps spoke for many New Englanders at the turn of the 19th century: "I have a most settled enmity to all ceremonies for the dead. Let their memories live but let their ashes be forgotten." His description of a graveyard in Portsmouth, New Hampshire, illustrates the social effects of this prevalent attitude. "Grave point has an antient [*sic*] graveyard in the greatest confusion and tho' the monuments of the best families are to be found in it they are in the utmost neglect."[10] Timothy Dwight, in his *Travels in New England and New York,* mentions the subject of graveyards several times and describes the one at Guilford, Connecticut, as being a typical town graveyard. It was simply an unenclosed, unkempt section of the town common where the graves and fallen markers were daily trampled upon by people and cattle.[11] In "The Burial Place" (1818) William Cullen Bryant explained that the Puritans did not bring to the New World the old English customs of decorating graves and adorning graveyards with vegetation:

> . . . Naked rows of graves
> And melancholy ranks of monuments
> Are seen instead, where the coarse grass, between
> Shoots up its dull spikes, and in the wind
> Hisses, and the neglected bramble nigh,
> Offers its berries to the schoolboy's hand. . . .[12]

The neglected graveyard was characteristic not only of New England but was common throughout the other colonies and states. In Philadelphia until the 1820s, for instance, sites for graveyards were simply temporarily vacant lots to serve the needs of the day which were soon obliterated

[9]This attitude began to abate toward the end of the 18th century. For symbolism in early New England graveyards and its changing trends see Allan I. Ludwig, *Graven Images: New England Stonecarving and its Symbols, 1650–1815* (Middletown, Conn.: Wesleyan Univ. Press, 1966); Edwin Dethlefsen and James Deetz, "Death's Heads, Cherubs, and Willow Trees: Experimental Archaeology in Colonial Cemeteries," *American Antiquity,* 31 (1966), 502–10; and Harriette M. Forbes, *Gravestones of Early New England and the Men who Made Them, 1653–1800* (Boston: Houghton Mifflin, 1927), pp. 113–25.

[10]*The Diary of William Bentley, D.D.* . . . (1905–14; rpt., Gloucester, Mass.: Peter Smith, 1962), III, 127, entry for Dec. 13, 1804; II, 389–90, entry for Dec. 4, 1801.

[11](1821–22; rpt. Cambridge: Belknap, 1969), II, 360.

[12]*The Poetical Works of William Cullen Bryant,* ed. Henry C. Sturges (1903; rpt. New York: AMS, 1969), pp. 34–35.

by the expanding city as if they had never existed.[13]   The condition of
burial grounds in the South was frequently worse because the decentrali-
zation of the population had, except in the few more settled areas, led to a
general replacement of community burial grounds by individual family
plots on private land. Many such family plots did not survive a change
in land ownership.[14]

The attitude of indifference concerning burial places was not limited to
the colonial or early national period of the United States, but was prevalent throughout Western Europe. This Western attitude was reflected in,
and probably augmented by, the international vogue for the poetic theme
of melancholy and the "graveyard school" of poets during the 18th century. In the English-speaking world the beginnings of the elegiac form
can be traced back to the 1640s, but the main works appeared in the first
half of the next century. The most important of these were: Thomas Par-
nell, "Night-Piece on Death" (1722); Edward Young, "Night Thoughts ..."
(1742); Robert Blair, "The Grave" (1743), and Thomas Gray, "Elegy in a
Country Churchyard" (1751). These poems stressed the finality of death
and the horrors of decomposition, while making only scant reference, if
any, to the comforting hopes of Christianity.[15] The general tenor of these
poems is well illustrated by Blair's "The Grave" which starts:

> . . . the task be mine,
> To paint the gloomy horrors of the tomb;
> . . . The Grave, dread thing!
> Men shiver when thou'rt named: Nature appal'd
> Shakes off her wonted firmness. Ah! how dark
> Thy long-extended realms, and rueful wastes!
> Where nought but silence reigns, and night, dark night,
> . . . The sickley taper,
> By glimmering through thy low-browed misty vaults
> (Furred round with mouldy damps, and ropey slime),
> Lets fall a supernumerary horror,
> And only serves to make the night more irksome.[16]

In America the funeral elegy initially appeared at about the same time
as it did in England, but it was confined to the Puritan culture of New
England, where it continued as a strong tradition into the 19th century.

[13]R. A. Smith, *Smith's Guide*, pp. 26–28.

[14]Philip A. Bruce, *Institutional History of Virginia in the Seventeenth Century* (1910; rpt.
Gloucester, Mass.: Peter Smith, 1964), I, 113–14.

[15]The two most recent monographs on the subject are John W. Draper, *The Funeral Elegy
and the Rise of English Romanticism* (1929; rpt. New York: Octagon, 1967) and Eleanor M.
Sickels, *The Gloomy Egoist: Moods and Themes of Melancholy from Gray to Keats* (1932; rpt.
New York: Octagon, 1969).

[16]Robert Blair, "The Grave" in George Gilfillan, ed., *The Poetical Works of Beattie, Blair,
and Falconer* (Edinburgh: James Nichol, 1854), p. 133.

In the Revolutionary era the elegiac form became more generally accepted in America and poets as diverse as John Trumbull and Philip Freneau wrote elegies.[17]

In the early years of the 19th century attitudes about death and burial began to change. People started to complain about the frequently revolting state of burial places. Timothy Dwight, for instance, continued his discussion of the Guilford, Connecticut, graveyard by declaring:

> Both remains and the memorials of the dead are presented to the mind in circumstances so gross and indicative of so little respect in the living as to eradicate every emotion naturally excited by the remembrance of the deceased, and to give to those which remain a coarseness and commonness destructive of all moral influence. Nor is it unreasonable to suppose that the proximity of these sepulchral fields to human habitation is injurious to health.[18]

During his visit to Westminster Abbey in the 1820s Washington Irving was disgusted by a French sculptor's recent work, a memorial to a Mrs. Nightingale, which stressed the finality of death in a grisly manner. He exclaimed:

> Why should we thus seek to clothe death with unnecessary terrors.... The grave should be surrounded by everything that might inspire tenderness and veneration for the dead, or that might win the living to virtue.[19]

The old gloomy poetic attitude toward melancholy and death culminated in America with Bryant's great poem "Thanatopsis" (1817). In Great Britain such poems as Robert Pollack's "The Course of Time" and Thomas Hood's "Ode to Melancholy," both published in 1827, seemed to mark the end of the "invocation to melancholy" and the graveyard-school approach to the subject. Thereafter, that poetic tradition seemed to die out about the same time that the rural cemetery movement began. Bryant's later poems concerning death and burial differ markedly from his "Thanatopsis." Such poems as "The Lapse of Time" (1825), "The Two Graves" (1826) and "The Past" (1828) generally stress the naturalness of death, its appropriateness as part of the life cycle and its moralizing influences.

A new attitude toward death and burial can also be seen in the mourning picture which was a popular genre of folk art in America during the first four decades of the 19th century. The graves and memorials depicted were not in crowded weedy fields, but were set amid beautiful foliage in rustic surroundings. The actual basis of the mourning picture was prob-

[17]John W. Draper, "The Funeral Elegy in the American Colonies," Chap. 6 of his *Funeral Elegy,* pp. 155–76.

[18]Timothy Dwight, *Travels,* II, 360.

[19]Washington Irving, *Sketchbook* (New York: New American Library, 1961), p. 173.

ably the family burial plots of the Southern plantation country. Certainly, the idea of the private cemetery was extant in the South long before it existed in the more settled Northern areas. Thomas Jefferson wrote up his plans for a private garden burial place for Monticello in 1771. His specifications describe the content of a typical mourning picture.[20] Probably the general idea of a rustic setting for burial received a great impetus from the popularity of the artistic motif of George Washington's grave—a typical private garden burial scene of the plantation country.[21]

By the beginning of the 19th century there were pressing social reasons for changes in burial customs. Because of the rapidly increasing population the old graveyards became so crowded that they were frequently little more than stinking quagmires—chronically offensive and occasionally serious public health hazards.

In New York City the problem was such that the Board of Health appointed a special committee to investigate the situation. The committee recommended that "intramural" (inner city) interments be prohibited, and it suggested that the existing city cemeteries be converted into parks "instead of remaining receptacles of putrefying matter and hot-beds of miasmata."[22] No effective legislation came from this report and the problem was allowed to ride until a yellow fever epidemic carried off 16,000 in the city in 1822. Since the disease was particularly virulent in the vicinity of Trinity Church burying ground the whole issue of intramural interments was revived. A couple of pamphlets strongly urging the closing of city graveyards appeared in 1822 and 1823, but again the city took no effective action.[23] The problem was finally rendered less acute by the creation of a "rural cemetery" in Brooklyn in 1838.

In Boston similar conditions prevailed. Although Boston did not experience New York's epidemic of 1822, the burial ground problem became prominent in the same year because several Boston churches petitioned the city for permission to bury in cellar vaults because of space limitations in existing graveyards. The report of the City Council's special committee to investigate the matter was an indictment against all forms of intramural burial. The author, Dr. Jacob Bigelow, called for the termination of all burials within the city to lessen the chance of some epidemic like the recent tragedy at New York. Moreover, he called for the exhumation of

[20]Edwin M. Betts, *Thomas Jefferson's Garden Book* (Philadelphia: Amer. Phil. Soc., 1944), pp. 25–27.

[21]There is, as yet, no comprehensive monograph on the mourning picture as an art genre.

[22]City of Boston, "Report of the Joint Special Committee on Intramural Interments, Document 96–1879" (Boston: n.p., 1879), p. 9.

[23]F. D. Allen, "Documents and Facts Showing the Fatal Effects of Interments in Populous Cities" (New York: n.p., 1822); and Felix Pascalis, "An Exposition of the Dangers of Interment in Cities" (New York: n.p., 1823); both cited in City of Boston, "Report," pp. 9–10.

those tombs "which are already sending forth no equivocal admonitions into some of our temples." He further recommended the establishment of a cemetery beyond the city limits, and suggested that "the cemetery at New Haven may serve as a model to be improved by any amendments which genius or experience may suggest."[24] As in the case of New York, Boston did not establish a new cemetery. In 1825 Dr. Bigelow on his own initiative would begin and lead the movement to establish a new cemetery outside the city. The new cemetery would be known as Mount Auburn and would be the effective prototype of the "rural cemetery." Following his own advice to the City of Boston, Bigelow improved (and made famous) the type of cemetery first constructed in New Haven in 1796.

The New Haven Cemetery, originally called simply the "New Burying Ground," now the Grove Street Cemetery, was the creation of the Federalist Senator James Hillhouse. He had considered making a family burying ground on his property, but realized that should the land be sold in the future the new owners might neglect or even obliterate the graveyard and his descendants would have no legal access to the plot. Since the standard type of town burying ground was hardly suitable to his purpose he conceived the idea of creating a "sacred and inviolable" tract of land in which not only his family but those of his fellow citizens as well could have a decent and permanent resting place. At Hillhouse's instigation some thirty citizens of the area joined him in purchasing a six-acre lot. The lot was "by its retired situation, better calculated to impress the mind with a solemnity becoming the repository of the dead." In addition to regular family plots the proprietors granted a number of gratuitous ones: "one to the president and fellows of Yale College, one to each ecclesiastical society then existing [in the city], one for the burial of strangers dying in the city, three for paupers, and one for people of color."[25] Since the type of cemetery was novel, the remaining plots did not sell readily, but through Hillhouse's perseverance enough people bought into the venture to insure its continued existence.

In contrast to its successor, Mount Auburn, the New Burying Ground was not noteworthy in its topography or vegetation, and it received only minor landscaping improvements. The tract was flat and mostly covered with shortlived poplar trees.[26] Despite the unexceptional setting the new

[24]"Remarks on the Dangers and Duties of Sepulture; or Security for the Living with Respect and Repose for the Dead" (Boston: Phelps and Farnham, 1823) pp. 64, 61.

[25]Aaron N. Skinner, "History of the City Burial Ground of New Haven" (New Haven: N. Green, 1863), pp. 4 (note), 3, 6.

[26]B. Edwards, "The Burial Ground at New Haven" (?   ) (Sept. 1833), 201–15, 202. This article is an extract from an unidentified periodical in the Beinecke Library, Yale University. It is not: *North American Review, Christian Examiner, American Quarterly Observer, American Quarterly Register, New England Magazine, American Biblical Repository, Biblical Repertory, Christian Spectator* or *Spirit of the Pilgrims.*

cemetery attracted much attention and was a major attraction for visitors to the New Haven area. Timothy Dwight asserted: "I have accompanied many Americans, and many foreigners into it; not one of whom had ever seen or heard of anything of a similar nature. It is incomparably more solemn and impressive than any spot of the same kind, within my knowledge; and if I am to credit the declaration of others, within theirs."

He further declared his belief that "the cemetery will extensively diffuse a new sense of propriety in disposing of the remains of the deceased."[27] The Scottish traveler, Basil Hall, who was generally contemptuous of most things American, admitted that the cemetery was "one of the prettiest burying places I ever saw," and stated that it was "certainly some improvement" over the standard "soppy churchyard, where the mourners sink ankle deep in a rank and offensive mould, mixed with broken bones and fragments of coffins."[28] By 1833 the fame of the cemetery was such that one writer could rhetorically demand: "And who has not heard of the beautiful cemetery of New Haven? It has been theme of more frequent praise among us than any other receptacle of the dead, save only Père la Chaise."[29]

Despite the author's claims, it would be Mount Auburn and not the New Burying Ground which would capture the public's imagination. In Boston in 1825 Jacob Bigelow organized a few people who were interested in promoting a garden cemetery to look for a suitable piece of land. A number of lots came under consideration, but finally they settled on 72 acres along the Charles River near Harvard College. The land was a pleasant, heavily wooded tract with a variegated topography of many little hills, valleys and streams. The highest point reached over a hundred feet above the river, and from this hilltop one could see Dorchester Heights, most of Boston, Cambridge and the College, and the river meandering off into the country toward the west. The area was generally known as "Stone's Woods" from its original owner, but Harvard students more frequently referred to it as "Sweet Auburn" because they associated their favorite picnic ground with Oliver Goldsmith's idyllic poem "The Deserted Village" (1770).[30] Apparently not many people had heard of the

[27] Timothy Dwight, *Travels*, I, 138.

[28] *Travels in North America in the Years 1827 and 1828* (Edinburgh: Adell, 1829), II, 201. His wife agreed with him: Una Pope-Hennessey, ed., *The Aristocratic Journey: Being the Outspoken Letters of Mrs. Basil Hall Written During a Fourteen Months' Sojourn in America* (New York: Putnams, 1931), pp. 113–14.

[29] B. Edwards, "Burial Ground," p. 201. For Père la Chaise see below, pp. 53, 54.

[30] The account of the formative stages of Mount Auburn drawn from Jacob Bigelow, *A History of the Cemetery of Mount Auburn* (Boston: J. Munroe, 1860), pp. 1–129 (hereafter cited as *HMA*). The origin of the term "Sweet Auburn" from Oakes I. Ames, "Mount Auburn's Sixscore Years," *Publications of the Cambridge Historical Society* (1951–52), pp. 77–95, 78.

success of the New Haven cemetery, so to promote his novel scheme Bigelow succeeded in combining the cemetery group with the recently incorporated Massachusetts Horticultural Society. He used the argument that the projected purchase of Stone's Woods would provide ample land for both interest groups. By August 1831 the combined forces had acquired enough subscribers to purchase the tract, which was renamed Mount Auburn.

As the enterprise was initially organized the Horticultural Society was the tail that wagged the dog because the act of incorporation was a revision of the Society's charter permitting it to create and maintain a "rural cemetery." (This was the origin of what became the generic term for the new type of cemetery.) However, the Horticultural Society was to get very little benefit from its dominant position in the joint endeavor. The initial apathy with which the public received the cemetery proposal was rapidly overcome when the public became aware of the extensive supervisory provisions of the rural cemetery. People would not have to worry about the remote graves of their loved ones and friends being subject to the depredations of suppliers to the medical profession or other forms of desecration because the new cemetery was to be effectively fenced and subject to constant supervision of a salaried staff consisting of supervisor, his secretary, a gatekeeper and a gardener. Also the cemetery was not created exclusively for the affluent upper class to which the founders of the institution all belonged. The founders made it clear to the public that Mount Auburn was open to anyone who wished to purchase a lot, and that it was a nonprofit organization in which the proceeds from plot sales would be spent exclusively in maintenance and improvements. The appeal of Mount Auburn to the lower classes was successful. Many farmers, mechanics and small businessmen applied to purchase plots on the proviso that they could be paid for in labor or articles used in the improvement of the place.[31] The cemetery proposal soon drew much more support than did the Horticultural Society's plans, which never materialized, and in 1835 the two groups formally split apart.[32]

The dedication of the new cemetery took place in September 1831. One of the little valleys was fitted out as a temporary amphitheater, and about two thousand people attended what was described as a solemn and mov-

---

[31]H. A. S. Dearborn, "A Report on the Garden and Cemetery, before the Annual Meeting of the Horticultural Society, September 30, 1831," in *HMA*, pp. 167–74, 178.

[32]Even though the two groups split up, one should not have the impression that the cemetery group was uninterested in the horticultural aspects of the cemetery. Mount Auburn instituted a long-term policy of diverse planting and cultivation for decorative and instructional purposes. The article by Oakes I. Ames, "Mount Auburn's Sixscore Years," discusses this in detail.

ing occasion.[33] The ceremony featured the Boston Unitarian and Whig establishment: the Rev. Henry Ware Sr., Harvard's Hollis Professor of Divinity, gave the introductory prayer; the Rev. John Pierpont, Unitarian minister of the Hollis Street Church, Boston, wrote a special hymn for the occasion; and Justice Joseph Story delivered a powerful address.

Story's address was a general indictment of prevailing burial customs and an announcement of the proper role of the cemetery as cultural institution. He declared that contemporary Christian attitudes and practices concerning burial were, unfortunately, not the equal of those of earlier heathen cultures, and to prove his point he briefly surveyed the burial customs of the Egyptians, Greeks, Hebrews and others. "Our cemeteries," he concluded, "rightly selected, and properly arranged, may be made subservient to some of the highest purposes of religion and human duty. They may preach lessons, to which none may refuse to listen, and which all that live must hear."[34]

With the establishment of Mount Auburn, the conception of the cemetery as an instructional institution and inculcator of morality became a more common theme in the contemporary discussions of the purpose of a rural cemetery than arguments concerning overcrowded facilities and health hazards. Time and again, the belief that "a rural cemetery is a school of both religion and philosophy" was reiterated.[35]

> The sweetest memorials of the dead are to be found in the admonitions they convey, and the instructions they give, to form the character, and govern the conduct, of the living.[36]

> It is not solely, nor even chiefly with reference to the feelings with which we regard our own last change, that we find reasons for these hallowed and beautiful places of repose. It is principally to their influence upon the living, in the elevating and purifying effect they exert. . . .[37]

In the new type of cemetery the plenitude and beauties of nature combined with art would convert the graveyard from a shunned place of hor-

[33]*Boston Courier,* cited in *HMA,* p. 15.

[34]"Address delivered on the dedication of the Cemetery at Mount Auburn, September 24th, 1831," in *HMA,* pp. 143–67, 153–56.

[35]Wilson Flagg, *Mount Auburn: Its Scenes, Its Beauties, and Its Lessons* (Boston: James Munroe, 1861), p. 37.

[36]Levi Lincoln, "An Address Delivered on the Consecration of the Worcester [Mass.] Rural Cemetery, September 8, 1838" (Boston: Dutton & Wentworth, 1838), p. 11.

[37]Oliver P. Baldwin, "Address Delivered at the Dedication of Hollywood Cemetery, 25th of June, 1849" [Richmond, Va.] (Richmond: MacFarlane & Ferguson, 1849), p. 9. See also Frederick C. Whitney, "Address Delivered at the Consecration of Evergreen Cemetery, August 7, 1850" [Brighton, Mass.] (Boston: John Wilson, 1850), pp. 12–13.

Plate 1: "Pilgrim Path," an 1840s view in Mount Auburn Cemetery conveying the characteristics and atmosphere of the "rural cemetery." Reprinted from Cornelia W. Walter, *Mount Auburn Illustrated in a Series of Views from Drawings by James Smillie* (New York: R. Martin, 1847). Courtesy of the Boston Athenaeum.

hor into an enchanting place of succor and instruction (see Plate 1). The world of nature would inculcate primarily the lessons of natural theology. The fullness of nature in the rural cemetery would enable people to see death in perspective so that they might realize that "in the mighty system of the universe, not a single step of the destroyer, Time, but is made subservient to some ulterior purpose of reproduction, and the circle of creation and destruction is eternal."[38]   In a lesson reminiscent of Gray's "Elegy" another moralist stated that if in our wanderings through the grounds we come across some flower blooming unseen in a remote spot we should experience "a feeling of the spontaneous goodness of God" and from this example: "Man should learn from Him, to be the same everywhere that he would choose to be in the sight of his fellows, and to have all his actions proceed from a deep, uncompromising conviction of duty, and love of what is right, rather than from a hope of reward."[39]

[38]"Mount Auburn," *New England Magazine* (Sept. 1831), 236–39.
[39]Nehemiah Adams, "Mount Auburn," *American Quarterly Observer,* 3 (July 1834), 149–72, 159–60.

Even the winds in the trees of the cemetery "represent the vicissitudes of life: but they inculate the lesson that there is no adversity that is not followed by a better day."[40]

Such teachings of nature would be complemented by the instructions of art. The traditional Western conceit that man was apart from and above nature was present even in the theory of the new cemetery. One commentator stated that the natural beauties of Mount Auburn were so admirably suited for its new purpose that "it is difficult to persuade oneself that man had no agency in forming it." Despite the natural perfections of Mount Auburn, the writer continued: "Nature under all circumstances was meant to be improved by human care; it is *unnatural* to leave it to itself; and the traces of art are never unwelcome, except when it defeats the purpose, and refuses to follow the suggestions of nature."[41]

The contributions of art would cultivate the faculty of taste, and they would serve to render the lessons of history tangible and to inspire the sentiment of patriotism. The most basic "improvement," of course, was simply the layout of the cemetery. At Mount Auburn a system of carriage avenues and graveled footpaths suitable to the topography was constructed. The avenues bore names of trees, footpaths of flowers. There was also selective thinning of trees for family plots. The minimum size family plot was 15 by 20 feet (and sold initially for $60.00). Each family plot could be fenced, but only in metal or stone, not in wood. The grave markers would have to be of stone, except that slate, the traditional material for headstones in the old burying grounds was specifically disallowed. There were no specific restrictions on the style of gravestones, but approval by the trustees according to their canons of taste was implied.

The function of monuments, according to Justice Story, was to show the living "much of our destiny and duty." The lives, events and examples of history are for most people lifeless on the printed page. "It is the trophy and the monument, which invest them with a substance of local reality."[42] A new awareness of history provided by the artistic memorials of a rural cemetery would reinvigorate the sense of patriotism. Governor Levi Lincoln cogently expressed this issue in his dedicatory address of the Worcester Rural Cemetery in 1838 when he declared that the generation of patriots who created the country is "all but forgotten." Time, mortality, the mobility of American society and the influx of new peoples have "left but few who can now claim affinity to the tenants of that ancient churchyard" (an old Worcester burying ground).[43] The new rural ceme-

---

[40]Wilson Flagg, *Mount Auburn,* p. 9.
[41]William B. O. Peabody, "Mount Auburn Cemetery," *North American Review,* 72 (Oct. 1831), 397–406.
[42]Story, "Address," p. 158.
[43]"Address," p. 14.

tery would give people more of a sense of historical continuity, a feeling of social roots, a "sense of perpetual home,"[44] and remind them that the standard of living and the blessings of a republic they owed to those who have gone before: "To the dead ... in our own beloved country, we owe, not only the foundations of the great fabric of our liberties, but those lessons of wisdom, justice and moderation, upon the observance of which alone can depend its stability."[45]

The rural cemetery would elevate and strengthen patriotism because: "The spot where their fathers and their friends are buried, if it possess those charms which impress the heart and gratify the taste, will never be forgotten, and the land which contains it, though it have no other attraction, will yet be dear [to the living] for this."[46]

In the early years of the rural cemetery movement the most important stylistic consideration concerning monuments was decreed by national self-consciousness. Gravestones and other monuments were supposed to be commensurate with the ideals of a republic. A typical admonition to the public urged Americans to remember that "we are members of a republic and that costly and highly decorative monuments and sculpture that may be seen in some of the cemeteries of Europe are not fit subjects for our imitation."[47] However, the trend toward more sophisticated monumental architecture and sculpture began soon after the founding of Mount Auburn. In the early 1840s the *Boston Evening Transcript* urged proprietors of Mount Auburn to employ the best American sculptors so that Mount Auburn would soon be "as remarkable for the treasures of art collected there, as it now is for its scenery." The rural cemetery movement supplied a great impetus to the development of sculpture in America.[48]

The architecture of the monuments in rural cemeteries was eclectic. Mount Auburn, for instance, had a Gothic chapel, a Gothic tower on top of the hill and an Egyptian gateway for the main entrance (see Plate 2). The symbolism employed was also electic. The grim symbolism of earlier times had long since disappeared. The symbol of the cross, hitherto used almost exclusively in Catholic cemeteries, began to appear on Protestant

[44]Edward P. Humphrey, "Address on the Dedication of the Cave Hill Cemetery near Louisville, July 25, 1848" (Louisville, Ky.: *Courier* Job Room, 1848), p. 12.

[45]Charles Fraser, "Address Delivered on the Dedication of the Magnolia Cemetery, 19th November, 1850" (Charleston, S.C.: Walker & James, 1850), pp. 4–5.

[46][Anon.], *Forest Hills Cemetery: Its Establishment, Progress, Scenery, Monuments, etc.* (Roxbury, Mass.: John Backup, 1855), pp. 12–13.

[47]Wilson Flagg, *Mount Auburn*, p. 230.

[48]*Boston Evening Transcript* quoted in Frederick A. Scharf, "The Garden Cemetery and American Sculpture," *Art Quarterly*, 24 (Spring 1961), 88–92, 84; and Oakes Ames, "Mount Auburn's Sixscore Years," pp. 90–91 for rural cemetery and sculpture. Edmund V. Gillon Jr., *Victorian Cemetery Art* (New York: Dover, 1972) provides many illustrations of rural cemetery sculpture.

Plate 2: The entrance to Mount Auburn Cemetery in the 1840s showing the Egyptian-style gateway and part of the massive iron boundary fence. Reprinted from Cornelia W. Walter, *Mount Auburn Illustrated in a Series of Views from Drawings by James Smillie* (New York: R. Martin, 1847). Courtesy of the Boston Athenaeum.

gravestones at Mount Auburn and elsewhere, but curiously symbols of Christianity were infrequently used.[49]   From the Revolutionary era into the 1840s the dominant style of monument was the sculptured marble block surmounted by an urn. This type of monument reflected the classical Greek revival much in vogue during those years because that was an architecture widely considered to be commensurate with republican principles. From the beginning of the rural cemetery movement to the Civil War period there was also a strong revival of Egyptian sepulchral architecture. The gateway to Mount Auburn was an Egyptian-style portico with motifs of winged globe and upside-down lotus flowers. Another piece of sculpture appearing often in the cemetery was a sphinx. The Egyptian-style main gateway was extensively copied in the rural cemetery movement and the Egyptian obelisk was a common gravestone. The Egyptian symbols of death—such as the winged globe, banded cylinder,

[49]Nehemiah Adams, *Mount Auburn*, p. 165.

reversed torches and lotus flowers, the circle-shaped serpent devouring its tail, and the sphinx—appeared frequently on gateways to individual family plots and on gravestones.[50] There were objections to the propriety of using ancient Egyptian burial architecture in Christian cemeteries, but as one apologist explained:

> Egyptian architecture is essentially the architecture of the grave.... Imposing and somber in its forms and mysterious in its remote origin, it seems particularly adapted to the abode of the dead, and its enduring character contrasts strongly and strangely with the brief life of mortals. Nor is it without the symbols of immortality, which the purer faith of the Christian can well appropriate and associate with the more sacred and divine promises of the gospel.[51]

Another characteristic of the rural cemetery, first extensively used in the Grove Street Cemetery, but later becoming universal, was the fencing of individual family plots. Iron railings were the preferred material, and in the next several decades there was a boom in ornamental ironwork. But by the late 1840s people started to complain that the cemeteries were becoming seas of fences—an unaesthetic development which was detrimental to the cemeteries' higher cultural purposes.[52] In the well-supervised rural cemetery such fencing served little practical purpose; it was merely symbolic of the national trait of possessive individualism. According to the opinion of a foreign couple who visited Mount Auburn in the 1850s: "The elegant iron rails, which divide the different small lots, are neither ornamental, nor ... reverential for the place. Exclusiveness little befits a cemetery; the idea of private property, carried even into the realm of the dead, where no one can own more than he covers, has something unnaturally strange [*sic*]."[53]

[50]For other examples see etching of entrance gate to Odd Fellows' Cemetery, Philadelphia in R. A. Smith, *Smith's Guide,* p. 30; frontispiece of gateway to Forest Hills Cemetery in *Forest Hills Cemetery;* Harriet Martineau, *Retrospect of Western Travel* (London: Saunders and Otley, 1838), II, 233. An Egyptian gateway was constructed for Grove Street Cemetery in the mid-1840s. For a photograph see Wendall D. Garett et al., *The Arts in America: The Nineteenth Century* (New York: Scribner, 1969), plate 48. There is a lithograph of the Egyptian gateway to Rochester's Mount Hope Cemetery pasted as an addendum to Pharcellus Church, "Address Delivered at the Dedication of Mount Hope Cemetery, Rochester, Oct. 2, 1838 (Rochester: David Hoyt, 1839) in Rundel Library, Rochester. For the Egyptian motif in gateways of individual family plots and gravestones see Harriette M. Forbes, "Symbolic Cemetery Gates in New England," *Old Time New England: Bulletin of the Society of Preservation of New England Antiquities,* 24 (Oct. 1933), 46–58, esp. Figs. 14 and 15, p. 56.

[51]*Forest Hills Cemetery,* pp. 79–80.

[52]For examples of the boom in the art of wrought iron see R. A. Smith, *Smith's Guide,* pp. 142–47, and Joy and Gorden Sweet, "Island Iron: Burial Plot Enclosures of Edgartown, Martha's Vineyard," *Magazine of Art,* 38 (Mar. 1945), 89–91. For criticism of internal fencing see Nehemiah Cleaveland, *Greenwood Cemetery: A History of the Institution from 1838 to 1864* (New York: Anderson and Archer, 1866), pp. 141–45.

[53]Francis and Theresa Pulszky, *White, Red, Black: Sketches of Society in America* (1853; rpt. New York: Negro Universities Press, 1968), III, 98–99.

The situation was somewhat alleviated in the 1850s when curbstones superseded iron railings as the preferred material for delimiting family plots. Spring Grove Cemetery (1845), Cincinnati, was the leader in abolishing internal fencing and the innovator in developing the rural cemetery into an aesthetically integrated park. This modification, the first major innovation on the idea of the rural cemetery, resulted in the concept of the "lawn cemetery" which became popular after the Civil War. In the 1880s the example of the lawn cemetery and the influence of the social gospel movement resulted in the removal of most internal fencing in rural cemeteries.[54]

The combination of nature and art in the rural cemetery and the acquisitions of time would create "legacies of imperishable moral wealth" which would provide a strong improving influence on all members of society.[55] The thoughts automatically inculcated by the decent cemetery would assuage the suffering of the mourner; it would make the young and careless pensive, the wise wiser; the vain would become aware of and correct their vanities, the avaricious would be rendered less grasping, ambition would be purified, the lessons of history would be remembered and patriotism enhanced, theological truths would be more easily perceived and morality would be strengthened. These themes appear in practically all of the discussions of the rural cemetery movement. The strong moralizing influence attributed, before the Civil War, to the contemplation of death was also the reason why death was such a common theme in the grade-school readers of the time.[56] Probably the mourning picture was supposed to serve the same function of the rural cemetery more accessibly in the home.[57]

To ensure the appropriate atmosphere custodial regulations were enforced. At Mount Auburn the cemetery was open from sunrise to sunset, carriages could not be driven faster than a walk, refreshments could not be brought in, no flowers could be picked and decorous behavior would be enforced at all times.[58] The supervisory provisions and propriety rules

[54]John B. Jackson, *American Space: The Centennial Years, 1865-1876* (New York: Norton, 1972), pp. 70-71. Los Angeles' Forest Lawn is in the Spring Grove tradition, not that of Mount Auburn. Harriette M. Forbes, "Symbolic Cemetery Gates," p. 48.

[55]Edward Humphrey, "Address," p. 11.

[56]Ruth Miller Elson, *Guardians of Tradition: American Schoolbooks of the Nineteenth Century* (Lincoln: Univ. of Nebraska Press, 1964), pp. 42, 43, 45.

[57]Aside from the frequency with which mourning pictures appear in folk art collections another indication of the popularity of the mourning picture is that Nathaniel Currier published a lithograph of one (no date) which was simply a standard form. The lithograph was a typical mourning picture, but the printed inscription on the gravestone stated only "In memory of," to be filled in by the purchaser. Copy in Webb Gallery, Shelburne Museum, Shelburne, Vt.

[58]"Regulations concerning visitors to the Cemetery," in *HMA*, pp. 252-54.

first instituted at Mount Auburn were extensively copied by the rural cemeteries which followed.

From the day of its dedication Mount Auburn began to attract attention. Since it was a much more ambitious endeavor from its beginning than the older Grove Street Cemetery, Mount Auburn rapidly and permanently eclipsed the first rural cemetery. After several years Mount Auburn's reputation was such that it began to be extensively copied, first in large cities, later in towns. Philadelphia was the first city to emulate Mount Auburn with the establishment of Laurel Hill Cemetery in 1836.[59] Brooklyn followed two years later with the opening of Greenwood Cemetery. Both of these were large enterprises as beautifully situated as Mount Auburn, and were subject also to a large amount of visitation and comment. Laurel Hill was a "sylvan eminence" about three miles up the Schuylkill River from the city limits; Greenwood was similarly located on a wooded, hilly area overlooking Gowanus Bay. From these examples the rural cemetery idea spread in the next two decades to become the dominant type of cemetery: Mount Hope at Rochester, New York; Greenmount at Baltimore; and Worcester Rural Cemetery at Worcester, Massachusetts, were also opened in 1838. And they were followed by such examples as: Allegheny Cemetery (1844) at Pittsburgh; Spring Grove (1845) at Cincinnati; Cave Hill (1848) at Louisville, Kentucky; Hollywood (1849) at Richmond, Virginia; and Magnolia (1850) at Charleston, South Carolina; to name but a few of the rural cemeteries built in the larger cities.

The rural cemeteries were mostly private nonprofit corporations. Mount Hope Cemetery of Rochester was the first municipally sponsored rural cemetery; the city bought the land for it in 1836. By the end of the 1850s one commentator declared that "there is hardly a city or town of any size in the union which does not possess its rural cemetery," and added that since the idea had been so universally adopted throughout the land it "may be fairly considered now one of our institutions."[60]

The press of population growth, public health considerations and changing attitudes also brought forth mortuary reforms in Europe during the first half of the 19th century. The first and most important European garden cemetery was Père la Chaise which was established in Paris in 1804. It became the customary burial ground for the upper classes of

---

[59]Prior to Laurel Hill there were several small private cemeteries in Philadelphia established in the 1820s, one of which, Ronaldson's (1826), came close to the ideal of the rural cemetery, but it had no perceptible influence on the rural cemetery movement. R. A. Smith, *Smith's Guide,* pp. 26–27.

[60]Henry M. Sargent, App. to 6th ed. of Andrew J. Downing, *A Treatise on the Theory and Practice of Landscape Gardening* (1859; rpt. New York: Funk & Wagnalls, 1967), p. 561.

France, renowned statesmen and artists. Over the years it acquired elaborate decoration. Because of its age, occupants and ornamentation Père la Chaise became the most famous garden cemetery in Europe during the 19th century. For the same reasons it was frequently, but erroneously, considered the model for Mount Auburn or other early rural cemeteries in America, and it was almost invariably the standard of comparison for European visitors to the American cemeteries.[61]

In Great Britain the first important garden cemetery was the Necropolis (1833) of Glasgow, which was inspired by Père la Chaise. The first significant garden cemetery in England was Abney Park established on the east side of London in 1840. This cemetery followed the example of Mount Auburn.[62]

There was a decided difference between Anglo-American and French cultural attitudes toward the new type of cemetery. The Americans and English sided together in giving an emphasis to the capacities of the garden cemetery for moral instruction, and they stressed the dominance of nature over art in the cemeteries. At the same time they criticized Père la Chaise for its aura of artificiality and vanities and for the French attitude of levity toward death.

One American complained that the hand of man was too evident in the landscape of Père la Chaise, which also "is the fault of Versailles."[63] The Rev. Mr. Archer, who delivered the dedication address of Abney Park, complained of the "fantastic" and "rich and elegant" monuments of Père la Chaise and claimed that Mount Auburn by comparison "lost none of its charms by grotesqueness of artificial decoration."[64] A reviewer of a couple of contemporary French guidebooks to the cemeteries of Paris cited with horror one author's unqualified comments about the Parisian cemeteries being the standard resorts for a Sunday outing, and their being surrounded by taverns for the benefit of revelers and mourners.[65] Harriet Martineau felt that the emphasis on art at the expense of nature created a very different atmosphere at Père la Chaise from that which existed at Mount Auburn. The sense of the continuity of life and of rebirth was absent at Père la Chaise: "In Père la Chaise every expression of mourning is to be found; few or none of hope.... There is no light

---

[61]For an account of Père la Chaise see "Cemeteries and Catacombs of Paris," *Quarterly Review*, 42 (Apr. 1819), 350–97. For European comparison of American rural cemeteries to Père la Chaise see Howard M. Jones, *American and French Culture, 1750–1848* (Chapel Hill: Univ. of North Carolina Press, 1927), p. 330.

[62]For sketch of Glasgow's Necropolis see John M'ure, *The History of Glasgow* (Glasgow: John Tweed, 1872), II, 735–42. For Abney Park see George Collison, *Cemetery Interment* (London: Longman, 1840).

[63]D. W. Cheever, "Burial Customs," *North American Review*, 93 (July 1861), 108–36.

[64]"Address," in George Collison, *Cemetery Interment*, pp. 288–301, 293–94.

[65]"Cemeteries and Catacombs of Paris," pp. 391–92.

from the future shining over the place. In Mount Auburn, on the contrary, there is nothing else. A visitor from a strange planet, ignorant of mortality, would take this place to be the sanctum of creation. Every step teems with the promise of life."[66]

But perhaps the Rev. Mr. Pierpont had the last word on the subject:

> How much better is Mount Auburn to muse in for the living, or to sleep in for the dead, than some few ages hence it may become, when opulence, and luxury, and fashion, and all the whims of humanity, and all the workings of time, shall have made it more like the great show place of the gay and vain French capital. Then indeed there will be over it a halo of glory; but will its charm for the heart remain the same?[67]

In both the United States and Great Britain formal theorizing about the social purposes of the rural cemetery was derivative from the institution, and not a causative influence. The first work which can be considered as a treatise on the rural or garden cemetery was a little book published in 1843 entitled *On the Laying Out, Planting, and Managing of Cemeteries*, by John C. Loudon who was the most important British landscape architect in the second quarter of the 19th century.[68] In the beginning of his book there is a short section on "The Uses of Cemeteries" in which he states that the main object was to provide a decent place to bury the dead without offending the sentiments or threatening the health of the living. "A secondary object is, or ought to be, the improvement of the moral sentiments and general taste of all classes, and more especially of the great masses of society." In addition to moral objectives, any burial place, properly designed and kept, "might become a school of instruction in architecture, sculpture, landscape-gardening, arboriculture, and in those important parts of general gardening, neatness, order, and high keeping [sic]." Also, the burying ground was traditionally "the country laborer's only library," and this function of instructing the lower classes in history and biography had not been superseded by the general increase in literacy and availability of printed matter.[69] After these brief comments the rest of the book is devoted to practical issues.

[66]Harriet Martineau, *Retrospect,* II, 230.

[67][John Pierpont], "Churchyard Sketches," *The Picturesque Pocket Companion and Visitors' Guide to Mount Auburn* (Boston: Otis, Broaders, 1839) pp. 207–8. For the differences in monumental architecture between Père la Chaise and Mount Auburn compare the engravings of Père la Chaise depicted in Joseph Marty, *Promenades pittoresque aux cimetieres'du Père LaChaise . . .* (Paris: Chailou, 1835) with those in Cornelia W. Walter, *Mount Auburn Illustrated in a series of Views from Drawings by James Smillie* (New York: R. Martin, 1847).

[68]John Gloag, *Mr. Loudon's England: The Life and Work of John Claudius Loudon and his Influence on Architecture and Furniture Design* (Newcastle-upon-Tyne: Oriel, 1970), pp. 17–23.

[69]Loudon, *On the Laying out, . . .* (London: Longman, 1843), pp. 1, 12–13.

In America the first practical handbook of cemetery construction was J. Jay Smith's *Designs for Monuments and Mural Tablets Adapted to Rural Cemeteries ... on the basis of Loudon's Work* (1846). The theory of this book was little more than verbatim quotations or extensive paraphrases of Loudon's work. Probably these books helped to spread the idea of the garden or rural cemetery, but such works were not important in the initial stages of the movement.

The beginning of the rural cemetery movement was not directly influenced by the landscape gardening movement much in vogue in Great Britain during the last three-quarters of the 18th century. Even though John Evelyn in his famous treatise on arboriculture, *Silva* (1662), had advocated an end to city burials and the desirability of garden cemeteries there was no mention in the movement's literature of improving burial places through landscape gardening. These writings range from Stephen Switzer's *Iconographia Rustica* (1718) through the works of Humphrey Repton (1752–1818), who was the major theoretician and last practitioner of the movement.[70] John C. Loudon (1783–1843) became involved in the theory and actual construction of garden cemeteries only in the last two years of his life, and his book became a standard reference on the subject only after the rural cemetery movement was well established. The first American work on landscape architecture was Andrew Jackson Downing's influential *A Treatise on the Theory and Practice of Landscape Gardening,* published in 1841, but it contained no mention of improving cemeteries. Formal theory and the landscape gardening movement, then, had little influence in creating the rural cemetery. The initial influences were more general moral, social and medical reasons.

The creation of rural cemeteries in America and the curtailment and closing of the older inner-city burial grounds undoubtedly improved living conditions in the cities and certainly rendered the circumstances of death less oppressive. For this reason alone the rural cemetery movement should be considered as another important reform initiated during the Jacksonian period. But this reform had other significance as well. Aside from the stimulation the rural cemetery movement provided to the arts of sculpture and wrought iron work, the new type of cemetery gave an impetus to the establishment of municipal parks. Even though Downing did not mention cemeteries in his *Treatise,* by the end of the 1840s he was using the example of the new cemeteries' success as one of

[70]John Evelyn, *Silva* (York: J. Dodsley, 1776), II, 625. Norman T. Newton, "The English Landscape Gardening School," Chap. 15 of his *Design on the Land: The Development of Landscape Architecture* (Cambridge: Belknap, 1971), pp. 207–20, esp. pp. 216 and 220. Newton states that the term "English Landscape Gardening School" may properly be used "only for Repton's work and what preceded it, back to Queen Anne's day" (p. 219).

his arguments for the development of urban parks: "Judging from the crowds of people in carriages, and on foot, which I find constantly thronging Greenwood and Mount Auburn, I think it is plain enough how much our citizens, of all classes would enjoy public parks on a similar scale." He further implied that the purposes of the rural cemetery would be enhanced with the establishment of public parks and gardens, because in their absence too many people went to the new cemeteries simply to enjoy themselves.[71] A quarter-century's prior experience of rural cemeteries helped to prepare the way for Central Park (1856) in New York City, the first modern municipal park in the United States.

The most important purpose of the new type of cemetery was its intended function as a cultural institution. The rural cemetery movement provided a partial answer to a frequent allegation by European visitors that the American landscape was, if not barbaric, at least amoral because it lacked the improving influence of a long, obvious heritage of historical associations supplied by ancient buildings, monuments, etc. The desirability of such a tangible heritage had been a felt need of a number of American intellectuals and artists at the time.[72] After the inception of the rural cemetery movement the moral instructional purpose of the new institution was stressed by the conservative religious, educational and Whiggish elements of American society which sought to mitigate what they considered to be the unfortunate social effects of an emerging mass society and culture. Complaints about the growing pervasiveness and tyranny of public opinion were the most common themes of native social criticism from the late 1820s through the 1830s, as well as being the subject of frequent foreign commentaries. Conservatives thought that an endemic social instability and cultural mediocrity were the main effects of a domineering uninformed public opinion.[73] The general names since given to the period such as the "Age of Jackson" and the "Age of the Common Man" acknowledge the dominance of the forces conservatives feared. In the effort to improve the level of public opinion and hence raise the moral character of the nation conservatives implemented or augmented various types of cultural reforms during the 1830s.

---

[71]"A Talk about Public Parks and Gardens," in Andrew J. Downing, *Rural Essays,* ed. George W. Curtis (New York: Leavitt & Allen, 1854), pp. 138–46, 144. The essay first appeared in Downing's magazine, *The Horticulturist* (Oct. 1848). See also Downing's "Public Cemeteries and Public Parks" in *Rural Essays,* pp. 154–59 and Hans Huth, *Nature and the American: Three Centuries of Changing Attitudes* (Lincoln: Univ. of Nebraska Press, 1972), pp. 66–69.

[72]Roderick Nash, "The American Wilderness," Chap. 4 of his *Wilderness and the American Mind* (New Haven: Yale Univ. Press, 1967), pp. 67–83; Hans Huth, *Nature and the American,* pp. 49–51.

[73]Stanley G. French Jr., "Some Theological and Ethical Uses of Mental Philosophy in Early Nineteenth Century America," Diss. Univ. of Wisconsin 1967, pp. 141–75.

This was the period of extensive academic institutionalization of moral philosophy from the McGuffey type of grade school readers through the tomes of the Scottish Realist philosophers, or their American expositors, in senior level college courses. The college course on moral philoshpy was considered the crowning element in undergraduate education.[74] Books on child nurture, etiquette and advice to adolescents began to appear in quantity at this time.[75] Conservative "judicial" literary criticism of the Federalist-Whig tradition was at a peak in the 1830s before it was challenged by the art and philosophy of the Romantic movement.[76] The lyceum movement got under way at this time, and Josiah Holbrook, its main promoter, thought that the lyceum was going to be the most effective expedient "for raising the moral and intellectual taste of our countrymen."[77] This was the period in which the principles of taste and eloquence of the Scottish Realist aesthetic philosophers began to be stressed in a junior level college course on "Rhetoric."[78]

The Scottish Realist school of philosophy which supplied much of the "Establishment's" criteria of morality and culture until the 1880s has often been considered as the peak of the Enlightenment rationalistic attitude, and as antithetic to the emotive and intuitive aspects of life usually equated only with Romanticism. But the Scottish school and its adherents held that moral and aesthetic "faculties" and the finer sentiments needed more than just didactic rationalism for their cultivation. As Justice Story succinctly expressed the issue in his address at Mount Auburn: "The truth, which strikes home, must not only have the approbation of . . . reason, but it must be embodied in a visible, tangible, practical form. It must be felt, as well as seen. It must warm, as well as convince."[79]

[74]Elson, *Guardians of Tradition;* George P. Schmidt, *The Old Time College President* (New York: Columbia Univ. Press, 1930); Wilson Smith, *Professors and Public Ethics* (Ithaca: Cornell Univ. Press, 1956).

[75]Bernard Wishy, *The Child and the Republic: The Dawn of American Child Nurture* (Philadelphia: Univ. of Pennsylvania Press, 1968); John and Virginia Demos, "Adolescence in Historical Perspective," *Journal of Marriage and the Family,* 31 (Nov. 1969), 632–38. Arthur M. Schlesinger Sr., *Learning How to Behave: A Historical Study of American Etiquette Books* (New York: MacMillan, 1947).

[76]Lewis P. Simpson, *The Federalist Literary Mind* (Baton Rouge: Louisiana State Univ. Press, 1962); William Charvat, *The Origins of American Critical Thought, 1810–1835* (Philadelphia: Univ. of Pennsylvania Press, 1936); Terence Martin, "The Instructed Vision," *Scottish Common Sense and the Origins of American Fiction* (Bloomington: Indiana Univ. Press, 1961).

[77]Quoted in Carl Bode, *The American Lyceum: Town Meeting of the Minds* (New York: Oxford Univ. Press, 1956), pp. 11–12.

[78]Warren Guthrie, "The Development of Rhetorical Theory in America," *Speech Monographs,* 13 (1946), 14–22; 14 (1947), 38–54.

[79]"Address," *HMA,* p. 157. For the importance of the emotive and intuitive aspects of life in the Scottish Realist tradition see Walter J. Bate, *From Classic to Romantic: Premises of Taste in the Eighteenth Century* (Cambridge: Harvard Univ. Press, 1949). For discussions

The inspiration and ideas associated with the rural cemetery movement obviously derived to an important degree from Romanticism, but defining the extent to which the rural cemetery owed its origins either to Romanticism or to the tradition of social philosophy which stemmed from Enlightenment presuppositions seems secondary to understanding the institution from the standpoint of the social significance attributed to it by contemporaries. It is apparent from their discussions that the rural cemetery through its intended capacity as cultivator of the finer emotions was another facet of the conservative cultural uplift movement during the Age of the Common Man.

---

of Americanized Scottish Realist philosophy see Daniel Walker Howe, *The Unitarian Conscience: Harvard Moral Philosophy, 1805–1860* (Cambridge: Harvard Univ. Press, 1970); Douglas Sloan, *The Scottish Enlightenment and the American College Ideal* (New York: Teachers College Press, 1971); and D. H. Meyer, *The Instructed Conscience: The Shaping of the American National Ethic* (Philadelphia: Univ. of Pennsylvania Press, 1972).

DEATH IN MEXICAN FOLK CULTURE

PATRICIA FERNÁNDEZ KELLY

We come only to sleep,
We come only to dream.
It is not true, it is not true
That to the earth we come to live.
We are to become as the weeds in every spring.
Our heart has greened and sprouted
Some flowers will our body give,
And then it shall forever wilt.

(Cant. Mex., f. 14v., lin. 3 ss. De Tenochtitlan)

MEXICO IS A COUNTRY WITH A DISTINGUISHED CULTURAL TRADITION DATING back three thousand years. Its historical route has been one of great achievements as well as of great tragedy, yet in its entirety it is possible to perceive the continued importance of the idea of death linked with religion, magic and, in later times, philosophy. The problem of death as a constant preoccupation of man in these three areas of human behavior is not limited to Mexico's past or present. On the contrary it probably constitutes, together with the idea of love, one of the most widespread concerns in the world. However, Mexico with its past rich with the memory of great and lost civilizations—civilizations in time blended with the European tradition in a historical cycle of colonialism and domination that in a sense has not yet ended—offers the researcher an abundance of material marked by its uniqueness and creativity.

Before surveying some of the characteristic ways the idea of death has been treated in Mexico, it is necessary to consider some more general matters. Where does the concern with death originate? It is reasonable to believe that this exclusively human question arises from another typically human trait: the capacity for self-awareness. It is only man who can observe the surrounding world while knowing at the same time that he can be observed. Many have pondered over the fundamental character of the reciprocity resulting from this perceptual act. Through complex mental processes man has separated his individual consciousness from the natural context. Unlike other animal species, man has attempted in a sense to withdraw from nature by means of an intricate net of symbols which transforms him into a unique observer of himself and everything about him. Not only does he grasp the mainstream of existence but also its painful termination and, incapable of accepting this fact in its definitive crudity, he evolves a complex structure of explanation which can only be understood against the background of the human conception of time.

It is of central importance to realize that far from defining an objective reality, categories of time shape the way in which human beings organize reality. The idea of death in the prehispanic civilizations of Mexico and in the contemporary folk culture cannot be fully comprehended without some mention of the peculiarities that time-notions have in specific contexts. For the natives of Mexico, time was a never-ending succession of cycles separated from one another by death and the destruction of the world, the order of which could only be restored through sacrifice. As with other highly religious cultures, they formulated a concept of life on earth as merely a fragment of what constitutes the existential totality of the cosmos. In addition, life on earth is often referred to as a dream, a fiction always posing the problematic question of what true life is:

> Will I depart in this manner?
> As the flowers which perished?
> Will nothing be left in my name?
> Will nothing remain of my fame here on earth?
> Let there at least be blossoms! at least songs!
>
> (Cant. Mex., f. 10r., lin. 17 ss De Huexotzinco. Anónimo)

In such an environment, death cannot represent merely the corruption of matter and the end of life for man; nor can it be seen only as a necessary step toward the granting of salvation or an eternity of happiness. It is rather conceived of as requisite to the prolongation of life. Nothing can exist in time if it has not previously passed through the process of death. Thus sacrifice, the generous donation of human blood, guarantees the permanence of the universe; man becomes an active agent in sharing in the responsibility of preserving cosmic order. Here lies the justification of the practice of human sacrifice, which in its purest expression does not constitute the brutal extermination of human life but rather the integration of it into a more real and permanent existence.

It is not difficult to understand the process that originates such a system of understandings when we reflect upon cultures as a whole, and when we notice that regardless of their complexity and sophistication they base their prosperity on the practice of agriculture. Tilling the earth as the establishment of a relationship with the natural environment represents a special experience. Indeed, there is nothing in nature which confirms the idea of death as a definitive end; when vegetation dies, it is only to come to life again the following spring. Thus death precedes life, which in turn must again be succeeded by death in a never-ending stream.

But where do these final conceptions of the prehispanic religions find their roots? The first observable indications of an interest in death appeared in Middle America around fifteen hundred years before Christ, in the form of funerary arrangements in which skeletons were buried in fetal positions or with the legs extended toward the west. Such remnants were frequently found in the company of vestiges of pottery and utensils that served as offerings or gifts.

The discovery of bone structures in crouched positions seems to indicate the presence of the belief in death as a return to the womb from which the child originally emerged. As for the orientation of the skeletons with their extremities turned west, it is not a surprise for the anthropologist. Other cultures in the world share the same custom, often associated with the idea that the dead must walk toward the region where the sun itself dies, where it sets every evening.

It is, however, the finding of offerings that more profoundly excites the imagination, as the custom seems to support the belief in the continuation of the daily needs of man even after his death. Accepting the continuing need for human essentials, an acknowledgment of the permanence of life, seems also to suggest that whatever follows death must be explained in accordance with familiar experiences. This tradition, as old as the existence of culture in Middle America, remains one of the significant patterns of behavior in present times.

Later, funerary rituals became more complicated in concept as well as in the technical and material preferences associated with the offerings. There have been discoveries of graves belonging to the Middle Preclassic period (ca. 1300–800 B.C.) in which human remains appear surrounded by a dazzling variety of finely polished jewelry worked in jade, obsidian, serpentine and other semiprecious stones, side by side with other graves characterized by their great simplicity. This contradictory abundance and scarcity of gifts seems to indicate a gradual and significant stratification of the social structure. One thing, however, is shared by the two burial systems: the proliferation of amulets in the form of delicate feminine figurines molded in clay, striking for the emphasis placed upon their sexuality by means of an exaggeration of the hips, breasts and navel. Some of these miniature masterpieces are shown holding infants in their arms and are covered with a reddish slip, or appear peculiarly bisected, thus exhibiting two heads or two faces on the same body. This intriguing division is further demonstrated by the frequent representation of bodies in which one half is painted red while the other is left without color.

Everything in these figurines speaks of life, particularly of the capacity of women to procreate, and they can be regarded as Mesoamerican counterparts of the European "venuses" of the Paleolithic era, possibly symbolic of the idea of the earth envisioned as a feminine entity. The fact that many of these sculptures have been found inside graves seems to specify their meaning. They are charms intended to facilitate the continuation of the vital forces after death. Aside from their obvious reference to life as shown through the exaggeration of the sexual elements, the frequency with which the number "two" appears in their composition poses an interesting question which can be addressed with the help of some other sculptures, particularly a miniature mask shown in the Museum of Anthropology in Mexico City. In it, half the face is covered with the appearance of living flesh while

Figure 1: Clay mask representing the duality of life and death. Preclassic Period (ca. 1500–200 B.C.) Central Mexico. Museo Nacional de Anthropologia.

the other half is a naked skull (Figure 1). Clearly a symbol of the unity resulting from the complementary character of life and death, it is only one of the many artistic works in which a sense of this duality is expressed.

Indeed, from a visual perspective, nature manifests itself in the form of complementary dualities: light and darkness, masculinity and femininity, the heavens and the earth, the visible and the invisible, warmth and cold, permanent and temporary, life and death. What is notable is the presence of all these opposing forces as integral parts of the unity within the universe, an idea which reached its summit in later cultures, particularly among the Aztecs.

Throughout the history of the prehispanic groups, the obsession with the contradiction of life and death remains as one of the most important religious preoccupations. Still, there is a point at which these gradually formulated traditions begin to take definite shape in a remarkably interesting way. This is the era known to archaeologists as the Classic period (ca. 200 B.C.–800 A.D.), specific evidence for which has been found in the southeastern region of Mexico where the Maya culture flourished.

Palenque is one of the most impressive sights in the world. It emerges from a patch of jungle, a conglomeration of finely built, monumental edifices still covered with white stucco and decorated with exquisite carvings in high relief. Among the temples, the most famous is the so-called "Temple of the Inscriptions," unique in Middle America because of the existence of an underground funerary crypt, inside which was found the dead body of an undoubtedly distinguished person buried approximately one thousand years ago. It seems, in fact, that the entire architectural structure was built with the deliberate purpose of preserving the noble tomb, which can only be reached by descending a steep staircase that connects the shrine above with the funerary enclosure below.

Inside the crypt is a monolithic burial casket carved and decorated on the sides as well as on the lid. It is the lid which particularly interests us when considering in detail the idea of death. On it we see the delicately carved figure of a man reclining in a fetal position. Behind him a tree of life (a ceiba or cottonsilk tree) stands erect with its branches supporting the sky. Underneath, the geometric mask of the monster of the earth serves as a pedestal while on top a Kuan bird symbolizes the heavens. To the sides of the plaque there are streams of water, and close to the nose of the reclining figure a small tube provides him with air. Both inside and outside the sarcophagus precious offerings were found that indicate the high social status of the man: necklaces made of patiently carved jade beads, enormous pearls, fragments of rock crystal, some impressive masks and particularly the dignified stucco heads of two young warriors, considered in our times among the masterpieces of Middle American art.

At first glance what surprises us about the relief is the magnificent technical ability which allowed the craftsman to produce such a fine and vital representation of the human body. Considered within the context of other Mesoamerican works, this one is exceptional for its approximation to visual reality. Even though it remains a highly stylized religious image surrounded by geometric designs, the figure of the man and the bird indicate a profound observation of nature as such, particularly of the structural subtleties of the human anatomy.

The Maya and other prehispanic groups did not cultivate portraiture to a significant extent. Probably this was so because their art was mainly intended to represent not so much the earthly visual reality as the supernatural, highly intellectual world which the eye cannot grasp. But it is possible to consider the relief on the lid of the casket as a re-creation of the man buried inside. Because of the position in which he is depicted, it seems that he has returned to the core of the earth in the form of a child. Nothing in the carving suggests the resigned acceptance of the man's death. On the contrary, efforts were made to provide, as a magical aid, all that was needed for the continuation of his life: water, air, the food of the earth and the sky above. If this were not a sufficient indication of the reluctance to perceive death as a definitive curtailment of existence, a fine umbilical cord creeping up the staircase connects the burial container with the carved representations of women on the façade of the building who hold babies in their arms. In synthesis this appears to be a monumental expression of the concepts according to which the man in his prenatal position may remain forever surrounded by a warm and living atmosphere which assures his future existence.

Another moment in the history of the prehispanic groups should be considered for its concern with death as a structural component of the universe. This is the period represented by the Aztec culture organized about the idea of war as the supreme activity of gods and men. It is known that the Aztec civilization flourished from an intricate fusion of previously existing influences, which were assimilated by later generations, with a tradition of aggressive nomads who arrived in the central highlands during the 13th century. These newcomers or "chichimecas," as they were labeled by the previous inhabitants of the region, already possessed, before migrating, a religion centered on Huitzilopochtli, the solar death deity who had emerged from the body of the earth. From this starting point, and after incorporating the influence of the existing sedentary groups of Central Mexico, the Aztecs evolved a complex and awe-inspiring religious system.

As a warfaring, sun-worshiping empire, they conceived the idea of the cosmos as the permanent and eternal manifestation of war among the gods, each representing a basic universal force. The sun itself became the perfect prototype of the victorious fighter who cyclically has to struggle against darkness in order to rise again each morning as the source of light. Only through war could the rhythmic structure of the universe be consolidated; only death assured the permanence of life.

The ancient concept of duality already expressed in the figurines of the preclassic era continued to be an important factor in the religion of the Aztecs. Accordingly, they accepted the existence of two great generative principles: Omecíhuatl ("Two-Lady") and Ometecuhtli ("Two-Lord"), one feminine and the other masculine, through whose union both gods and men had been created. We should use the term "principles" rather than "gods" because their artistic representation was not permitted; they had no shape or form and thus remained as abstract notions. Still their contact had produced the life of four main deities who inhabited the four cardinal regions of the world: Huitzilopochtli, the solar god of death, Xipe Totec, the flayed god of spring, Tezcatlipoca, the deceiving god of war, and Quetzalcoatl, the cultural hero who had taught men the value of fire and the practice of agriculture. In this religious pattern, the gods opposed each other in their diverse characteristics.

Among all the representations related to death, the monstrous image of Coatlicue ("She with the skirt made of snakes"), the Goddess of Earth, is of particular interest (Figure 2). In the magnificent sculpture which is exhibited in the Museum of Anthropology in Mexico City, Coatlicue represents more than a single deity; she is a synthesis of the religious beliefs of the Aztecs. Completed in the year "onetochtli," corresponding in our own calendar to the year 1454, the representation takes the form of a monolith carved in basaltic stone, and could be regarded as a prehispanic counterpart of the idea of "mother earth" in the Western tradition. However, there are a number of elements that transform it into something exceptional. From a structural point of view, the sculpture shows a geometric pattern, frontally dividing the mass into four horizontal planes: the legs, the skirt, the breasts, and the head in the shape of two large snakes which stare at the same time forward and to the sides. Considered vertically it is a perfectly symmetrical cruciform design in which each of its extremes seems to point to each of the four cardinal regions previously mentioned. From the numerical point of view it is important to remember that "four," the mystical digit, is a multiple of "two," the sign that symbolizes the intrinsic duality of the cosmos.

The legs of the goddess are seen in the form of gigantic eagle claws clenched to the underworld or Mictlan engraved on the soles of her feet. There lived Mictlantecuhtli, one of the deified representations of death in the company of an owl, a symbol of darkness. The legs of the sculpture are also decorated with spiral motifs that appear to represent snails, which in the mythology of the Aztecs were references to Huitzilopochtli.

Between the extremities hangs a monumental snake whose head touches the ground. This element has been interpreted as a phallic symbol and if, in fact, the sculpture as a whole is to be considered as a feminine entity, its

Figure 2: The goddess Coatlicue ("she with the skirt made of snakes"). Aztec Period (1325–1521 A.D.). Museo Nacional de Anthropologia.

synthetic character would not be complete without an allusion to the masculine forces that shape nature.

The second part of the body, formed by a skirt of snakes which gives its name to the image, represents a mundane level of existence, while the breasts, decorated with a necklace formed of human hearts and opened hands, has been interpreted as a reference to sacrificial death. In this particular area of the sculpture we are once again made conscious of death by the presence of the impressive half-living skull which decorates the belt that separates the skirt from the necklace. As mentioned before, human sacrifice, particularly in the form of the removal of the heart, is one of the distinctive features of the Aztec religion. Hearts were symbolized by the eagle and this in turn was also one of the symbols of the deified sun, Tonatiuh. Thus, hearts and blood, the two finest possessions of mankind, constituted the food that preserved the sun and allowed it to move in the sky. This idea is clearly expressed in some of the sacred manuscripts left to us by the Aztecs:

> And four days passed by, and the sun was in the sky.
> All upon the earth feared amid eternal shadows.
> Went the hawk to ask: the gods wish to know the reason why you don't move.
>
> And the sun answered,
> Do you want to know why?
> I want the blood of humans,
> I wish to have their sons, I desire to possess their offspring.

In this fashion, death through sacrifice was one of the privileges reserved for those destined for higher fates. Warriors whose hearts had been removed in order to provide life for the sun were regarded as gods and obtained exclusive honors shared only by two other kinds of dead: those killed in war and women who had died in childbirth. This last belief is of a particular interest, as it is based upon the idea that when giving birth to a child, women were transformed into warriors who struggled so that a new life could begin. When dying in childbirth, they became the eerie Cihuateteo or deified women who accompanied the sun in its journey through the heavens (Figure 3).

In these successive levels of existence, the breast of Coatlicue is followed in the upper section by the forked snake which represents duality incarnated in unity. The head is the symbol of the Omeyocan ("Two-Place"), the region where men and gods alike had taken shape and the source to which everything must return. Thus in a final consideration, Coatlicue becomes a synthesis of the many dualities that form the universe: the mundane and the celestial, femininity and masculinity, the Omeyocan and the Mictlan, life and death. Even though the grandiosity of the sculpture can hardly be comprehended in this superficial description, it remains one of the most im-

Figure 3: Stone "cihuateteo" (deified woman who died in childbirth). Aztec Period (1325–1521 A.D.). Museo Nacional de Anthropologia.

pressive manifestations of man's attempt to explain the contradiction of life and death in his surrounding world.

Finally, it is necessary to remember the Aztec poetry in which the idea of death, especially death in war, is continuously glorified:

> Where are you to go? Where are you to go?
> To war, to the divine water where our mother Itzpapalotl gives color to men.
> In the battlefield dust rises within the water of the bonfire:
> The heart of the God Camaxtle suffers, oh Macuil Malinalli!
> As a flower is the battle and you shall hold it in your hands.
>
> (Cant. Mex., f. 70 r., lin 19 ss. De Tenochtitlan, ca. 1495)

Again, in a different fragment, the glory of sacrifice is remembered:

> Oh Giver of Life!
> Your sacrifice is like emeralds and turquoises.
> It is the happiness and wealth of princes
> To die at the edge of the obsidian,
> To die in war.
>
> (Romances de los Señores de Nueva España, f. 42)

If we have restricted ourselves to the consideration in a rather superficial manner of some of the characteristics of the death ideologies in the history of ancient Mexico, it is mainly with the purpose of pointing out the permanence of some traits and in general the sense of continuity of the idea of death within contemporary Mexican folk culture.

The exquisite and awe-inspiring artistic work described was destined to disappear as an active agent in the official history of Mexico, a history shaped after the bloody conquest that subjugated the native peoples to a position of degradation and oppression. The victorious war songs were followed by dramatic epilogues in which the anguish and despair of the Indians at the sight of their own humiliation became manifest.

The polytheistic religions were replaced by Christianity and the voice of the indigenous Mexican was dimmed forever. Its former power was lost, but a murmur was to remain. The cultural collision came accompanied by a process of ethnic intermeshing commonly known as "mestizaje" and the three hundred years which followed, characterized by political, economic and social colonialism, represent a slow and painful fusion of different cosmic visions and ways of behavior, some belonging to the European tradition and some which had already existed in the prehispanic world.

Without doubt, the Christian tradition has left Mexico a priceless collection of artistic and literary testimonies which document its own interpretation of death. But the fusion of the European cultural patterns with the pre-existing Mexican beliefs offers a third and perfectly individualized complex of practices and ideas. This process of religious fusion is probably the most distinctive feature of contemporary Mexican folk tradition.

However, in a highly stratified country such as Mexico generalizations are dangerous. Even the term "folk culture" is difficult to define. In a broad sense, and for the purposes of this essay, folk culture can be understood as the unification of those traditional forms of behavior which are shared by the majority of the members of the underprivileged socioeconomic strata. As is evident, such a definition has important limitations. First it is necessary to note that it includes the Indian groups that inhabit the territory, a population of about ten million who have scarcely been touched by the dubious privileges of "civilization." There are many important differences between the traditions of these groups and those shared by the inhabitants of the rural provinces which have a constant contact with the urban centers, and between these and the marginal areas of the cities. In a rigorous sense neither is it feasible to restrict the definition of folk culture to the socially and economically underprivileged groups, in view of the fact that many of the customs and beliefs considered as folkloric are also shared to a lesser degree by members of the middle and upper classes of Mexico. There are, however, important variations in meaning.

Such differences are closely linked with a process of desacralization of the traditions involved. We might therefore suggest the hypothesis that an important process of secularization exists in the transit of customs related with death from the way in which they are conceived in the more autochthonous groups (where they cannot be understood outside the framework of religion and magic) to the way in which they are comprehended in an urban atmosphere of different social groups (as colorful customs whose original religious or magical significance is no longer meaningful or has been forgotten).

It is difficult to choose from among the many traditions related with the idea of death those which represent most clearly the typical conceptions that prevail in Mexico. It has often been said that in this country people deal with death sacrilegiously, mocking it as if it were something which deserved to be treated with humor. Whether this view is accurate or exaggerated, it seems clear that death is often the main protagonist in many of the folkloric festivities. Among these none are as well known or as impressive as the celebrations that take place in commemoration of All Souls' Day: the day of the dead.

In Mexico this date is surrounded by a variety of activities which begin with the preparation of specific kinds of food: one of these, "calabaza en tacha," is a preserve made by combining small pieces of pumpkin with sticks of sugarcane, haws, aromatic spices and a peculiar brown sugar called "piloncillo." There is also the so-called "pan de muerto" or bread of the dead consisting of loaves prepared with wheat flour and decorated with stylized bones and tears of the same dough. To these are added a remarkable variety of meals spiced with chili and vegetables typical of each region, placed in bowls and dishes made of black ceramic as a sign of mourning. Among the special sweets which are produced only for this occasion are the famous "calaveras de azúcar," an amazing ensemble of human skulls of all sizes and shapes, made in sugar, decorated with colorful paper and labeled with an assortment of names. When looking at them in the showcases of the sweet shops one cannot help recalling the ancient Aztec tzompantlis, special stone structures where the skulls of the men who had died in sacrifice were exhibited. In our times it is an All Souls' Day custom to purchase one of these sugar sculptures labeled with the name of the buyer or with the name of a friend; these are then given as gifts to be eaten, an act that often puzzles those who are not acquainted with ancient Mexican traditions.

But the preparation of food is only a preliminary activity for the most typical of Mexican customs: the fabrication and decoration of family altars where the dead are honored. These altars or "ofrendas" for All Souls' Day consist of tables or shelves on which the pictures of dead relatives are placed, surrounded by garlands of zempazúchitl flowers, the yellow blossoms which since prehispanic times have accompanied the festivities of the dead. At the feet of these images the food is carefully arranged, often side by side with alcoholic beverages. The table itself is spread with paper mats resembling a colorful and dramatic mosaic. The practice of honoring the dead at home is complemented with the tradition of going to the cemeteries to spend the night after the graves have been decorated with the yellow flowers, candles and dishes. The atmosphere is one of great solemnity while the murmur of prayers offered by those waiting for the coming of the beloved dead float up to the evening sky. The following morning the vigilants walk away with the food, which is then to be eaten by their families.

It is worth reflecting upon the significance of this preparing of food for the dead that afterward is eaten by the living, as it indicates that for the participants in this tradition, existence evolves on two different levels: one natural and the other supernatural. Everything that exists shares in both aspects: one essential, the other transitory. As the dead belong to the former, it is the essence of the food which they digest, while the living benefit only from the material substance. Thus the widespread notion that the food, after being offered to the dead, is "flavorless," that is, without the essence, which has been taken by the dead. These same customs suggest another conclusion: that of the idea of the dead as members of a group of which they never entirely cease to be a part. It is not necessary to point out the similarities of these traditions and the prehispanic cultural patterns already evident in the archaeological findings to which we have previously made reference. In both there seems to exist the assumption that the dead and the living must satisfy similar needs even if the former now belong to a supernatural stage of existence.

The above practices are found throughout Mexico, in small villages as well as in the cities. There are other traditions, however, which are less well known, such as those typical of the Huichol tribes, living scattered and isolated in the mountains of the states of Jalisco, Nayarit and Sinaloa. These are indigenous groups that have had very little contact with the cities and therefore preserve, almost untouched, their prehispanic traditions. They are known to anthropologists for their annual processions to the sacred land of Viricota, in the state of San Luis Potosí for the purpose of collecting peyote or "jícuri," the holy weed which in their mythology is identified with Kauyumarie, the deer, with the sun Taoyopá, and with fire, all of which they worship.

The Huicholes believe that every human being has a soul or kupúri residing in the upper part of the head. When the person dies, the kupúri leaves the body in the form of a small cloud or whirlwind. Five days after the person has died, a ceremony takes place in which the marakamé, that is, the shaman of the group, captures the soul in the shape of a small shining insect by shooting arrows at it. According to this tradition, the soul does not wish to be caught, but as the marakamé exerts enormous effort to convince it, it eventually agrees to return in order to bid farewell to its relatives who have brought gifts and offerings for the occasion. As the kupúri is captured, everyone greets it, and farewells are exchanged amid tears until the shaman once again frees it.

In the five days that elapse between the death of the person and the return of the kupúri, the soul has to engage in a variety of dangerous adventures in order to purge itself of the sins committed during its lifetime, and finally it deposits them at the foot of the ancestral tree. Only afterward can it return to earth to see its relatives for the last time. In its journey the soul manifests itself in the form of a skeleton, while the marakamé himself must accompany the spirit in order to reconstruct every one of the episodes of its mortal life. After the final departure of the kupúri, five years must pass before, according to custom, it can reappear in the form of fragmented rock crystal, regarded thereafter as a repository of wisdom (Figure 4).

Figure 4: Huichol "nearika" (yarn and beeswax on wood) showing a "marakamé" attempting to rescue the soul of a dead man. State of Jalisco, Mexico. Instituto Nacional Indigenista.

Besides the celebrations in commemoration of All Souls' Day, there is another date in the religious calendar when the idea of death manifests itself with great dramatic force. This is during the rituals held for Holy Week, the most important part of the year for devout people, a period of remembrance of the sacrifice of Jesus for the salvation of mankind. In most parts of Mexico these ceremonies also demonstrate the prototypal syncretism we have observed in the prehispanic and European traditions.

Easter Week is preceded by the forty days of Lent, reserved for austerity, abstinence and meditation, and culminates in a variety of processions of masked penitents who, wearing crowns of thorns, whip their bodies in order to obtain absolution for their sins. These practices, striking for their pathos, seem to many observers to be the remnants of superstition and ignorance. Rather than ignorance, however, such traditions merely reflect a distinctive way of perceiving the world as a cosmic experience according to which the human creature accepts the validity of penitence, humiliation and degradation of the body as a means of obtaining a more permanent gift of mercy granted by the majesty of God. It is not difficult to understand the importance and the purpose of a promise of salvation to a people permanently oppressed by the sorrow and misery of their daily existence.

Throughout Mexico the commemoration of the sacrifice of Christ is accompanied by theatrical representations in which biblical episodes are re-enacted. In places such as Ixtapalapa in Mexico City, the crucifixion of Jesus—played by a young penitent, on top of Cerro de la Estrella, an old shrine in existence even before the Spanish culture arrived in Mexico—is one of the most impressive religious episodes of the year. Such theatrical ceremonies involve the participation of as many as fifty thousand people who gather to observe the procession of "The Three Falls" and the Passion of Christ. Few observers fail to be moved by this scene, as among the milling thousands dark-skinned centurions on horseback attempt to control the mobs while groups of barefoot penitents dressed in purple and wearing crowns of thorns carry their heavy crosses.

Similar, but with distinctive features of their own, are the celebrations that take place among the Cora tribes of the mountains in the state of Nayarit. The small village of Jesús María has for the Cora Indians much the same function and meaning as did that of the ceremonial center in the prehispanic world. Here the tribespeople gather during the year on several occasions marked for their religious significance. Of all the festivities that are held here, none is as memorable as the celebration of Holy Week—a celebration so complex and multifaceted that only certain of its more solemn and momentous aspects can be treated here. What distinguishes this holiday most strikingly from others is the presence of a group of men known as "demonios" or "judios" whose purpose is the killing of Christ.

From the moment on Ash Wednesday when they are whipped by a long rope symbolizing the evil forces of a snake, their purpose is the destruction of Christ. Consequently they represent evil, while Jesus incarnates all that is good and pure in the cosmos. The spirit of the festival is captured in the ritual hunting of Jesus which takes place on Good Friday. This performance reproduces step by step the hunting of the deer, a common practice among the members of the group, and can be easily recognized as a remnant of ancient magic customs in which the hunting has to be simulated in order to assure the killing of the animal in reality. Many similar examples are found in other countries and in different eras. What is remarkable about this particular ritual hunting is the fact that it penetrates the celebration of the sacrifice of Christ in such a way that his death is not considered a fact until he is pursued as a deer. Further, among the Cora Jesus does not die on one single occasion but rather at least three different times, for he is identified with other pre-existing deities: the fire, the sun and the deer, all of whom die with him on this solemn occasion.

While emphasis is generally placed upon the idea of the death of Christ in the folk traditions of Mexico, his Resurrection is almost forgotten. This seems peculiar in view of the orthodox Catholic beliefs according to which the death of Christ gains full meaning only with his Resurrection. Once again we must look for the explanation of the importance placed on the death of Christ in popular custom by examining the culture's autochthonous roots.

The apparent pessimism of these celebrations must be considered along with the impressive religious images that accompany them. The varied and silent processions carried out as acts of penance would not be complete without the presence of many wooden sculptures which recreate the moments of agony, resignation and misery that characterize the passion of Christ. Noted for their pathos and expressionistic realism, they remain one of the most distinctive elements of Mexican tradition and give clear indication once again of the continuing vitality of prehispanic culture in which bloody sacrifice and agonizing penitence were common.

It is evident, then, that death is a permanent concern, a daily presence, especially in a country like Mexico in which problems ranging from the difficulty of providing medical services to the persistence of ignorance and oppression accentuate its meaning. The death of an individual, no matter how poor, is always accompanied by elaborate family traditions. As in other areas of social behavior, vigils represent a moment when social solidarity becomes manifest, and often they are transformed into parties in which food and alcoholic beverages flow freely. In many parts of Mexico it is the custom to wash the dead body with water which is later used in the preparation of the meal. This meal is eaten with the purpose of helping the

dead remove the burden of his sins: "ayudar al muertito con sus pecados."
This burden remains a matter of concern for the members of the family,
while at the same time the deceased continues to be regarded as an active
participant in the group.

In the case of the dead being a young child, there are variations which de-
serve mention. The burial of a child is rarely accompanied by expressions of
pain or sadness. On the contrary, there must be joy and happiness in view of
the fact that the child, not having sinned, will immediately join God. What
better fate could await a human? Certainly not a life full of poverty, misery
and deprivation. A child when dying becomes an important protector of his
family, a miniature saint who carries their petitions directly to God. When
buried, children are therefore considered as little angels, "angelitos," and
thus they are attired in robes similar to those seen on the images of saints.
In this case, as well as in the case of adults, processions escorting the dead
to the graveyard are accompanied by music.

Obviously, then, funerals are in themselves a matter of great aesthetic
and cultural interest. The great archaeologist Miguel Covarrubias has left
us an invaluable testimony of such an occasion that clearly illustrates a
custom that, with variations, can be found everywhere in Mexico, and that
deserves quoting at length. Referring to the funeral of an old woman from
Tehuantepec in the state of Oaxaca, Covarrubias writes:

> When the woman entered into the death agony, all close relatives were present
> and a prayer expert had been sent for. The deep sigh that escaped her was re-
> garded as a sign that the soul had left her body. A violent reaction shook the
> members of the household, strangely calm and collected before, particularly the
> women, her daughters and sisters, who gave vent to wild outbursts of despair and
> screams. . . . Soon the neighbors and distant relatives came to the house to
> embrace and sympathize with the mourners, as well as to deposit their alms. . . .
>
> The corpse was then dressed in her best clothes, . . . and her hair was carefully
> combed and then placed, not on a bed or mat, but on the bare ground in front of
> the house altar, its head resting on a little pillow placed over two bricks. It was
> provided with four candles of pure beeswax and with vases of tuberoses, as well as
> with an incense brazier. A male prayer-expert (rezador) knelt in front of the
> corpse to pray, alternately censing the saint's altar and the body. A litany was
> recited and the women chanted. . . .
>
> As there was enough money available, the wake proceeded throughout the
> night, and everybody came to help. A table was set for the elders and the company
> was served coffee, bread, mezcal (a kind of liqueur) and cigarettes. When
> everything was ready, the funeral procession started for the cemetery in the cool
> of the late afternoon, preceded by a brass band playing sad or farewell music. . . .
> The procession marched through the principal streets, the coffin flanked by
> solemn men in their Sunday clothes, the elders in red felt and silver-braided hats.
> Immediately behind followed the husband and sisters and daughters of the old

lady, in a state of utter despair, dramatic in their black clothes, unkempt hair, and trailing shawls, crying and wailing, carried, or rather dragged by the arms on the shoulders of friends. . . .

At the cemetery . . . the coffin was nailed and lowered into the grave. At this point it is the custom for the nearest women relatives of the deceased to give a final and most violent display of despair. . . .

The mourners returned home to initiate the prayers (rezos) said every evening for nine days after the burial before an earth and sand replica of the grave. This symbolic grave was erected over the ground where the corpse had lain in front of the saint's altar, and was covered with flowers, with a candle at each of its four corners. In Tlacotepec, a beautiful little village by a spring in the neighborhood of Ixtepec, it is customary to plant grains of corn all over the grave, which is watered every day, so that the corn sprouts, and by the ninth day it has become a miniature cornfield. This charming custom has no purpose, according to the people of Tlacotepec, beyond an aesthetic one, but it is significant that they believe that, though the body is gone, the spirit of the deceased remains with the family for these nine days, some people going so far as to assure one that during that time the dead lives under the saint on the alter.

Every day the flowers on the make-believe grave are replaced with fresh ones, and those wilted are saved in a basket. At the end of nine days the mound is dismantled; the earth and flowers are collected, carried away, and thrown into the river, the churchyard, or cemetery. It is not until then that the house may be swept. Black bows are hung on the gate and windows, where they remain until they fall to pieces, and for nine months the family must observe deep mourning. Women wear only black costumes with white ruffles on the bottom of the skirt, but it is enough for men to wear black ribbons on their left arms for a while.[1]

In contrast to the somber, often pessimistic character of much of its funerary ritual, Mexico is also well known, paradoxically, for the humorous nature with which her people regard death. In the end death is to be seen with a touch of humor in order that the psychological burden it implies may be lessened. Not only a smile but outright laughter and mockery distinguish some of the most typical manifestations of Mexican folklore concerning death; but it is a bitter gaiety that philosophically recognizes the fact that the definitive character of death can only be successfully confronted with gestures of indifference and scorn. Among these cultural gestures the "calaveras," verses that celebrate the death of a still-living person and his arrival in hell or heaven, are typical. Politicians and other prominent figures are favorite victims of this morbid joke. But power or prestige are not prerequisites for receiving, as a gift for All Souls' Day, a verse in which one's death has been humorously related. Apparently unique to Mexican culture, the "calaveras" are seen as a particularly effective antidote for the anguish that all men must feel when contemplating the termination of their life.

[1]Miguel Covarrubias, *Mexico South* (New York: Knopf, 1946), pp. 390–94.

Figure 5: Cardboard All Soul's Day Mask. Mexico City.

Figure 7: Funerary police car. Wire and paper. Mexico City.

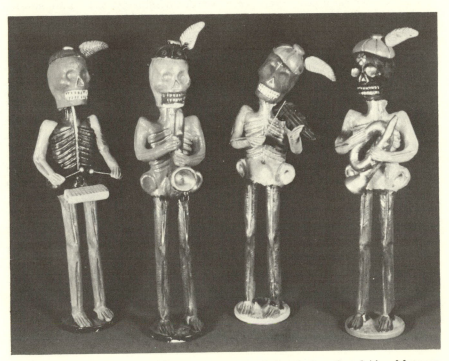

Figure 6: A band of "mariachis" (musicians). Colored clay. San Isidro Metysec, Estado de Mexico.

The Mexican acceptance of death is perhaps best understood by observing the almost infinite collection of toys which are inspired by it, and which are intended purely to give pleasure to children (Figure 5). As with all popular creations, they are made in perishable materials, by anonymous artisans who do not hesitate to artistically transform a group of skeletons into a band of "mariachis" (the musical ensembles which are hired to entertain on holidays or serenades) wearing their colorful hats and playing their traditional instruments (Figure 6). It is also possible to encounter festive arrangements in cardboard, clay and even sugar, of funeral processions in which, by means of an ingenious mechanism, the deceased is made to spring periodically out of the casket, stimulating the hilarity of those who contemplate him (Figure 7).

These complex and diversified folkloric traditions—the poetry and songs, the masks and sculpture—inevitably suggest the enormous tenacity and wisdom of a people and a culture whose oppressed situation has not been an obstacle for the expression of a unique and creative philosophy of life and death. But ultimately we return to the exquisite poetry of the native Mexicans:

Not for a second time do we come to earth,
Oh, princes! rejoice and bring flowers.
We are going to the kingdom of death;
Only in transit are we.

It is true, it is true that we shall go,
It is true that we are forced to leave.
It is true that we shall abandon the blossoms, the songs and the earth.
Yes, it is true that we shall leave.

Where are we to go?
Will we still be alive or shall we be dead?
Is there a place where existence will prevail?

On earth, only the beautiful song and the lovely flower is our wealth and adornment.
Let us rejoice in both!

(Cant. Mex., f. 61 n., lin. 27 ss. Anónimo de Tenochtitlan)

GATES AJAR:
DEATH IN MORMON THOUGHT
AND PRACTICE

MARY ANN MEYERS

THE IDEA OF DEATH RAISES QUESTIONS WHICH LIE AT THE CORE OF ALL religious and philosophical systems of thought. As Peter Berger suggests, death presents the ultimate threat to a socially constructed reality.[1] If the function of a belief system is to give meaning to the exigencies of collective history and individual biography, the fundamental test of a world view is how it deals with death. Indeed as Berger and Thomas Luckmann wrote in an earlier work, it is in "the legitimation of death that the transcending potency" of a symbolic universe most clearly manifests itself.[2]

For most of us operating in the Judaic-Christian tradition, death is a profound mystery—at once unique and universal, a crucial and unrepeatable episode in the life of man, shadowy and haunting, what Paul Tillich called the "darkness of the no more."[3] Confronting it can be an anomic experience, terrifying and often cruel. It is worth remembering, however, that in modern America we are removed from the reality of death to a degree unimaginable in frontier communities. Quite apart from the state of medical progress in the antebellum West, the imminence of death was heightened for the first generation of Mormons by the dearth of doctors, the nearly total absence of hospitals, the probability of Indian attacks, and the risks to health attendant upon a rough outdoor existence where food was sometimes scarce and man was often at the mercy of the elements. To these perils, moreover, there must be added the life-threatening experiences of persecution and open group conflict, and the hazards of a 1,400-mile migration across the plains.

Thomas O'Dea reports that by the end of 1846, less than a year after the

---

[1] *The Sacred Canopy,* (Garden City: Doubleday-Anchor, 1969), p. 23.
[2] Peter L. Berger and Thomas Luckmann, *The Social Construction of Reality* (Garden City: Doubleday-Anchor, 1967), p. 101.
[3] Paul Tillich, "The Eternal Now" in *The Meaning of Death,* Herman Feifel, ed. (New York: McGraw-Hill, 1959), p. 33.

Saints' exodus began, there were some 600 graves in the cemetery at Winter Quarters.[4] How many Mormons died along the trail before reaching the Great Basin may never be known, but one witness, Mrs. Benjamin G. Ferris, the wife of a government official who served briefly in Utah, paints a grim picture of the toll taken by the trek to Zion. Traveling toward Salt Lake, Mrs. Ferris met a discouraged widow who had turned back with her last surviving children. The woman plaintively asked Mrs. Ferris if she would pause by a child's grave somewhat farther west. "Alas!" the usually caustic Mormon critic says:

> It will be difficult to distinguish the resting place of this poor child, in the multitude of graves that line the road. The further we go, the more frequent they become; and we are fast growing callous to the mortality and suffering, of which they furnish such abundant evidence. What a history they unfold! Some are found close to the way-side, as if its poor tenant had been hurriedly and carelessly inhumed by strangers; others appear a little further off upon a slight mound, or under a solitary tree, as though its occupant had been laid in its lonely resting place by surviving friends amid tears and anguish—its future guardian, the roving red man—its future requiem, the howling of the wolf.[5]

In the journals and diaries of many Mormons one finds consummate human sorrow revealed in the face of death, and the natural anxiety of pilgrims for whom Zion is still a distant promise. Hosea Stout, for example, recorded the tragic circumstances which claimed three children and his wife in a five-month period in 1846, yet it is evident he retained a tenacious hold on the Mormon vision. "How often," Stout wrote,

> I beheld my family one by one yielding up the Ghost and bereaving me of every earthly prospect with the melancholy reflection that there was yet more soon to follow. How often in sorrow and anguish have I said in my heart: When shall my trials and tribulations end? But amid all these adverse changes, these heart-rending trials, not once . . . have I regreted that I set out to follow the council [sic] of the people of God and to obey the voice of the spirit to flee the land of the Gentiles.[6]

The faith which sustained the Mormons in the darkest hours of their pilgrimage was grounded in what O'Dea has called an "extra-Christian evolutionism."[7] The Saints conceived of the universe as an on-going process, and pervading every other tenet of their theology was an unquestioning faith in the reality of eternal progression. The Mormons' beliefs about death cannot be understood apart from their conviction, expressed over and over again, that improvement was inevitable if man kept working towards it.

[4]O'Dea, *The Mormons* (Chicago: Univ. of Chicago Press, 1957), p. 80.
[5]*The Mormons At Home* (New York: Dix and Edwards, 1856), pp. 55f.
[6]*On the Mormon Frontier* (Salt Lake City: University of Utah Press, 1964), 1:213.
[7]O'Dea, p. 95.

For the Saints, life on earth encompassed neither the beginning nor the end of human existence. Joseph Smith taught that "the mind or intelligence which man possesses is co-eternal with God Himself."[8] According to the doctrine of pre-existence, Mormons believed "eternal man lived a personal life before the earth-life began."[9] God earned the title of Father by taking "intelligence . . . which was not created nor made"[10] and begetting spirits, which then spent their premortal life with Him.[11]

The Saints did not speculate upon how long man lived in his first estate. They insisted, however, that "intelligent spirits have possessed, from the beginning, a consciousness of the world in which they found themselves," though memory of its initial experiences had fled the mortal mind.[12] In their premortal existence, Mormons said human souls felt pain and pleasure, and through their activities in that realm, they made varying degrees of progress.[13] In one particular, however, "they were all alike: by their faithful efforts, they had earned the right to take another step onward and share in the earth experience."[14]

The origin myth holds that when God saw that the spirits "were ready for further light," He "came down among them to discuss their future."[15] Explaining that "familiarity with gross matter" was necessary for "real mastery over the universe," He presented them with a plan whereby they could acquire the requisite experience by putting on bodies which would be subject to death.[16] Should the spirits agree to the deity's development plan—and as *free* spirits it was their privilege to accept or reject it—a technical necessity was for someone to break a law and thereby bring immortal souls under the bondage of mortality. A further requirement, then, would be for someone to raise bodies from their graves inasmuch as these "tabernacles," when reunited with eternal souls, would "become mighty helps in the endless search for truth."[17] God proposed Adam for the first task and Jesus was chosen (or volunteered) for the second.[18] But before the grand design could

---

[8]"The King Follett Discourse," a sermon preached at the funeral of Elder King Follett (1844), in *The Vision, or, The Degrees of Glory,* Ned B. Lundwall, ed. (Independence, Mo.: Zion Printing and Publishing, 1945), p. 23.

[9]John A. Widtsoe, *Rational Theology* (Logan, Utah: General Priesthood Committee, 1915), p. 14.

[10]*Doctrine and Covenants,* 93:29.

[11]See Brigham Young, *Journal of Discourses* (Liverpool: F. D. Richards, 1854–75), 1:50; 4:216; and 11:43.

[12]Widtsoe, p. 28.

[13]Ibid.

[14]Ibid., p. 128.

[15]Ibid., p. 33.

[16]Ibid., p. 30. Cf. *Doctrine and Covenants,* 93:33f.

[17]Ibid., p. 31.

[18]*Journal of Discourses,* 3:256. Cf. John Taylor, *The Meditation and Atonement* (Salt Lake City: Deseret News Company, 1882), p. 97.

be voted upon, Satan interjected himself into the discussion. Aspiring to un-merited power, the Son of the Morning proposed that during their earthly sojourn, men be forced to do his will in return for a guarantee of salvation.[19] Jesus, however, promptly objected to any sort of compulsive redemption on the grounds that "it interfered with the essential right of intelligent beings to act for themselves."[20] Arminianism won. The assembled spirits approved God's plan without Satan's amendment, and the rebuffed angel then led an open rebellion for which he and his followers were expelled from heaven.[21] "The hosts who accepted the plan," meanwhile, "girded themselves with the necessary strength to begin the pilgrimage."[22]

Before they could embark on their new careers, of course, the spirits needed a place in which to acquire the desired familiarity with gross matter. God provided it by assembling materials found in the universe.[23] The spirits also needed tabernacles. God formed these for Adam and Eve, com-manding them then "to multiply and replenish the earth." At this point, the Mormon myth accounting for the origin of death shades into the familiar Eden story, with one significant variation: the Fall of Man is a *felix culpa* not because it made possible the "coming of so great a redeemer," but be-cause it opened the door to eternal progression.

The Saints did not share the orthodox Christian belief that by his disobedience Adam corrupted the whole human race. In their view, he served the great law of development by playing the technically necessary role of "law breaker." By begetting children, moreover, Adam and Eve set in motion the process by which waiting spirits might become "personages of tabernacle."[24] Definition of the scope of the Atonement, a burning theological issue in nineteenth-century America, was really peripheral to the Mormon's conception of Christ's saving act. Their emphasis was not upon the Son's accomplishment in bringing about a reconciliation between God and man in the sense of defeating the objective power of sin or in the sense of making satisfaction for sin or in the sense of freeing man from his fear of God, thus enabling him to respond personally to God's love.[25] The principle and inestimable value of Christ's suffering, dying and rising again was, according to Mormon belief, that these acts purchased a resurrected body for man. By releasing human souls from the bondage of death, Jesus made it possible for them to "become the fathers and mothers of lives, and

[19]James E. Talmage, *Articles of Faith* [1890] (Salt Lake City: Deseret News, 1919), p. 65.
[20]Widtsoe, p. 35.
[21]Ibid., p. 65. Cf. *Doctrine and Covenants*, 24:36f and *Journal of Discourses*, 3:369.
[22]Widtsoe, p. 36.
[23]Ibid., p. 45.
[24]*Journal of Discourses*, 7:268.
[25]See Van A. Harvey, *A Handbook of Theological Terms* (London: Allen and Unwin, 1966), pp. 30f. for a discussion of traditional ways of viewing the atonement.

be capable of perpetual and eternal progression."[26] He "saved" man mainly in the negative sense that he removed a principal impediment to continual development, namely, the prospect of perpetual incorporeity.

The Saints' consummation myth, like their origin myth, is firmly rooted in the visions received by Joseph Smith. He taught that as a direct result of the sacrifice of Jesus Christ, every member of the human race will one day acquire a resurrected body. The Book of Mormon says: "This restoration shall come to all, both old and young, both bond and free, both male and female, both the wicked and the righteous." (Alma 11:44) The Saints believed in two general resurrections—termed first and final, or the resurrection of the just and the resurrection of the unjust. The first was inaugurated by Christ's resurrection at the time of which many departed saints came forth from their graves.[27] It will be completed at the Parousia when immortal bodies will be put on by three specific classes of dead persons: those who have kept faithfully the laws of God as made known to them, children, and the heathen who died in ignorance groping for light. The final resurrection will be deferred until the end of the millennium and will occur in connection with the Last Judgment.[28]

Mormons were as explicit about the nature of the resurrection as they were about the sequence of the resurrection. President John Taylor said that "all must come forth from the grave . . . in the selfsame tabernacles that they possessed while living on the earth. Bone will come to its bone and flesh and sinew will cover the skeleton, and at the Lord's bidding breath will enter the body and we shall appear, many of us, a marvel to ourselves."[29] Brigham Young said that though the mortal particles "be deposited in the depths of the sea, and though one particle is in the north, another in the south, another in the east, and another in the west, all will be brought together again in the twinkling of an eye."[30]

The Mormon conception of the millennium appears as hopeful and expectant as any postexilic eschatology found in Jewish apocalyptic literature. The Saints believed that in connection with Christ's second coming the earth would undergo "a change in its physical features, climate, soil, productions; and in its political, moral and spiritual government."[31] It would become a virtual Garden of Eden where Mormons would be "the owners of the soil, the proprietors of all real estate, and other precious things; and the kings, governors, and judges of the earth."[32] As lords of

[26]Talmage, p. 141.

[27]Cf. *Matthew* 27:52.

[28]See Talmage, pp. 396–401.

[29]Sermon delivered at the funeral of Ann Tenora and George Callister, published in the *Deseret News*, 26 (March 21, 1877).

[30]*Journal of Discourses*, 8:28.

[31]Parley P. Pratt, *Key to the Science of Theology* (Liverpool: F. D. Richards, 1855), p. 133.

[32]Ibid., p. 134.

creation, they would be able to turn their energies from getting and spending to concentrate exclusively upon building temples and officiating in them for those who died ignorant of the restored gospel. The tempo of missionary activity in the spirit world would be stepped up until "man is sealed to man" in a "perfect chain of priesthood from Adam to the winding-up scene."[33]

For all its physical splendor and spiritual satisfactions, however, the earth in the millennium would be but another preparatory stage occupied briefly by souls eternally progressing. After a thousand years of peace would come the judgment—an event Mormons said was "divinely foreordained" and at which "every man will be called to answer for his deeds; and not for his deeds alone but for his words also, and even for the thoughts of his heart."[34] It would be Jesus, they believed, who would sit in the magistrate's seat on the Dies Irae, and He would consign men either to salvation or damnation.[35] In general, according to the revelation received by Joseph Smith, there would be three degrees of glory and a place of everlasting fire.[36]

The Saints were loath to predict anyone's condemnation to hell, but acceptance of universal salvation would have vitiated their cherished principle of free will. Although it was often conceived of as a tide, in theory there was nothing compulsive about eternal progression. It was possible that given individuals might turn their backs on the law of development; these few would suffer the wrath of God. The unforgiveable sin was committed by "those who have received the truth, or had the privilege of receiving it, and then rejected it. All will be saved," said Brigham Young, "except the sons of perdition."[37] In this category clearly fell Mormon apostates, probably conscious persecutors of the Saints,[38] and perhaps also unrepentant adulterers and those who had shed innocent blood and not atoned with their own.[39] These were the damned, and their fate was to be "everlasting punishment."[40] It would have been "better for them," said Joseph Smith, "never to have been born."[41]

---

[33]*Journal of Discourses,* 15:138.

[34]Talmage, p. 57. Cf. Book of Mormon, 2 Nephi 9:16.

[35]Ibid., p. 59.

[36]Mormon beliefs about the final state of man are derived principally from a vision Joseph Smith reportedly received on February 16, 1832. An account of it can be found in *Doctrine and Covenants,* 76. See also Book of Mormon, 2 Nephi 9:16.

[37]Sermon delivered April 5, 1860, published in the *Deseret News,* 10 (May 16, 1860).

[38]See O'Dea, p. 131.

[39]George A. Smith, *Answers to Questions* (Salt Lake City: Deseret News Office, 1872), pp. 44f. Nineteenth century Mormons seemed to hold that there were limits to the propitiatory effects of Christ's sacrifice in relation to actual sin. According to their doctrine of blood atonement, the transgressions of adultery and murder could not be expiated by any other means than the shedding of the blood of the transgressor.

[40]*Doctrine and Covenants,* 76:44.

[41]*Doctrine and Covenants,* 76:32.

The majority of the earth's inhabitants, according to the Mormons, were destined for the lowest realm of glory known as the telestial kingdom.[42] Its inhabitants would include those who refused to receive the gospel of Christ but still did not deny the Holy Ghost through the ministrations of other spirits.[43] In this category the prophet puts "liars, and sorcerers, and adulterers, and whoremongers."[44] They would be blessed neither with the presence of the Father nor the Son; still the glory of their kingdom would surpass all understanding.[45]

The middle kingdom was called the terrestial. The inhabitants of this realm were described as those who "died without the law;" those who "received not the testimony of Jesus in the flesh, but afterwards received it," and "honorable men of earth who were blinded by the craftiness" of others. These spirits were destined to receive the presence of the Son, but not the fullness of the Father.[46]

The Saints' term for the highest kingdom was celestial, and they located it on a sanctified and crystalized earth where God and Jesus would dwell forever.[47] Minimum requirements for admission to this realm would include faith, repentance, baptism by immersion and reception of the Holy Ghost by the laying on of hands.[48] What more would be necessary to enter this kingdom was nowhere specified, but the Mormons believed it would contain various degrees of glory.[49] Consigned to the lower celestial estate would be Latter-day Saints who had not entered into the covenant of marriage on earth. Developed coterminously with a mounting emphasis on the desirability of polygamy, this doctrinal addition to Smith's codified consummation myth held that "the fulness of exaltation" would be denied bachelors, for they would have forfeited the right to wives and children in the afterlife. The highest degree of glory, then, was reserved for those Mormons who married for time and eternity. They would beget children without pain,[50] and more:

> . . . the great creative principle, the mechanical work which was performed by our Father and God in constructing creations, and in redeeming and glorifying them; the great principle of knowledge from which our Father and God can call forth from a shapeless mass of dust an immortal tabernacle, into which enters an immortal spirit, all these principles of wisdom, knowledge and power will be given to his children, and will enable them to organize the elements, form creations, and

[42]*Doctrine and Covenants,* 77:109.
[43]*Doctrine and Covenants,* 76:82–86.
[44]*Doctrine and Covenants,* 76:103.
[45]*Doctrine and Covenants,* 76:89.
[46]*Doctrine and Covenants,* 76:72–77.
[47]*Doctrine and Covenants,* 76:62.
[48]*Doctrine and Covenants,* 76:51–53.
[49]*Doctrine and Covenants,* 131:1.
[50]See Orson Pratt, "The Three Glories" (1873), in Lundwall, pp. 36ff.

call forth from the dust intelligent beings, who will be under their charge and control.[51]

In the celestial kingdom, the Saints expected to become gods.

From the beginning Mormons retained the traditional Christian view of death as a separation of body and soul. To a degree which was unique among Western religions, however, they viewed the spirit world as a place of conscious activity and decision-making where spirits continued to perfect their knowledge of the law. Although Robert Mullen attributes to Joseph Smith the observation that "forever playing harps around the throne of God is a poor prospect,"[52] and at King Follett's funeral, the Mormon leader expressed the belief that the spirits of his friends and relatives "exist in a place where they converse together,"[53] this conception of a dynamic afterlife was not greatly emphasized until after the prophet's death. Indeed, the *Book of Mormon* refers to "the state of the soul between death and the resurrection" as "a state of rest."[54] Whereas eleven years after Smith's assassination, Parley Pratt described the Spirit world as a "place of preparation, instruction or education, where spirits are chastened or improved."[55]

A possible explanation for what appears in Mormon writing as an increasingly detailed scenario for postmortem existence is that the Saints could not, in the last analysis, "let go" of so charismatic a leader as Joseph Smith. Unwilling to entertain the idea that through death the prophet should be lost to them forever, the Mormons recreated the community of Saints beyond death. Exclusion was followed by a new integration. As Durkheim's student, Robert Hertz, observed in a discussion of the social functions of beliefs about death, the afterlife could be pictured as a state free of "external constraints and physical necessities which, here on earth, constantly hinder the flight of collective desire" precisely because it was a realm of the ideal.[56]

On the twelfth anniversary of the martyrdom, the *Western Standard* commented that the murderers "did not realize that they were removing [Joseph and Hyrum] to a sphere of far more extended usefulness, where they could more effectively help—because [they were] unfettered and untrammeled—to roll forward the designs of God in relation to this latter dispensation."[57] Dismissing the possibility that spirits of the faithful departed

[51]Pratt, "The Increased Powers and Capacities of Man In His Future Estate" (n. d.), in Lundwall, p. 82.

[52]Quoted by Robert Mullen, *The Latter-day Saints: The Mormons Yesterday and Today* (New York: Doubleday, 1966), p. 25.

[53]Smith in Lundwall, p. 24.

[54]Book of Mormon, Alma 40:11–12.

[55]Pratt, p. 126. Cf. Book of Mormon, Alma 40:11–14.

[56]Robert Hertz, *Death and the Right Hand,* translated by Rodney and Claudia Needham (London: Cohen and West, 1960), p. 77.

[57]*Writings from the Western Standard* (New York: Paladin Press, 1969), June 27, 1844.

had nothing better to do than "sit and sing . . . away to everlasting bliss,"[58] Brigham Young wrote that "Father Joseph . . . and every other good Saint is just as busy in the spirit world as you and I are here. They are preaching, preaching all the time, and preparing the way for us to hasten our work in building temples here and everywhere."[59] At the funeral of Jedediah Grant, he said: "Brother Grant . . . is at work for the benefit of Zion, for that is all the business that Joseph and Elders of this Church have on hand";[60] and on the same occasion, the *Standard* observed: "We will not repine at his departure for the Lord . . . has removed him to a higher, more extensive and glorious sphere where he can move foreward the cause of Zion in mightier power than he possibly could upon earth."[61] Eliza R. Snow expressed the same sentiment in a poem:

> Some say that Jedediah's gone to rest.
> They mean mortality, not *him*. To rest?
> No; J. M. Grant could never rest, and leave
> His fellow-laborers here to tug and toil—
> Spend and be spent, to move the mighty ship
> Of Zion on. No, no: that never was
> His calling. He will never rest, until
> Zion's redeem'd—Jerusalem built up—
> Iniquity destroyed, and Satan bound.
> He'll not relax in faith and diligence
> Until his brethren shall with him partake
> The promis'd blessings of a glorious rest.
> He boldly fought the pow'rs of darkness here
> And he'll oppose them there, with all his might;
> Till Satan and his hosts are overcome—
> Till truth and righteousness on earth shall reign.[62]

The nature of spirit world activity, according to Mormon doctrine, involved bringing the message of the restored gospel to those multitudes who had no opportunity to hear it during their earthly existence. Taking as their Biblical text the Petrine passage about Christ "preaching unto the spirits in prison" between His crucifixion and resurrection (I Peter 3:18–20), the Saints taught that the task incumbent upon all Mormons after death was to prepare "the way to redeem the nations of earth" by calling to repentance "disobedient spirits" and presenting the tenets of Mormonism to all those ignorant of them.[63] Thus prepared, countless Catholics, Protestants, Jews,

---

[58] *Journal of Discourses,* 12:313.
[59] Ibid., 3:369f.
[60] Ibid., 12:313.
[61] *Writings From the Western Standard,* Jan. 17, 1857.
[62] *Deseret News,* 4 (Dec. 10, 1856).
[63] *Journal of Discourses,* 3:369f. Cf. Talmage, p. 63.

Muslims, infidels and members of the most primitive societies on earth would be in a position to accept or reject baptism vicariously received for them by Saints on earth.

Joseph Smith taught his followers that "the greatest responsibility in this world" lain upon them by God was "to seek after" their dead.[64] Mormons believed that this vicarious work was absolutely essential in order that the departed might be duly admitted into their church and allowed to share in endless possibilities for progression. Baptism of the dead was considered an "ordinance and preparation that the Lord ordained and prepared before the foundation of the world, for the salvation of the dead who should die without a knowledge of the gospel."[65] The Saints cited a Biblical basis for the ritual in I Corinthians 15:29: "Else what shall they do which are baptized for the dead, if the dead rise not at all? Why are they then baptized for the dead?" O'Dea suggests that the ordinance was reflective of "a curious desire to bind past generations to the present and not cast aside, as lost, those who came before the miraculous restoration . . . It seems," he says, "that at the very time when Mormonism was in fact and in belief immensely widening the chasm that separated the converted from the general run of their fellows, there was needed some countermotion, some symbolic link between the separated and their own past in terms of relatives and ancestors."[66]

Vision experiences played a critical part in the Mormons' understanding of the nature of death. Certainly one of the first such experiences to befall a Mormon after Joseph's death was that which Parley Pratt reported having as he was returning to Nauvoo after hearing of the murder. "The Spirit of God came upon me," the apostle said; and he reported it saying: "Lift up your head and rejoice; for behold! it is well with my servants Joseph and Hyrum. My servant Joseph still holds the keys of my kingdom in this dispensation, and he shall stand in due time on the earth, in the flesh, and fulfill that to which he is appointed."[67]

A vision of the final judgment was reported by John D. Lee,[68] and at the funeral of Jedediah M. Grant. Heber Kimball told the congregation that Grant had confided in him, saying:

> I have been into the spirit world . . . and, of all the dreads that ever came across men, the worst was to have to again return to my body, though I had to do it. O! the order and government that were there! When . . . I saw the order of righteous

---

[64]Smith in Lundwall, p. 26.

[65]*Doctrine and Covenants,* 128:5.

[66]O'Dea, p. 57.

[67]Parley P. Pratt, *Autobiography,* P. P. Pratt, ed. (Salt Lake City: Deseret Book Co., 1972), p. 333.

[68]*A Mormon Chronicle* (San Marino, Calif.: The Huntingdon Library, 1955), 1:252f.

men and women; beheld them organized in several grades, and there appeared to be no obstruction to my vision; I could see every man and woman in their grade and order. I looked to see whether there was any disorder there, but there was none; neither could I see any death nor darkness . . . or confusion.[69]

The appearance of individual spirits was apparently a fairly common phenomenom. Austin E. Fife has recounted his grandmother's tale of a visitation from a victim of the Mountain Meadows massacre who returned to look upon her baby.[70] David King Udall told of the appearance of his sister some months after her death, an experience which he says impressed him "with the reality of life after death," and which was a comfort to him throughout his life.[71] And far removed from these personal encounters was President Wilford Woodruff's report of a visit from the signers of the Declaration of Independence, who, he said, chastised him for neglecting to "redeem them," and spurred him on to more vigorous baptizing of the dead.[72]

The prophet himself was said to have appeared to a number of Mormons. Brigham Young reported a visit during an illness in which Joseph told him that "the mind of man must be open to receive all spirits, in order to be prepared, to receive the spirit of the Lord." On this occasion, too, Young had a glimpse of pre-existing souls. "I saw," he said, "how we were organized before we took tabernacles."[73] Woodruff related that the prophet visited him "a great deal" after his death. The first time was during a storm at sea; the last time in a vision which suggested something of the bustle of post-mortem existence:

In a night vision I saw him [Joseph] at the door of the temple of heaven. He came and spoke to me. He said he could not stop to talk with me because he was in a hurry . . . I met half a dozen brethren who had held high positions on earth and none of them could stop to talk with me because they were in a hurry . . . By and by I saw the Prophet again, and I got the privilege to ask him a question. "Now," said I, "I want to know why you are in a hurry. I have been in a hurry all through my life but I expected my hurry would be over when I got into the kingdom of heaven, if I ever did." Joseph said, 'I will tell you, Brother Woodruff, every dispensation . . . has had a certain amount of work to do to prepare to go to the earth with the Savior when He goes to reign on earth. Each dispensation has had ample time to do this work. We have not. We are the last dispensation, and so much work has to be done and we need to be in a hurry in order to accomplish it."[74]

[69]Remarks made at Grant's funeral, 1856, in Lundwall, pp. 71f.
[70]"Popular Legends of the Mormons." *California Folklore Quarterly*, 1 (April, 1942), pp. 121f.
[71]*Arizona Pioneer Mormon* (Tucson: Arizona Silhouettes, 1959), p. 9.
[72]"Testimony," in Lundwall, pp. 100f.
[73]Quoted in Stout, 1.238.
[74]In Lundwall, pp. 101f.

Mystical experience of this sort reinforced the Saints' thanatological beliefs, and they seem to have been as critical as any physical encounters with dying in shaping the Mormons' attitudes toward death. Clearly death was not a release from striving.

It was, however, portrayed as a release from suffering, as shown in numerous Mormon accounts of the passing of kith and kin. In an 1857 edition of the *Deseret News,* a prototypic obituary reads: "She is spared the bitter sorrow of all who linger here."[75] In his autobiography, Parley Pratt described his wife's death as a deliverance from "this world of sorrow and pain."[76] At the death of a child, John D. Lee composed the following lines:

> Death has transplanted My child
> Beyond the Reach of Sin & Guile
> Where every faithful Saint must go
> & leve the scenes of Earth below.
> From Death to Life we Must pass through
> & bid this Sinful World adiew.
> Our Father's Mansion then we'll gain
> Beyond the reach of Grief & Pain.
> Then for that day let us prepare
> To meet our Friends and kindred there
> That we to Earth May come again
> To Spend the Great Millenium.[77]

Recognition of the right of the bereaved to mourn and of their need of consolation is found in the funeral sermons preached by Mormon leaders throughout the last half of the nineteenth century. But what emerges far more strongly in these discourses is a kind of Pauline admonition that lamentation is inappropriate for Saints. "Mourning for the righteous dead springs from ignorance and weakness that are planted within the mortal tabernacle," Brigham Young said. "Could we have knowledge and see into eternity, if we were perfectly free from weakness, blindness and lethargy with which we are clothed in the flesh, we should have no disposition to weep or mourn."[78]

An almost ritual line in published death notices tells us that the departed "died strong in the faith of a glorious resurrection."[79] Confidence in God's justice is also a common attitude among the Mormons, and it can be traced through several moving passages in John D. Lee's diaries from the time of his excommunication in 1870 to his execution in 1877, when the Saints offered up his life as a one-man reparation for the Mountain Meadows

---

[75] 7 (April 29, 1857).
[76] *Autobiography,* p. 166.
[77] Lee, 2:94.
[78] *Journal of Discourses,* 4:131.
[79] *Deseret News,* 9 (Aug. 31, 1859).

massacre in which many Mormons evidently participated. On the day of his death, Lee wrote: "I am on the brink of eternity . . . I feel resigned to my fate. I feel as a summer morn. I have done nothing wrong; my conscience is clear before God and man. I am ready to meet my Redeemer and those that have gone before me, behind the veil . . . I do not fear to die; I trust in God . . . I do not fear eternity . . . I ask the Lord . . . if my labors be done, to receive my spirit."[80]

If countless Mormons, even such as Lee, faced death calmly with a sure and certain faith in the promises of their religion, still others "cheerfully met that power termed [by others] 'King of Terrors.' "[81] Their attitude was grounded in their belief that life beyond the grave would offer further and appropriate opportunities for personal development toward godhood. At the death of President George A. Smith, poet Eliza Snow wrote:

> He is not dead; yet death has done its work;
> It came, but not in ghastliness—it as
> A kindly porter set the Gates Ajar,
> And he stepped forth, leaving the tenement
> A breathless corpse, that slumbers in the tomb;
> 'Twas worn and weary and it needed rest.
> No faith, nor prayers, nor heart yearning of
> The loving and beloved, could longer bind
> The mighty spirit in an earthly form.
> And now, disrobed of frail mortality's
> Encumbrances, he joins the mighty host
> Of valiant veterans of the cross, who're all
> Co-operating with the saints on earth;
> And with the band he'll shout triumphant strains.[82]

Snow's metaphor for death, "a kindly porter," seems especially telling, for seldom in the writings of Mormons does one find even the suggestion that death is an enemy. Nowhere in many sad accounts of children dying does one come across any embittered references to lives cut short or promises unfulfilled. Classically, the Saints view death as a passage. It is a spatial transition, but, as we have seen, the life they glimpse beyond the "Gates Ajar" is exceedingly active and protean.

The serenity with which Mormons approached death in general is reflected in the plan they evolved for dealing with particular deaths. Like every society, members of the Church of Jesus Christ of Latter-day Saints

---

[80]Quoted in Appendix to Lee's *The Mormon Menace* (New York: Home Protection, 1905), pp. 367f.

[81]Comment upon the death of Brigham Young's sister, Fanny Young Murray, *Deseret News*, 9 (June 29, 1859).

[82]*Deseret News*, 24 (Sept. 29, 1875).

developed a ritual for disposing of the body, aiding the bereaved in their reorientation to the community, and publicly commemorating the completion of a life. Anthony F.C. Wallace has argued that it is a people's belief system which serves "to explain, to rationalize, to interpret and to direct the energy of ritual performance," and an exploration of Mormon funerary practices clearly supports this hypothesis in the case of the Saints.[83]

In general, the Mormon rituals associated with death were derived from the simple and dignified practices of New England ancestors.[84] Determined to avoid what they considered the "popish error" of saying prayers over the dead, the Puritans held funerals which were models of austerity. The ceremony consisted mainly of friends and relatives gathering together at the tolling of a bell, carrying the dead solemnly to the grave, and after the burial, returning to the church to hear a sermon. By the middle of the eighteenth century, however, New England funerals usually began in church, where prayers were offered and sermons read over a pall-covered bier. The procession to the grave was on foot, and here another brief collect was recited before commitment of the body to the earth. Considerably more elaborate death rituals had evolved, even in New England, by the last half of the nineteenth century. Funerals were characterized by a pomp and rigidity that echoed the ostentation of the late Middle Ages, and were undoubtedly derived from Victorian England. That the Saints did not adopt this exceedingly ceremonious behavior may be due, in part, to cultural isolation, but a more important reason why Mormons eschewed funerary grandeur can be found in their beliefs about death and its place in what they conceived as an everlasting continuum.

Detailed information about the Saints' funeral practices can be derived from a number of contemporary, as well as later, accounts of the assassination of Joseph and Hyrum Smith.[85] The murder, in the jail at Carthage, Illinois, on June 27, 1844, was witnessed by Willard Richards, who arranged for the care of the bodies. Because the anti-Mormon population was fleeing the town precipitously out of fear of reprisal, Richards had some difficulty finding anyone to carry the corpses to the local hotel, but at the last, after

[83]*Religion: An Anthropological View* (New York: Random House, 1966), p. 103.

[84]See Robert M. Habenstein and William M. Lamers, *The History of American Funeral Directing* (Milwaukee: Bulfin Printers, 1962), for a discussion of funerary practices in medieval Europe and in Colonial, eighteenth century, and nineteenth century America.

[85]See Fawn M. Brodie, *No Man Knows My History* (New York: Alfred A. Knopf,1966), p. 396f; J. H. Kennedy, *Early Days of Mormons* (New York: Scribner's, 1888), pp. 250ff; William A. Linn, *The Story of the Mormons* [1902] (New York: Russell and Russell, 1963), p. 307; Henry Mayhew, *The Mormons or Latter-day Saints* (London: Office of the National Illustrated Library, 1851), p. 168; T. B. H. Stenhouse, *The Rocky Mountain Saints* (1872) (Salt Lake City: Shepherd Book, 1904), pp. 168 and 174f; and Samuel W. Taylor, *Nightfall at Nauvoo* (New York: Macmillan, 1971), pp. 268–271.

offering firm assurances of protection, he persuaded the innkeeper and his family to transport the bodies and prepare them for removal to Nauvoo the next day.

The mortal remains of the Brothers Smith were brought to Nauvoo by wagon in rough oak boxes that had been covered by a horse blanket and prairie grass to try to forestall decomposition of the corpses under the summer sun. The Nauvoo Legion had stood at arms from ten in the morning until three in the afternoon awaiting the cortege, and when it arrived they escorted it to Mansion House, followed by ten thousand grieving Saints. At the prophet's residence, Richards and four other prominent Mormons addressed the crowd, urging them to leave vengeance to God.

After the people had dispersed, the rude coffins were carried into the dining room of the mansion, where three men washed the bodies, plugged the gunshot wounds with cotton soaked in camphor, dressed the corpses and arranged them by a window. Family and friends were then permitted to look upon the remains of Joseph and Hyrum. Before a public viewing the next day, however, the bodies were removed from the rough boxes, and placed in ones covered with black velvet, lined with white cambric and fastened with brass studs. Over the face of each dead man was a hinged lid holding a square of glass. Twenty thousand Saints filed past the biers, but by then it had been nearly two days since the murder and putrefaction had begun. Only the constant burning of a mixture of tar, vinegar and sugar made it possible for the crowds to pass through the viewing room.

In the evening, a solemn procession walked to the Nauvoo cemetery beside the coffins. The throng watched silently as they were lowered into graves. But it was to be a few hours yet before the bodies of Joseph and Hyrum Smith were committed to the earth. Because they feared desecration of the brothers' remains, Mormon leaders had filled the pine boxes with bags of sand, reserving the actual corpses for private interment. They were buried at midnight in the basement of the unfinished Nauvoo House, after which stone chips and rubbish were carefully strewn to cover the spot.[86] The oak boxes in which the bodies had been brought from Carthage then were sawed into pieces and distributed among Joseph's friends, many of whom made them into canes and prized them as relics.

The "missing" ingredients in the funeral of Joseph and Hyrum Smith obviously are a sermon and a prayer. And while these elements became part of the Saints' death rituals under later and more leisurely circumstances, there is a "secular" quality about the Nauvoo rites which was not dissipated in

---

[86] But even this was not to be the prophet's final resting place. Stenhouse wrote that the body was reburied beneath a brick path behind Mansion House, exhumed once again, and interred finally in Missouri. Brodie insists that after being removed from Nauvoo House, the body was reburied under "the summer cottage" at Emma's request.

time. The grief expressed in Illinois, in Nebraska, and in Utah is consummately human. The Saints manifested no sign of spiritual anguish in the face of death. They made no appeal to God for mercy on the departed or upon themselves.

Deaths occurring on the trail in the course of the Mormons' long march to Zion could not, of course, be observed with ceremony. Graves were shallow trenches marked by upright stones. Once settled in Utah, however, the Saints did attend to death in a more traditional manner. From its beginning in 1850, the *Deseret News* published death notices. Rarely displayed prominently, obituaries for ordinary Mormons might occupy only a line or two, while obituaries for church leaders were longer and followed a prescribed pattern. They gave the date and cause of death, contained an account of the deceased's last illness, mentioned his parents, listed his survivors, then recounted his spiritual biography, including details of his baptism, confirmation, ordination and missions. The notice might invite friends to attend a funeral service, or if the ceremony had taken place, note that a particular elder or bishop had delivered an "appropriate address."

It seems clear from the writings of Mormons and their close observers that ordinarily Saints were buried in their endowment garments. Thomas Stenhouse noted that they were carried to their graves "clothed with the robes of the priesthood, such as they hope to be seen in when they burst the bands of death."[87] Brigham Young left specific instructions that his body be "dressed in [his] Temple clothing."[88] Lee related that his wife was laid in her coffin in "priestly attire" which "was made of the finest linen."[89]

The quality of these clothes apparently was enough to tempt at least one grave robber. Stenhouse related that an assistant grave-digger, "an Italian by birth," was found to have disrobed the dead when a search of his house revealed a collection of burial garments. "The fearful grief of mothers at the thought of their sweet ones lying naked in their graves is beyond description," the chronicler observed, noting that Brigham preached a timely sermon assuring the women that "the power of the Lord was equal to everything," and that, "in the morning of the resurrection" they would greet their little ones "arrayed in suitable garments." The fate of the grave robber is unknown, but Stenhouse said he was considered "a monster."[90]

By the second half of the nineteenth century, both the traditional wooden coffin and more recently developed metal caskets were used in the United States as burial receptacles.[91] The common Mormon choice seems to have been wood, and it is interesting to note that both Brigham Young and

[87]Stenhouse, p. 482.
[88]*Deseret News,* 26 (Sept. 5, 1877).
[89]Lee, 2:17.
[90]Stenhouse, p. 482.
[91]See Habenstein and Lamers, p. 281.

George A. Smith left directions as to the size and construction of their burial cases.[92] These requests, together with the lack of any advertisements for ready-made coffins in the *Deseret News* in the period between 1850 and 1875, suggest that burial receptacles were made to order upon death. In fact, Lee wrote that his wife's coffin had been made and "neatly painted" within twenty-four hours of her passing, though he noted that he had had the "lumber previously dressed up."[93]

The custom of viewing the remains of the dead apparently was observed mainly in the case of the Mormon elite. In most circumstances, the ritual was limited to an hour or two and immediately preceded the funeral itself. Obsequies ordinarily were held in the deceased person's home if it was of sufficient size to accommodate the mourners; otherwise the ceremony took place in a public meeting house or school. In Salt Lake, an assembly hall called the Bowery was used, as was the Tabernacle itself after its completion in 1867. The latter especially seems to have been reserved for the obsequies of the leaders of the church. There is no indication that funerals ever have been held in Mormon temples.

As frequently noted by students of culture, partaking in funeral rites give participants a renewed sense of belonging to a social whole. A not incidental function is to acknowledge kinship relationships beyond the immediate family. In every ceremony there are two broad categories of participants: relatives of the dead person and his fellows in the community. The multiple social identities of the deceased are revealed by the various classes of mourners; their presence shows him as husband, father, friend, soldier, civic, and religious leader. In late nineteenth century Mormon death rites, the foremost parts in the category of participants who were not bereaved kinsmen were taken by members of the church hierarchy. It was customary for a member of the Melchizedek priesthood to speak at funerals. The delivering of eulogies seems to have been a common duty of elders; at the obsequies of the Mormon elite, the main participants regularly included the President, his two counselors, and members of the Quorum of Twelve.

From newspaper descriptions of various ceremonies one derives a picture of the typical positioning of participants at the funerals of leading Saints. At those rituals taking place in the Salt Lake Tabernacle, the family of the dead person usually was seated around the coffin. On the stands facing the congregation were the General Authorities. With the President in the center, members fanned outward in descending order of rank. The bier was not the focus of attention; rather it was the church hierarchy, and indeed the funeral sermons delivered by Mormon leaders were the chief elements of the ceremony itself.

[92]*Deseret News,* 24 (Sept. 8, 1875) and 26 (Sept. 5, 1877).
[93]Lee, 2:17.

The reading of Scripture appears to have been an uncommon practice in Mormon obsequies. The usual "comforting words" were not those of the psalmist, Paul, or even Joseph Smith. They were instead those of Latter-day orators who made the occasion of death an opportunity to deliver "much good instruction to the living."[94] Introductory panegyrical descriptions of the life and works of the departed served to transport the dead, in the emotions of the mourners, from the secular realm to the realm of the sacred. The heart of the Mormon funeral sermon was a restatement of beliefs about the spirit world as a place of conscious activity:

He is not lost. He has only gone to perform another part of the mission which he has been engaged in all his life, to labor in another sphere for the good of all mankind, for the welfare of the souls of men.[95]

From the labors of the flesh they rest, but their work continues. Rest is a change, but not a cessation from labor . . . Having done a great, a glorious work in the flesh, [he] now joins his labors with them in the more extensive labors of the priesthood, the redemption of the hosts of the dead.[96]

The idea of a literal, material resurrection was reinforced:

The very body that lies there in that coffin will be raised at the first resurrection . . . we will see him in the flesh just as we have seen him . . . here; only he will be made pure, holy and immortal. And when we are made pure we shall associate together.[97]

Every component particle of his body, from the crown of his head to the soles of his feet, will be resurrected, he, in the flesh, will see God and converse with Him; and see his brethren and associate with them and they will enjoy a happy eternity together.[98]

Commonly the funeral was portrayed for those attending it as an occasion of joy.

Hymns of rejoicing customarily were sung, and prayer, usually in the form of an opening prayer and a benediction, was part of the rite.[99] Rarely were the words of these printed in the *Deseret News,* but the few texts it did run indicate that, in general, the Saints' funeral collects fell into two cate-

[94]*Deseret News,* 18 (Sept. 8, 1969).

[95]D. H. Wells, at the funeral of Heber C. Kimball, published in the *Deseret News,* 17 (July 1, 1868).

[96]Wilford Woodruff, at the funeral of Brigham Young, published in the *Deseret News* 26 (Sept. 5, 1877).

[97]Brigham Young, at the funeral of George A. Smith, published in the *Deseret News,* 24 (Sept. 8, 1875).

[98]Brigham Young, remarks made at the funeral of Heber C. Kimball, published in the *Deseret News,* 17 (July 1, 1868).

[99]A favorate was: Weep, weep not for me, Zion:/ Rejoice new and sing ye aloud;/ Pray, pray and Judah's fierce lion/ May quickly descend in a cloud./ Haste, haste; oh quickly descend in a cloud.

gories: 1) requests that God inspire the funeral orators and open the hearts of the congregation to their counsel; and 2) petitions for His blessing upon the surviving Saints, particularly the deceased person's family, including, and specifically, a man's widows. Nowhere were there requests for God's mercy upon the departed soul.

Processions to the place of the funeral, and from there to the grave, were common practices. Stout referred to a Masonic procession for a man who was a Master Mason, and apparently military escorts were provided at the death rites of Mormons who had served in the United States army during life.[100] Bands occasionally accompanied a cortege to the grave.

It is hardly surprising, in light of the Saints' emphasis upon a material resurrection, that interment, rather than cremation, was the accepted Mormon manner of disposing of the dead. Once settled in the Great Basin, family plots seem to have been common, and given the size of early Mormon families, these often were large. Simple stone markers most often designated the sites of graves, though more elaborate monuments sometimes were erected in memory of the Mormon elite.

Unlike the prophet Joseph, Hyrum Smith and Parley Pratt, the second president of the Mormon Church died of natural causes at the end of a long life. Brigham Young passed away at seventy-six leaving seventeen wives and forty-four children among his survivors. In contrast to the funeral of the Saints' first president, his successor's occurred under circumstances which allowed for pageantry and the leisure to "celebrate" death.

Young's funeral was to all intents and purposes an affair of state.[101] The morning after he died, his body was conveyed by bearers from his home to the Salt Lake Tabernacle. The procession included the male members of his family and several of the Council of Twelve. The corpse was encased in a coffin with a "metallic covering" which was constructed with a glass panel to permit the faithful to view the mortal remains of their fallen prince.

The president's body lay in state for twenty-four hours, during which time an estimated eighteen to twenty-five thousand persons passed by the floral-wreathed coffin to pay their last respects. Saints from outlying districts came by wagon, and the railroad also conveyed many mourners, facilitating their presence at the obsequies by running special trains to Salt Lake City and offering reduced rates. An organist and an orchestra provided music throughout the viewing. They played a funeral march especially composed for the occasion as well as such traditional pieces as Mendelssohn's "Funeral March" and Handel's "Dead March in Saul."

The tabernacle itself was decorated with strands of flowers. The organ,

---

[100]See Stout, pp. 29f.
[101]See the *Deseret News,* 26 (Sept. 5, 1877) for a detailed account of Brigham Young's funeral.

the stands and the front of the platform were draped in black. The coffin, which was completely closed before actual services began, was placed on a plain catafalque in front of the stands and in view of the whole congregation. Mourners were seated in reserved and unreserved sections of the building, the front pews being set apart for relatives, high priests, members of the seventies, and elders. On the stands were the General Authorities, seated in their accustomed places, as well as visiting presidents, counselors and High Council members from stakes throughout the territory, ward bishops, the Salt Lake City Council, a glee club, a band, and, finally, representatives from the local and national press.

Brigham Young's funeral instructions called for singing, a prayer, and a few words spoken by friends. At the actual ceremony this modest request was elaborated upon, and the services consisted of hymns sung by a 220-voice choir, an opening prayer offered by Apostle F. D. Richards, a benediction read by Apostle Orson Hyde, and eulogies delivered by Second Counselor D. H. Wells and Apostles William Woodruff, Erastus Snow, and George Cannon. Their common theme was that while a great leader was dead, his gifts and energies were not lost to the Mormons. As Brigham worked for Zion in the spirit world, the speakers said, so must the Saints on earth continue in their righteous labors. Cannon related that he had heard the president say he should count "the day of his release from his mortal existence as the happiest day of his life."

At the conclusion of the tabernacle ceremony, a procession wound its way through the streets of Salt Lake to Brigham's "white house," where the Mormon leader was buried in the Young family's private graveyard, in accordance with directions he had drafted four years before his death. A stone vault had been built to receive the coffin, and there Brigham's body was laid to rest with a final hymn and dedicatory prayer. In keeping with his instructions, a simple tombstone was erected to mark the grave.

Brigham Young's death rites were described in the *Deseret News* as the "grandest and most impressive" the reporter who covered them had ever witnessed.[102] Indeed, his funeral *was* a social event of great importance primarily because of the superb opportunity it afforded to reinforce roles and relationships in the community of Saints. In the last analysis, however, the rituals observed in connection with the president's death had scant religious significance. Their place in the Mormon's sacred scheme reflects, it seems clear, the Saints' view of death as a mere episode in man's progression toward godhood. It is not salvation, but everlasting development which was the church's overriding concern, and in this emphasis nineteenth century Mormonism can be seen as a radically secular faith.

The central motifs of the Mormon world view are notions of pre-exis-

[102] Ibid.

tence and of continued, conscious postmortem activity. These ideas stand in stark contrast to the traditional Judaic-Christian view that at some time between conception and birth, the human soul bursts upon "the sky of reality without even a glimmer of anticipation," and that self-affirmation and self-realization achieve absolute termination in death.[103]

By and large in the Western intellectual tradition, the word death has signified the end of man's ability to make decisions—to render actual what was previously a mere possibility. In religious terms, this means that at death man loses the ability to act in his own behalf in securing salvation or avoiding damnation. Death brings him, as a moral person, to a kind of consummation—that is, to a position where, as Karl Rahner has said, the decisions for or against God, which he has made during his earthly existence, become final and unalterable.[104] The last of the Last Words were "Father, into Thy hands I commend my spirit," and both Catholics and Protestants generally have held that when life ends, the destiny of the soul rests wholly with God. Collects for the dead are appeals to Him, whose property is always to have mercy, not to deliver the souls of the faithful departed into the hands of the enemy, nor forget them, but bid His angels receive them—and grant them eternal rest.

As we have seen, petitions on behalf of the dead had no place in Mormon funeral ceremonies. The Saints believed that after death, as indeed before birth and during his earthly sojourn, man's fate, that is, his progress, depended upon his comprehension of the great laws of the universe and his diligence in observing them. They posited a spirit world in which earthly relationships are not only maintained, but in which individuals retained the ability to make certain choices—specifically, and crucially, the ability to accept or reject baptism performed in their behalf by the living, and the will and energy to continue missionary work among the unredeemed. Life, the Saints often said, is a probationary period; it is, from their point of view, a provisional effort open to revision at a later date.[105]

Given their conception of the universe as moving to its immanent consummation along a unique path in time, more orthodox Christians consider death a crucial event. Although it does not signify the end of individual existence, neither does it connote a mere passage from one form of existence to another. Death is a genuine end, for when it occurs, man's role in history is over. It is also a genuine beginning; death marks the individual's assumption of his eternal part. Ontological dualism is inescapable since man is both person and nature, liberty and necessity, spirit and matter.

The Mormon view of death is that of a mere episode in man's progression

[103]Jaroslav Pelikan, *The Shape of Death* (New York: Abingdon Press, 1961), p. 35.
[104]*On the Theology of Death* (New York: Herder and Herder, 1961), p. 36.
[105]See *Doctrine and Covenants*, 74:73.

"from grace to grace, from exaltation to exaltation."[106] Development, moreover, is ever onward and upward. John Widtsoe wrote:

> . . . in each estate, with each onward step, a profounder knowledge of the laws of nature is attained. When conscious, active wills are thus at work, the new knowledge makes possible a more perfect adaptation of man to law. The more completely law is obeyed, the greater the consciousness of perfect joy. Throughout eternal life, increasing knowledge is attained, and with increasing knowledge comes the greater adaptation to law, and in the end an increasingly greater joy.[107]

What of man's natural horror before the reality of his impending death? "To obtain or give greater joys, smaller pains may often have to be endured."[108] While the Mormons manifested great concern for the unbaptized and unsealed dead, death itself was, for the Saints, a minor event. As John Taylor said: "For a man of God to bid adieu to the things of this world is a matter of comparatively small importance."[109] Death was not an event of salvation or damnation according to whether it was encountered in faith or in disbelief; it was, in the Mormon's view, a prescribed, logical step in the individual's march toward godhood.

Paul counseled the Thessalonians not to mourn as those who had no hope (I Thessalonians 4:13), but the Church always has acted as if there is a mourning appropriate to believers which acknowledges that, however strong one's faith, death is, at the last, inscrutable. Because the Mormons posited a known and knowable universe in which they could calculate the outcome of events, death, for them, lost its dark and hidden character. The Saints' funeral practices reflected death's lack of significance in their belief system when it is viewed as a transformation of state, and finally, death's lack of mystery.

[106] Smith in Lundwall, p. 19.
[107] Widtsoe, p. 31.
[108] Ibid., p. 34.
[109] John Taylor, remarks made at the funeral of Heber C. Kimball, published in the *Deseret News,* 17 (July 1, 1868).

THE REVERSAL OF DEATH: CHANGES IN ATTITUDES TOWARD DEATH IN WESTERN SOCIETIES* ·

PHILIPPE ARIÈS

Translated by Valerie M. Stannard

THIS STUDY COULD HAVE BEEN ENTITLED "THE CONTEMPORARY crisis of death," if Edgar Morin had not already given this title to one of the chapters in his book *L'homme et la mort devant l'histoire.*[1] Indeed, Morin's very words and ideas apply here: "Panic-stricken confrontation in an atmosphere of anguish, neurosis, and nihilism," which takes "the form of a veritable crisis of individuality in the face of death" and probably also, as we shall see *in fine,* a crisis of individuality itself.

Edgar Morin intentionally limited himself to "death in books": "literature, poetry, philosophy, that is, . . . the non-specialized sector of civilization, or more correctly, the sector specialized in generalities." In this case the subject matter was evident: literature and philosophy have never been completely silent on the subject of death and dying, and have sometimes been known to be extremely loquacious; today we know how any discourse on the subject of death becomes confused and expresses one of the many forms of a pervasive anxiety.

Since Edgar Morin's book was published in 1951, a new literature has appeared, the history and sociology of death, which is no longer general but specialized, and is no longer merely a discourse on death. To be sure, in those days there were a few pages by Emile Mâle and art historians on the iconography of death, there was the excellent book by Huizinga on the decline of the Middle Ages, and there was Roger Caillois' essay on American attitudes toward death, but there was as yet really no history or sociology of death.[2]

*Translation of Philippe Ariès, "La mort inversée. Le changement des attitudes devant la mort dans les sociétés occidentales," *Archives Européennes de Sociologie,* 8 (1967), 169–195.

[1] *L'homme et la mort . . .* (Paris: Correa, 1951).

[2] Johan Huizinga, *The Waning of the Middle Ages* (Garden City, N.Y.: Doubleday, 1954); Roger Caillois, *Quatre essais de sociologie contemporaine* (Paris: Perrin, 1951).

It is strange how the human sciences, so outspoken regarding family, work, politics, leisure, religion and sex, have been so reserved on the subject of death. Scholars have kept silent, acting like the men that they are and like the men that they study. Their silence is only a part of this great silence that has settled on the subject of death in the 20th century. Although literature has continued its discourse on death, with, for example, Sartre or Genet's *"mort sale,"* ordinary men have become mute and behave as though death no longer existed. The chasm between the discussion of death in books, which is still prolific, and actual death, which is shameful and not to be talked about, is one of the strange but significant signs of our times. This silence is the main subject of this essay. As is usually the case with silence, it has gone unnoticed and therefore unknown; only during the past few years has it been the subject of discussion.

A history of death was begun with Alberto Tenenti's two books, *La vie et la mort à travers l'art du XVᵉ siècle,* which appeared in 1952, one year after Edgar Morin's essay, and *Il senso della morte e l'amore della vità nel Rinascimento.*[3]

A sociology of death was begun in 1955 with Geoffrey Gorer's comprehensive article, "The Pornography of Death."[4] Next came the collection of interdisciplinary studies (anthropology, art, literature, medicine, philosophy, psychiatry, religion, etc.), edited by Herman Feifel under the title *The Meaning of Death,* which had been presented at a colloquium organized by the American Psychological Association in 1956. The mere idea of a colloquium on death testifies to the awakening interest in this hitherto forbidden topic. Indeed it seems that, with regard to the forbidden topic of death, today's sociologists are following the example of Freud concerning the forbidden topic of sex. Thus it is that the current taboo regarding death is being threatened in an indirect way by social scientists. Literature remains conservative and continues with the old themes, even when it takes the form of their opposites.

On the other hand, sociology and psychology are supplying the first signs that contemporary man is rediscovering death. And far from suppressing these scholarly works, newspapers and popular weekly magazines have given them a great deal of attention. A literature of social criticism has followed, which first became popular with Jessica Mitford's book, *The American Way of Death.*[5] Today hardly a month passes without the French, British or American press reporting on a book concerned with death, or some observed curiosity regarding it. Death is now becoming what

---

[3] *La vie et la mort* . . . (Paris: Colin, 1952); *Il senso della morte* . . . (Turin: Einaudi, 1957).

[4] Reprinted as an appendix to his book, *Death, Grief, and Mourning* (New York: Doubleday, 1965).

[5] *The American Way of Death* (New York: Simon & Schuster, 1963).

it had ceased to be since the very end of the Romantic era, the subject of an inexhaustible supply of anecdotes—a fact which would lead one to suspect that the newspaper-reading public is becoming interested in death, perhaps initially because of its seemingly forbidden and somewhat obscene nature.

The new sociology of death, then, marks not only the beginning of a scientific bibliography on death, but very likely also a turning point in the history of attitudes toward death. Sociology, however, is not very conscious of history: Edgar Morin was led to treat the death of philosophers as history, because his philosophic and literary documents were already a part of history—for a long time of the history of ideas, for only a few decades, of social history. On the other hand, common attitudes toward death, such as are being discovered today by sociologists, psychologists and doctors, seem so unprecedented, so bewildering, that as yet it has been impossible for observers to take them out of their modern context and put them into historical perspective. Nevertheless, that is what this article proposes to do, around three themes: the dispossession of the dying person, the denial of mourning, and the invention in the United States of a new funerary ritual.

1. The Dying Man is Deprived of His Death

For thousands of years man was lord and master of his death, and the circumstances surrounding it. Today this has ceased to be so.

It used to be understood and accepted that a man knew when he was dying, whether he became spontaneously aware of the fact or whether he had to be told. It seemed reasonable to our old storytellers that, as the plowman in La Fontaine says, man would feel his approaching death. In those days death was rarely sudden, even in the case of an accident or a war, and sudden death was much feared, not only because there was no time for repentance, but because it deprived a man of the experience of death. Thus death was almost always presaged, especially since even minor illnesses often turned out to be fatal. One would have had to be mad not to see the signs, and moralists and satirists made it their job to ridicule those foolish enough to deny the evidence. Roland "feels that death is taking all of him," Tristam "felt that his life was draining away, he realized that he was dying." Tolstoy's peasant replied to the goodwoman who asked him if he were all right: "Death is here"; for Tolstoy's peasants died like Tristam or like La Fontaine's plowman, having the same resigned, comfortable attitude toward it. This is not to say that the attitude toward death was the same throughout all this long period of time, but that it survived in some social strata from one generation to the next despite competition from other styles of death.

When the person involved was not the first to become aware of his fate, others were expected to warn him. A papal document of the Middle Ages made this a task of the doctor, a task he for a long time carried out unflinchingly. We find him at Don Quixote's bedside: "He took his pulse, and was not happy with the results. He therefore told him that whatever he did, he should think of saving his soul, as his body was in grave danger." The *artes moriendi* of the 15th century also charged with this task the "spiritual" friend (as opposed to "carnal" friends), who went by the name—so repugnant to our modern fastidiousness—of *nuncius mortis*.

As man progressed through time, the higher up the social and urban ladder he climbed, the less he himself was aware of his approaching death, and the more he had to be prepared for it; consequently, the more he had to depend on those around him. The doctor renounced the role that for so long had been his, probably in the 18th century. In the 19th century he spoke only when questioned, and then somewhat reticently. Friends no longer had to intervene, as in the time of Gerson or even Cervantes, because from the 17th century on, it was the family that took care of this—a sign of development in family feeling. An example of this can be seen in the de La Ferronnays household in 1848. Mme. de La Ferronnays had fallen ill. The doctor announced that her condition was dangerous, and "one hour later, hopeless." Her daughter wrote: "When she came out of the bath . . . she suddenly said to me, while I was thinking of a good way to tell her what the doctor thought: 'but I can't see anything any more, I think I'm going to die.' She immediately recited an ejaculatory prayer. 'Oh, Jesus,' " the daughter then remarked, " 'what a strange joy I felt from those calm words at such a terrible time.' " She was relieved because she had been spared the distress of making a nevertheless indispensable disclosure. The relief is a modern characteristic, the necessity to disclose the truth is ancient.

Not only was the dying man not to be deprived of his death, he also had to preside over it. As people were born in public, so did they die in public, and not only the king, as is well known from Saint Simon's famous pages on the death of Louis XIV, but everyone. Countless engravings and paintings depict that scene for us. As soon as someone "was helplessly sick in bed," his room filled with people—parents, children, friends, neighbors, fellow guild members. The windows and shutters were closed. Candles were lit. When passersby in the streets met a priest carrying the *viaticum*, custom and piety demanded that they follow him into the dying man's room, even if he was a stranger. The approach of death transformed the room of a dying man into a sort of public place. Pascal's remark, "man will die alone," which has lost much of its impact on us since today man almost always dies alone, can only be understood in this context. For what Pascal meant was that in spite of all the people crowded around his bed, the dying man was alone. The enlightened doctors of the end of the 18th century, who believed in the qualities of fresh air, complained a great deal about this bad habit of crowding into the rooms of sick people. They tried to have the windows opened, the candles snuffed, and the crowd of people turned out.

We should not make the mistake of thinking that to be present at these last moments was a devout custom prescribed by the Church. The enlightened or reformed priests had tried, long before the doctors, to do away with this crowd so that they could better prepare the sick person for a virtuous end. As early as the *artes moriendi* of the 15th century it had been recommended that the dying man be left alone with God so that he should not be distracted from the care of his soul. And again, in the 19th century, it sometimes happened that very pious people, after yielding to the custom, asked the numerous onlookers to leave the room, all except the priest, so that nothing would disturb their private conversation with God. But these were rare examples of extreme devotion. Custom prescribed that death was to be marked by a ritual ceremony in which the priest would have his place, but only as one of many participants. The leading role went to the dying man himself. He presided over the affair with hardly a misstep, for he knew how to conduct himself, having previously witnessed so many similar scenes. He called to him one by one his relatives, his friends, his servants, "even down to the lowliest," Saint-Simon said, describing the death of Mme. de Montespan. He said farewell to them, asked their pardon, gave them his blessing. Invested with sovereign authority by the approach of death, especially in the 18th and 19th centuries, the dying person gave orders and advice, even when this dying person was a very young girl, almost a child.

Today nothing remains either of the sense that everyone has or should have of his impending death, or of the public solemnity surrounding the moment of death. What used to be appreciated is now hidden; what used to be solemn is now avoided.

It is understood that the primary duty of the family and the doctor is to conceal the seriousness of his condition from the person who is to die. The sick person must no longer ever know (except in very rare cases) that his end is near. The new custom dictates that he die in ignorance. This is not merely a habit that has innocently crept into the customs—it has become a moral requirement. Vladimir Jankélévitch confirmed this unequivocally during a recent colloquium of doctors on the subject: "Should we lie to the patient?" "The liar," he stated, "is the one who tells the truth. . . . I am against the truth, passionately against the truth. . . . For me, the most important law of all is the law of love and charity."[6] Was this quality then lacking prior to the 20th century, since ethics made it obligatory to inform the patient? In such opposition we see the extent of this extraordinary reversal of feelings, and then of ideas. How did this come about? It would be

---

[6] *Médecine de France,* 177 (1966), 3–16, repr. in Jankélévitch, *La mort* (Paris: Flammarion, 1966).

too hasty to say that in a society of happiness and well-being there is no longer any room for suffering, sadness and death. To say this is to mistake the result for the cause.

It is strange that this change is linked to the development in family feelings, and to the emotional centrality of the family in our world. In fact, the cause for the change must be sought in the relationship between a sick person and his family. The family has no longer been able to tolerate the blow it had to deal to a loved one, and the blow it also had to deal to itself, in bringing death closer and making it more certain, in forbidding all deception and illusion. How many times have we heard it said of a spouse or a parent: "At least I had the satisfaction of knowing that he never felt he was dying"? *This "not feeling oneself dying" has in our everyday language replaced the "feeling one's impending death" of the 17th century.*

In point of fact, it must happen quite often—but the dead never tell—that the sick person knows quite well what is happening, and pretends not to know for the sake of those around him. For if the family has loathed to play *nuncius mortis,* a role which in the Middle Ages and at the beginning of modern times it was not asked to play, the main actor has also abdicated. Through fear of death? But death has always existed. Only it used to be laughed at—"What haste you are in, O cruel goddess!"—while society compelled the terrified dying man nevertheless to act out the great scene of farewells and departure. Some say this fear is innate, but its suppression is equally innate. The fear of death does not explain why the dying man turns his back on his own death. Again we must seek for the explanation in the history of the family.

The man of the late Middle Ages and the Renaissance (as opposed to the man of the early Middle Ages, like Roland, who still lives in Tolstoy's peasants) insisted on participating in his own death, because he saw in his death the moment when his individuality received its ultimate form. He was master over his life only insofar as he was master over his death. His death was his, and his alone. However, beginning with the 17th century he no longer had sole sovereignty over his own life and, consequently, over his death. He shared his death with his family, whereas previously his family had been isolated from the serious decisions he, and he alone, had to make regarding his death.

Last wills and testaments are a case in point. From the 14th century to the beginning of the 18th century, the will was one way for each person to express himself freely while at the same time it was a token of defiance—or lack of confidence—with regard to his family. Thus, when in the 18th century family affection triumphed over the traditional mistrust by the testator of his inheritors, the last will and testament lost its character of moral necessity and personal warm testimony. This was, on the contrary, replaced by such an absolute trust that there was no longer any need for written wills. The last spoken wishes became at long last sacred to the survivors, and they considered themselves to be committed from then on to respect these wishes to the letter. For his part, the dying man was satisfied that he could rest in peace on the word of his close ones. This trust that began in the 17th and 18th centuries and was developed in the 19th century, has in the 20th century turned into alienation. As soon as serious danger threatens one member of a family, the family immediately conspires to deprive him of information and thus his freedom. The patient then becomes a minor, like a child or a mental defective, to be taken into charge and separated from the rest of the world by his spouse or parents. They know better than he what he should do and know. He is deprived of his rights, specifically the formerly essential right of knowing about his death, of preparing for it, of organizing it. And he lets this happen because he is convinced that it is for his own good. He relies on the affection of his family. If, in spite of everything, he does guess the truth, he will pretend to not know it. Death used to be a tragedy—often comic—acted out for the benefit of a man who was about to die. Today, death is a comedy—always tragic— acted out for the benefit of a man who does not know he is about to die.

Without the progress of medicine the pressure of family feeling would probably not have been sufficient to make death disappear so quickly and so completely. Not so much because of the real conquests made by medicine as because, as a result of medicine, in the mind of the sick man death has been replaced by illness. This substitution first appeared in the second half of the 19th century. When the dying peasant in Tolstoy's *Three Deaths* (1859) was asked where he hurt, he replied: "I hurt all over, death is here; that's what it is." On the other hand Ivan Ilych (1886), after overhearing a conversation that could leave him in no doubt, continues to think obstinately of his floating kidney, of his infected appendix, which can be cured by the doctor or the surgeon. The illness has become the focus of illusion. His wife treats him like a child who is disobeying the doctor's orders: he is not taking his medicine properly, that is why he is not getting better.

Moreover, it is clear that, with the advancements in therapeutics and surgery, it has become increasingly more difficult to be certain that a serious illness is fatal; the chances of recovering from it have increased so much. Even with diminished capacities, one can still live. Thus, in our world where everyone acts as though medicine is the answer to everything—where even though Caesar must die one day, there is absolutely no reason for oneself to die—incurable diseases, particularly cancer, have taken on the hideous, terrifying aspects of the old representations of death. More than the skeleton or mummy of the *macabres* of the 14th and 15th centuries, more than the leper with his bell, cancer today is death. However, the disease must be incurable (or thought to be so) in order for death to be allowed to come forward and take on its name. The anguish this releases forces society to hurriedly intensify its customary demands of silence, and thus to bring this overly dramatic situation to the banal level of an afternoon walk.

People die, then, in secret—more alone than Pascal ever imagined. This secrecy results from refusing to admit the imminent death of a love one by concealing it beneath the veil of a persistent disease. There is another aspect of this secrecy that American sociologists have succeeded in interpreting. What we have been inclined to view as avoidance, they have shown to be the empirical establishment of a style of dying in which discretion appears as the modern form of dignity. It is, with less poetry, the death of Mélisande, a death of which Jankélévitch would approve.

A study has been made by Barney G. Glaser and Anselm L. Strauss in six hospitals in the San Francisco Bay Area of the reactions toward death of the interdependent group of the patient, his family and the medical personnel (doctors and nurses).[7] What happens when it is known that the patient is nearing his end? Should the family be notified, or the patient himself, and when? For how long should life be prolonged by artificial means, and at what point should the individual be permitted to die? How does the medical staff behave toward a patient who does not know, or who pretends not to know, or who does know that he is dying? These problems no doubt arise in every modern family, but within the confines of a hospital, a new authority intervenes: the medical authority. Today people are dying less and less at home, more and more in hospitals; indeed, the hospital has become the modern place for dying, which is why Glaser and Strauss' observations are important. However, the scope of their book goes beyond empirical analyses of attitudes. The authors have discovered a new ideal way of dying which has replaced the theatrical ceremonies of the Romantic era and, in a more general way, of the traditional public nature of death. There is a new model for dying which they explain almost naively, comparing it with their concrete observations. Thus we see taking shape a "style of dying," or rather an "acceptable style of living while dying," an "acceptable style of facing death." The accent is placed on the word "acceptable." It is essential, indeed, that the death be such that it can be accepted or tolerated by the survivors.

If doctors and nurses (the nurses with more reticence) delay for as long as possible notifying the family, if they are reluctant ever to notify the patient himself, the reason is that they are afraid of becoming caught up in a chain of sentimental reactions that would bring about a loss of self-control, their own as much as that of the patient or the family. To dare to speak of death,

---

[7] *Awareness of Dying* (Chicago: Aldine, 1965).

to admit death into social relations, is no longer, as in former times, to leave the everyday world undisturbed; it brings about an exceptional, outrageous and always dramatic situation. Death used to be a familiar figure, and moralists had to make him hideous in order to create fear. Now the word has only to be mentioned to provoke an emotive tension incompatible with the equilibrium of everyday life. "An acceptable style of dying," then, is one that avoids "status-forcing scenes," scenes that tear the person out of his social role, that violate his social role. These scenes are patients' crises of despair, their cries, their tears, and in general, any demonstrations that are too impassioned, too noisy or even too moving, that might upset the serenity of the hospital. This would be the "embarrassingly graceless dying," the style of dying that would embarrass the survivors, the opposite of the acceptable style of dying. It is in order to avoid this that nothing is said to the patient. Basically, however, what is essential is less whether the patient does or does not know, but rather, that if he does know he should have the good taste and the courage to be discreet. He should behave in such a manner that the hospital staff can forget that he knows, and can communicate with him as though death were not hovering about them. Communication is, in fact, an equally necessary factor. It is not enough for the patient to be discreet, he must also be open and receptive to messages. His indifference might set up the same "embarrassment" among the medical personnel as would an excess of demonstration. There are, then, two ways to die badly: one consists of seeking an exchange of emotions; the other is to refuse to communicate.

The authors very earnestly cite the case of an old woman who conducted herself very well at first, according to convention: she cooperated with the doctors and nurses, and fought bravely against her illness. Then one day she decided that she had fought enough, the time had come to give up. She closed her eyes and did not open them again; in this way she was signifying that she was withdrawing from the world, and was awaiting her end alone. Formerly this sign of introspection would have surprised no one and would have been respected. In the California hospital, it drove the doctors and nurses to despair, and they quickly sent for one of the patient's sons to come by plane, he being the only person capable of persuading her to open her eyes and not to go on "hurting everybody." Patients also sometimes turn toward the wall and remain in that position. This is recognizable, not without emotion, as one of man's oldest gestures when he feels death approaching. The Jews of the Old Testament died this way and, even in the 16th century, the Spanish Inquisition recognized by this sign an unconverted Marrano. Tristam died in this way: "He turned toward the wall and said: 'I can hold on to my life no longer.'" Nevertheless, in our time the doctors and nurses of a California hospital saw in this ancient gesture nothing but an antisocial refusal to communicate, an unpardonable renouncement of the vital struggle.

We should realize that the surrender of the patient is censured not only because it demoralizes the medical personnel, representing as it does a failure to meet a moral obligation, but also because it supposedly reduces the capacity for resistance of the patient himself. It thus becomes as much to be feared as the "status-forcing scenes." This is why, today, American and British doctors are less often hiding the seriousness of their case from terminal patients. This year British television broadcast a program on cancer patients who had been apprised very accurately of their situation; this broadcast was intended as an encouragement to tell the truth. The doctors probably think that a man who has been told, if he is stable, will be more willing to undergo treatment in the hope of living to the full his last remaining days and, when all is said and done, will die just as discreetly and with as much dignity as if he had known nothing. This is the death of the good American, as described by Jacques Maritain in a book designed for the American public: he is led by the medical personnel "to think in a sort of dream, that the act of dying amid happy smiles, amid white garments like angels' wings would be a veritable pleasure, a moment of no consequence: relax, take it easy, it's nothing." This is also, with a little less of the commercial smile and a little more music, the humanistic, dignified death of the contemporary philosopher: to disappear "*pianissimo* and, so to speak, on tiptoe" (Jankélévitch).

2. The Denial of Mourning

We have seen how modern society deprives man of his death, and how it allows him this privilege only if he does not use it to upset the living. In a reciprocal way, society forbids the living to appear moved by the death of others; it does not allow them either to weep for the deceased or to seem to miss them.

Mourning was, nevertheless, until our time the supreme form of grief, and it was both right and necessary to express it. The old word for grief (in French *douleur*), *dol* or *doel,* has remained in our language, but with the restricted meaning of mourning (in French *deuil*). But even before it had been given a name, grief over the death of a loved one was the most violent expression of the most spontaneous feelings. During the height of the Middle Ages, the most hardened warriors or the most illustrious sovereigns broke down before the bodies of their friends or relatives, like—as we would say today—women, and hysterical women at that. Here we see King Arthur swoon several times in succession, beat his chest, claw at his face "so that the blood gushed forth." There, on the battlefield, we see the same king who "fell from his horse in a faint" before the body of his nephew, "then, crying all the while he began to search for the bodies of his friends," like Charlemagne at Roncevaux. Finding one of them, "he struck his palms against one another, crying that he had lived long enough. . . . Removing the helmet from the dead man, and looking at him for a long time, he then kissed his eyes and his frozen mouth." So many spasms and fainting fits! So many passionate embraces of already cold cadavers! So many desperate clawings, so many torn clothes! But aside from a very few inconsolable spirits who retreated into monasteries, once the great demonstrations of grief were over, the survivors took up their lives where they had left off.

Beginning in the 13th century, the demonstrations of mourning lost their spontaneity and became ritualized. The great displays of the early Middle Ages were from then on simulated by professional mourners. Such mourning is still carried on today in the southern and Mediterranean areas of France. Romancero's Le Cid demands in his will that there be no mourners at his funeral, as was the custom, nor flowers nor wreaths. The iconography of tombs from the 14th and 15th centuries shows processions of mourners in black robes around the exposed body, their heads hidden under cowls and penitents' hoods. Later, we can learn from last wills and testaments in the 16th and 17th centuries that the funeral cortèges were mainly composed of a crowd similar to the professional mourners: mendicant friars, paupers, children from the almshouses, all of whom were dressed for the occasion in black robes supplied by the inheritors, and who received some bread and a small amount of money following the ceremony.

One might wonder whether the closest relatives took part in the obsequies. Friends were given a banquet—an occasion for carousing and overindulgence, which the Church tried to abolish; in time these banquets became mentioned less often in the wills, except in cases where they were specifically forbidden. One notices in the last wills and testaments that sometimes the testator insisted on the presence of a brother or a son—usually a child—in his funeral procession. He would offer a special legacy as a reward for this much sought after attendance. Would this have been the case if the family always followed the procession? We know without doubt that women never attended funerals in the *ancien régime*. It seems most likely that, beginning with the late Middle Ages and the ritualization of mourning, society imposed a period of seclusion on the family, even keeping it away from the funeral, and replacing it by numerous priests and by professional mourners, monks and nuns, members of guilds, or ordinary people attracted by the distribution of alms.

This seclusion had two purposes: firstly, to allow the truly unhappy survivors to shelter their grief from the world, to allow them to wait, like a sick man who rests, for their pain to be alleviated. Henri de Campion mentions this in his *Mémoires*. In June 1659, de Campion's wife "gave up . . . the ghost, having delivered to the world a daughter who died five or six days after her. I was heart-broken and fell into a pitiable state. My brother . . . and my sister . . . brought me to Conches; I stayed there for seventeen days and then returned to Baxferei to put my affairs in order. . . . Being unable to remain in my house, which constantly reminded me of my sorrows, I took a house in Conches where I remained until 2 June 1660 [that is to say, until the *bout de l'an,* until the first anniversary of his wife's death], at which time, seeing that my sorrow would not leave me, I returned to my home in Baxferei with my children and lived there in great sadness."

The second reason for the seclusion was to prevent the survivors from forgetting the departed too soon; it excluded them, during a period of penitence, from the social relations and pleasures of secular life. This precaution was helpful in defending the unfortunate dead from being replaced too hastily. Nicolas Versoris, a Parisian bourgeois, lost his wife from the plague "the third day of September [1522] one hour after midnight." The next-to-last day of December in the same year, he was betrothed to a doctor's widow, whom he married as soon as he was able, on January 13, 1523, "the first festal day after Christmas."

The 19th century brought no softening in the severity of seclusion. In houses where there was a death, men, women, children, servants, and even horses and bees were separated from the outside world by a screen of crapes, veils and black cloth. However, this seclusion was more voluntary than forced and no longer were close friends and family forbidden to take part in the dramatic obsequies, to make pilgrimages to the graves, or to take part in the cult of remembrance so characteristic of the Romantic era. It was no longer obligatory for women to be excluded from the funeral services. They were accepted first by the bourgeoisie; the nobility remained faithful to the customs of exclusion for a longer period of time, and it was many years before the well-bred wife could participate in her husband's death. Nevertheless, even among the nobility, the women began attending their husband's, son's or father's burial, at first in secret, hidden in a corner of the church or in the gallery, with the approval of the Church. The traditional customs of seclusion were forced to come to terms with the new feelings of glorifying the dead and worshiping their tombs. The woman's presence, nonetheless, did not in any way alter the concept of seclusion in mourning: entirely veiled in black—a *mater dolorosa*—in the eyes of the world she was merely a symbol of inconsolable sorrow. However, seclusion was transferred from the physical level to the moral level. It served less to protect the dead from oblivion than to emphasize how impossible it was for the living to forget them and to live as they had before. The dead no longer required society's protection against the indifference of their close ones, any more than, as we saw earlier, the dying needed last wills and testaments to enforce their final wishes.

So we see that the increase in family feeling had, by the end of the 18th and beginning of the 19th centuries, combined with the traditional concept of seclusion to make mourning not so much an enforced quarantine as a right to demonstrate extreme grief, in defiance of conventional proprieties. This was, then, a return to the spontaneity of the high Middle Ages while maintaining the ritual constraints that followed in the 12th century. If one were to draw a "mourning curve," there would first be a peak stage of frank, violent spontaneity until somewhere around the 13th century, then a long phase of ritualization until the 18th century, and then in the 19th century a period of impassioned, self-indulgent grief, dramatic demonstration and funereal mythology. It is not inconceivable that the paroxysm of mourning in the 19th century is connected to its prohibition in the 20th, in the same way that in the postwar years the *mort sale* of Remarque, Sartre and Genet seems to be a reaction against the extremely noble death of the Romantic era. This is the meaning of Sartre's gesture, more ridiculous than scandalous, of "passing water" on Chateaubriand's tomb. There had to be a Chateaubriand in order for there to be a Sartre. It is the same kind of relationship that links contemporary eroticism to Victorian sexual taboos.

In the mid 20th century the ancient necessity for mourning—more or less spontaneous, or enforced, depending on the century—has been succeeded by its prohibition. During the course of one generation the situation has been reversed: what had always been required by individual conscience or social obligation is now forbidden; what had always been forbidden is now required. It is no longer correct to display one's grief, nor even to appear to feel any.

The British sociologist Geoffrey Gorer deserves the credit for having unearthed this unwritten law of our civilization. He was the first to understand that certain facts which had been neglected or misinterpreted by humanists were in fact part of an overall attitude toward death that was characteristic of industrial societies. In the autobiographical introduction to his book, Gorer tells of the personal way he discovered that death had become the principal taboo of the modern world. The sociological investigation that he organized in 1963 on the subject of attitudes toward death and mourning in England only confirmed, clarified and enriched the ideas he had already outlined in his noteworthy article, based on personal experience, "The Pornography of Death."

Gorer was born in 1910. He recalls that his entire family went into mourning at the death of Edward VII. He was taught to take off his hat when funeral processions passed by in the street, and to treat people in mourning with special consideration. Such practices seem very strange to

British people today! But when in 1915 his father perished in the wreck of the *Lusitania,* he in his turn was treated like a special person, with unusual gentleness. People spoke to him softly, or became silent in his presence as though they were dealing with an invalid. However, when, encouraged by the feeling of importance this mourning gave him, he told his schoolteacher that he would never be able to play again nor to look at flowers, she shook him and ordered him to stop being "morbid." The war permitted his mother to take a job where she found relief from her sorrow. Before the war, social convention would not have allowed her to work, "but later," remarks Gorer, "she would not have had the support of the ritual of mourning," which she had respected and which protected her. So Gorer came into contact with the traditional manifestations of mourning in his childhood, and they must have made an impact on him for he was to remember them later. After the war, when he was a young man, he had no further experiences of death. Once only, and then by chance, he saw a corpse in a Russian hospital he was visiting in 1931, and this unusual sight made an impression on him. This lack of familiarity with death is very definitely a general phenomenon, a long-unnoticed result of increased longevity: J. Fourcassié has shown how the youth of today can reach adulthood without ever seeing anyone die. Nevertheless, Gorer was surprised to find that, among the subjects of his investigation, more people than he would have suspected had in fact seen a dead person. Those who had already seen a corpse hastened to forget the fact and spontaneously adopted the behavior of those who had never seen one.

After the death of his sister-in-law, he was surprised that his brother, a noted physician, sank into such a state of depression. At that time intellectuals were already beginning to abandon the traditional funeral ceremonies and outward manifestations of mourning, which they considered superstitious, archaic practices. However, Gorer did not then see the connection between his brother's pathological despair and the absence of ritual mourning. This was to change in 1948, when he lost a friend, who left behind a wife and three children. "When I went to see her, two months after John's death, she told me, with tears of gratitude, that I was the first man to stay in the house since she had become a widow . . . she had been almost completely abandoned to loneliness, although the town was full of acquaintances who considered themselves friends." Gorer then understood that the changes that had taken place in the ritual of mourning were not insignificant, anecdotal occurrences. He realized the importance of the phenomenon and its serious effects. It was a few years later, in 1955, that he wrote his well-known article.

The final, decisive proof came a few years later. In 1961 his own brother, the physician, who had remarried, became ill—he was stricken with cancer.

Naturally, the truth was hidden from him, and it was only decided to inform his wife Elizabeth because she, not knowing that her husband was ill, might be annoyed with his behavior and impatient with him for pampering himself. Contrary to all expectations, the cancer spread quickly, and Gorer's brother died quite suddenly in his sleep. Everyone was pleased that he had been fortunate enough to die without knowing what was happening to him. And since this was a family of intellectuals, there was no wake, no displaying of the body. Because the death had taken place at home, the body had to be laid out. There were specialists to do this, former nurses who thus occupied their days of retirement. When these two old women arrived, it was "Where is the patient?" There was no longer any death, or any corpse—only a patient who kept his status as patient in spite of the biological change he had undergone, at least so long as he could be seen and be recognized. The laying out of a body is a traditional rite; however, its meaning has changed. Formerly the purpose was to arrange the body in the position representing that era's ideal image of death, that of a recumbent effigy, its hands crossed, waiting for its life in the afterworld. It was in the Romantic era that men discovered the special beauty that death imposes on a human face, and the purpose of the final solicitudes was to free this beauty from the death agonies that spoiled it. But in either case, the intention was to retain an image of death—a beautiful corpse, but a corpse. When the two old women had finished with their "patient" they were so pleased with their work that they invited the family to come and admire it: "the patient looks lovely now." This is not a dead person you see here, this is an almost-living person. Our fairy fingers have given him back the appearance of life. We have taken away the ugliness of the death agony from him, but have not replaced it with the majesty of a recumbent effigy or with the saintly beauty of the dead; he still has the charm of life, he is still nice, "lovely."

In these days the purpose of laying out a body is to hide the appearance of death and to retain the body's familiar, cheerful attitude of life. It should be noted that this tendency was not very pronounced in Gorer's England, and that this family of intellectuals did not share in the nurses' enthusiasm. However, in the United States, the laying out of a corpse has gone as far as embalming and displaying in "funeral homes."

This family of British intellectuals was not seduced either by the beliefs of another age or by the gaudy ostentation of American modernism. The body was to be cremated. However, in England and no doubt also in Northern Europe, cremation has taken on a particular meaning, which is made very clear in Gorer's investigation. The choice for cremation is no longer made, as it was for so many years, to defy the Church and ancient Christian customs. Nor is the choice made solely for reasons of convenience and saving space: the Church being inclined to accept these reasons in memory of a time when ashes, as for example those of Antigone's brother, were respected as much as human bones. In modern England cremation suggests more a sign of one's modernity, an assurance of rationality, and finally a denial of the afterlife. However, these reasons are not immediately or clearly apparent from the spontaneous statements given by the subjects of the investigation. Out of 67 cases in the investigation there were 40 cremations against 27 burials. The reasons for the choice of cremation came down to two. Firstly, cremation was considered to be the most complete method of disposing of the dead. This is why one woman, whose mother had been cremated and who thought the process was "cleaner, more hygienic," nevertheless rejected it for her husband because it was "too final"; she had him buried.

The second reason is an offshoot of the first: cremation does away with the cult of cemeteries and the making of pilgrimages to graves. This is not a necessary consequence of cremation. Indeed, crematorium administrators have done their best to permit families to venerate their dead just as in traditional cemeteries; there is a remembrance room where one can place a memorial tablet to serve the same purpose as a tombstone. However, of the 40 cases in the investigation, there was only one case with a name engraved on such a tablet, and only 14 with a name written in the memory book, whose pages are turned every day to permit commemoration of deaths occurring on that date—an intermediate solution between complete obliteration and the perpetuity of a memorial tablet. For the other 25 cases, no visible trace was left. The reason that the families did not use the facilities at their disposal is that they saw cremation as a sure means of escaping from the cult of the dead.

It would be a serious mistake to attribute this refusal to worship and remember the dead to indifference or insensitivity. On the contrary, the results of the investigation and Gorer's autobiographical testimony indicate how much the survivors suffer and how long they remain distressed. In order to be convinced of this, let us go back to Gorer's narrative, to the time of his brother Peter's cremation. The widow, Elizabeth, attended neither the cremation nor the Anglican service that preceded it—a concession to convention, since the deceased had no religion. Her absence was not due to the ritual interdictions of the old style of mourning, nor to lack of feeling, but to the fear of "cracking" and to a new form of modesty. "She could not bear the thought that she might lose control and other people observe her grief." The new conventions required that one hide that which formerly had to be shown, even simulated: one's grief.

There were even more imperative reasons for keeping the children away from such a traumatizing ceremony. Already in France, where old customs die hard, children of the bourgeoisie and the middle classes (families of

white-collar workers) scarcely ever take part any more in the burials of
their grandparents; old people, grandparents several times over, are sent
out of this world, without the presence of any little grandchildren, by adults
who are as rushed and ill at ease as they are emotionally upset. This sight
struck me forcefully after I had just finished reading, in the central archives,
some 17th century documents in which the testator, who was often still
indifferent regarding the presence of his close relatives, insistently demanded that a grandchild follow his funeral procession. During the same
period a portion of all mourners was recruited from among foundlings or
children aided by almshouses. And in the numerous representations of the
dying man in his bedchamber surrounded by a crowd, the painter or en-
graver never forgot to include a small child.

So Elizabeth and the children stayed at home in the country on the day of
the cremation. Geoffrey joined them in the evening, broken from fatigue and
emotion. His sister-in-law, very much in control of herself, met him and
told him that she had spent a very good day with the children, that they had
picnicked in the fields and watched the grass being mown. Elizabeth, who
was an American from New England, spontaneously and courageously
adopted the behavior that her fellow-countrymen had taught her and that
the English expected of her. She was supposed to act as if nothing had happened so that everyone else could act the same way, and social life could
continue without being interrupted, even for a single moment, by death. If
she had dared to show any signs of grief in public she would have been
ostracized by society, as a loose woman would have been in former times.
But in any case, in spite of these safeguards Elizabeth's friends had, as a
precautionary measure, so to speak, avoided her at the beginning of her bereavement. She confided to her brother-in-law that at first she had been
kept at a distance "as though she were a leper." She was accepted only
when it was safe to assume that she would not betray any emotion. In fact,
this isolation led her to the brink of a nervous breakdown: "at the period
when she most needed help and comfort from society she was left alone." It
was then that Geoffrey Gorer conceived the idea of his investigation into the
modern denial of mourning and its traumatizing effects.

It is easy to see how these things happened. According to Gorer, it began
with the disappearance of the social rules, which laid down the ritual conduct to be observed during mourning and which awarded a special status
during this time, both to the family and to society in its relations with the
family. The author gives perhaps too much importance to the role of the
two world wars in accelerating the change. Little by little the new social
conventions took hold, in a spontaneous way, however, and without anyone
being aware of their newness. Even today, in fact, they have not been for-
malized in the same way that the old customs were, though their power is no

less constraining for that. Death has become a taboo, an unnameable thing (the expression appears in a completely different context in Jankélévitch's book on death), and, as formerly with sex, it must not be mentioned in public. Nor must other people be forced to mention it. Gorer shows forcefully how, in the 20th century, death has replaced sex as the principal prohibition. Children used to be told that they were born in a cabbage leaf, but they took part in the great farewell scenes in the bedroom or by the bedside of a dying man. However, by the second half of the 19th century, the presence of children was beginning to make people feel uneasy and they tended, not to forbid it but to shorten it. At the deaths of Emma Bovary and Ivan Ilych, the old custom of presenting the children was definitely respected, but they were made to leave the room immediately afterward because it was thought that the distortions of the death agony would inspire them with too much horror. Although removed from the deathbed, the children still had their place at the funeral ceremonies, clothed in black from head to toe.

Today even the youngest children are acquainted with the facts of love and birth, but when they no longer see their grandfather and they ask why, they are told in France that he has gone on a very long trip, and in England that he is resting in a beautiful garden filled with honeysuckle. It is no longer the children who are born in cabbages, but the dead who disappear among the flowers. The relatives of the dead are thus forced to feign indifference. Society demands from them a self-control corresponding to the propriety or dignity that it imposes upon the dying. The essential thing both for the dying man and the survivors is to not let any emotion show through. Society as a whole behaves in the same manner as the hospital staff. If the dying man must overcome his anxiety and collaborate obligingly with the doctors and nurses, the unhappy survivor must hide his grief, refuse to withdraw into a solitude which would betray him, and must continue without a pause his life of social contacts, work and leisure—otherwise he would be avoided, and this avoidance would have an entirely different consequence from the ritual seclusion of traditional mourning. This seclusion was accepted by all as a necessary transition, and included such equally ritualized behavior as obligatory visits of condolence, "letters of consolation," the "succor" of religion. Today this exclusion carries the implication of a reproof, similar to the treatment accorded those who have lost social status, the contagiously ill or sexual deviants: those who insist on grieving are shunned in the same way as those who are social misfits. He who wishes to be spared this ordeal must therefore wear a mask in public and take it off only in the utmost privacy: "one does not cry," says Gorer, "except in private, as one undresses or goes to bed in private," in secret, "as if it were an analogue of masturbation."

Today's society refuses to accept the bereaved as a sick man to be comforted. It refuses to associate the idea of mourning with that of sickness. The old-style courtesy was more understanding, perhaps more "modern" in this regard, more sensitive to the pathological effects of repressed mental suffering. In our cruel times Gorer recognizes the beneficial effects of the ancestral customs which protected a man stricken by the death of a loved one. During his mourning "he has more need of society's help than at any other period of his life since his childhood and early youth, and yet it is then that society withdraws its aid and refuses him assistance. The price of this failure in misery, loneliness, despair, and morbidity is extremely high." The prohibition of mourning pushes the survivor into losing himself in his work or, on the contrary, to the brink of insanity, into pretending to live with the dead person as if he were still there, or, further, into taking his place, imitating his gestures, his words, his eccentricities, and sometimes, in the height of neurosis, into copying the symptoms of the disease that carried him off. Thus we see the reappearance of strange manifestations of extreme grief, which seem new and modern to Gorer, but which are nevertheless familiar to a historian of customs. He will have met them before as the excessive demonstrations which were accepted, recommended, even simulated, during the ritual period of mourning in traditional societies. However, he must admit that the demonstrations are similar in appearance only. Formerly, the purpose of these demonstrations was to liberate; and even when, as happened very frequently in the Romantic era, they overstepped the bounds of convention and became pathological, they were not rejected as shocking, but were tolerated kindly. A striking example of this indulgence appears in one of Mark Twain's novels, where all the friends of the deceased willingly agree to support the illusions of the widow, who has not accepted the death and who, at every anniversary, imagines and acts out the impossible return. In a current context, these friends would refuse to participate in such an unhealthy comedy. Where Mark Twain's rough heroes showed tenderness and indulgence, modern society can see only embarrassing, shameful morbidity, or mental illness to be cured. One comes to wonder then, with Gorer, whether a large part of today's social pathology is not rooted in the removal of death from everyday life, in the prohibition of mourning and of the right to weep for one's dead.

3. The Invention of New Funerary Rites in the United States

From the preceding analyses, it would be tempting to conclude that the prohibition surrounding death today is a structural characteristic of contemporary civilization. The elimination of death from speech and other familiar forms of communication, along with the high priority given well-being and material consumption would thus be part of the pattern of industrial societies. One might say that this is generally true of the vast area of modern society that covers Northern Europe and America, but that it meets with resistance wherever the old ways of thinking still exist, such as in Catholic countries like France or Italy, in Protestant countries like Presbyterian Scotland, and among the populace of technocratic countries. The concern for total modernity, in fact, depends as much on social as geographic conditions and, even in the most developed regions, it is still restricted to the educated classes, whether believers or atheists. Wherever this concern has not penetrated one finds the continued presence of the romantic attitudes toward death that were born in the 18th century and developed in the 19th—the cult of the dead and the veneration of cemeteries. Nevertheless, one might say, these survivals are deceptive, because even though they still affect the largest segment of the population, they are doomed: as the outdated thinking to which they are tied declines, so inevitably will they. The pattern of future society will be imposed on them and will complete the elimination of death that has already begun in bourgeois families, both progressive and reactionary. This evolutionist sketch of death is not entirely false, and it is probable that the denial of death is too much a part of the pattern of industrial civilization not to expand along with it. On the other hand the sketch is not completely true, for pockets of resistance have occurred where they were least expected, not in the archaic religious fervors of the old countries, but in the most fertile center of modernity, the United States of America. And yet America was the first country to lessen the tragic sense of death. It was in America that observations could first be made on the new attitudes toward death. They inspired the satirical humor of the English Catholic novelist Evelyn Waugh in *The Loved One,* which was published in 1948.[8] In 1951 they attracted the attention of Roger Caillois, who interpreted these attitudes as a hedonistic avoidance of the issue. "Death is not to be feared, not because of any moral obligation to overcome the fear it causes, but because it is inevitable and because in fact there is no reason to dread it—only it must absolutely not be thought about, much less spoken about."[9]

Everything that we have described in the preceding pages is true of America: the alienation of the dying person, the suppression of mourning, everything except the actual burial itself. Americans have been loath to simplify the ritual of the funeral ceremony and the burial to the extent of Gorer's English model. In order to understand this peculiarity of American society, we should go back in our earlier account of the death of modern

---

[8] *The Loved One* (London: Chapman and Hall, 1948).
[9] Caillois, *Quatre essais . . .*

man to the moment of the last breath. Up to the last breath and after the burial, that is, during the so-called mourning period, everything happens the same way in both England and America. This is not so during the intermediate period. The enthusiastic attitude noted earlier of the ex-nurses who laid out the body ("it looks lovely now") died out almost immediately in English circles since it was not shared by the family nor encouraged by society. The main thing, in England, is to make the body disappear, in a respectable way, of course, but quickly and completely, thanks to cremation.

In America quite the opposite is true. The laying out of the body is the beginning of a series of complicated and sumptuous rites: embalming the body in order to restore to it the appearance of life; laying the body out for viewing in the room of a funeral home where the deceased, surrounded by flowers and music, receives a last visit from his relatives and friends; solemn funeral ceremonies; burials in cemeteries designed like parks, adorned with monuments and intended for the moral edification of visitors who are more tourists than pilgrims. There is no need here to go into a long description of these funerary customs, so well known from Waugh's caricature that has recently been made into a film, and from the criticism of Jessica Mitford in her book *The American Way of Death*. However, there is a danger that this literature, that is both moralistic and polemical, will lead to a false interpretation. By suggesting either commercial exploitation and pressure of interests, or a perversion of the cult of happiness, it conceals from us the real meaning, which is the denial of the absolute finality of death and the repugnance of physical destruction without ritual and solemnity. This is why cremation is so rare in the United States.

American society is very attached to its new funerary rites, which its own intellectuals (Jessica Mitford is a voice of the intellectual circles) and Europeans see as ridiculous; they are so attached to them that the taboo on death is at this point broken. In American buses there are advertisements that read: "The dignity and integrity of N. . . Funeral costs no more. . . . Easy access. Private parking for over 100 cars." Obviously, death here is also an article of consumption. But what is remarkable is that it could become one—as well as a subject for advertising—in spite of the prohibition that is operative in all other facets of social life. The American does not treat the deceased, once they are dead, in the same way that he treats death in general, or in the same way that he treats the dying or the survivor. In this one respect he does not follow the general path of modernity. He leaves the dead their special place in society that traditional civilizations had always kept for them but which industrial societies have reduced to almost nothing. He maintains the solemn farewell to the dead, which, in the other countries of the technological modern world is carried out with suspicious haste. One factor that has probably accelerated this nonconformist reaction is the fact that people in America today die more and more frequently in hospitals and less and less frequently at home. The French, whose hospitals still bear traces of the 17th century, when patients were subjected to the humiliating and coarse treatment of vagrants and criminals, are familiar with the coldrooms where bodies are preserved like meat; they are in a good position to understand why the increasing use of hospitals would make it even more necessary to have a period of contemplation and solemnity between the mass morgue and the final burial.

This ceremonial solemnity could take place in the home, as in former times. But the new prohibitions on death conflict with the idea of bringing the body back into excessively close contact with the living: European intellectuals are showing less and less desire to keep the body when the death occurs at home, either for reasons of hygiene or, more usually, for fear of not being able to bear the nearness of the body and therefore of emotionally "cracking." So in the United States they have devised the plan of putting the body in a neutral place, which would have neither the anonymity of the hospital nor the excessively personal nature of the house—in other words, the funeral home, run by the funeral director somewhat like a hotel specializing in dead guests. The stay at the funeral home is a compromise between the respectable but hasty and radical deritualization of Northern Europe and the archaic ceremonies of traditional mourning. In the same way the new funeral rites created by the Americans are a compromise between their repugnance for having no solemn time for reflection after death and their general respect for the taboo on death. This is why these rites seem so different from any we have known before and, as a result, seem so ridiculous. The Americans have, however, rediscovered some of the traditional elements. The half-closed coffin showing the upper half of the body (the head and bust) is not an invention of American morticians. They borrowed it from the Mediterranean customs that are still observed in Marseilles and Italy, and that date back at least to the Middle Ages: a 15th century fresco in the Saint-Petrone Church in Bologna depicts the relics of Saint Mark preserved in a coffin of this type.

However, the meaning of the funeral-home rites has completely changed. In the "slumber rooms" of the funeral homes it is not the dead who are being glorified, but the dead transformed by the mortician's art into the almost-living. The old embalming procedures were used mainly to pass on a little of the incorruptibility of saints to illustrious, respected men who had died. Since one of the miracles that proves the saintliness of a man is the extraordinary incorruptibility of his corpse, by helping to make a body incorruptible one was setting it on the road to sainthood, participating in the sanctification.

In modern America the purpose of the chemical preservation techniques is to play down the death of the person and to create the illusion of a living being. This almost-living person will receive his friends one last time, in a flower-laden room and to the sound of sweet or serious—never gloomy—music. The idea of death, as well as of any sadness or pathos, has been banished from this farewell ceremony. As Roger Caillois saw it: "Dead bodies completely dressed from head to toe, who continued to have a physical personality and who came there as though for a walk along the river." The fact remains, however, that this last illusion could be dispensed with, that the sectors of English society described by Gorer have dispensed with it, and that American intellectuals as represented by Jessica Mitford would like to dispense with it. The resistance in America probably stems from very deeply rooted characteristics.

The idea of turning a deceased person into a living one in order to pay tribute to him one last time may seem to us to be childish and ridiculous, intertwined, as it often is in America, with commercial concerns and advertising jargon. It is, however, proof of a rapid and precise adjustment to complex and contradictory feelings. It is the first time that a society has in a general way honored its dead while refusing them the status of death. It was done during the 15th to 17th centuries, but only for a single category of death—that of the king of France. Upon his death, the embalmed king was clothed in his coronation purple and laid on a ceremonial bed similar to a judge's couch, as though he would wake up at any moment. Banquet tables were set up in the chamber, no doubt connected with funeral banquets, but primarily they served as a sign of the denial of mourning. The king had not died; he was receiving his court for the last time, dressed in his ceremonial garb, like a rich Californian in the slumber room of a funeral home. The idea of the continuity of the crown imposed a funerary ritual which, in spite of the time that has passed, is on the whole similar to that in contemporary America—a compromise between the respect that is due the deceased and the refusal to accept the unnamable idea of death.

Americans, as convinced of the legitimacy of their "way of death" as they are of their "way of life," and of course of their funeral directors, have given their rituals a second justification which is very interesting because, in an unexpected way, it deals with Gorer's hypotheses on the traumatizing effects of the denial of mourning. This fact is reported by Jessica Mitford: "Recently a funeral director told me of a woman who needed psychiatric treatment because her husband's funeral was with a closed casket [the word "coffin" is not used any more], no visitation and burial in another state with her not present." In other words, the funeral of a British intellectual. The psychiatrist confided to the funeral director that this case had taught him a great deal about the consequences of a lack of ceremony at funerals. "The patient was treated and has recovered and has vowed never to be part of another memorial type service," that is, a service that is simply a short commemoration of the deceased.

Funeral directors, whose profits are threatened by the movement toward more simple funeral ceremonies, have taken refuge in the opinions of psychologists, who have deemed that elegant, flowery funerals dissipate the grief, replacing it with gentle serenity. The funeral and cemetery businesses, they say, have a moral and social function, that of "softening" the sorrow of the bereaved, and preparing monuments and memorial parks to bring happiness to the living. Modern American cemeteries fulfill the same role as the planned necropolises of French designers at the end of the 18th century, after a royal edict had forbidden burials to take place within cities. New cemeteries had to be planned and there was a profusion of literature describing what they should be like (and what Père Lachaise—the model for modern cemeteries in Europe and America—would be like): one is struck by the resemblance between these 18th century texts and the prose, cited by Jessica Mitford, of both modern funeral directors and the American moralists who support them. America is rediscovering the style and tone of the Enlightenment—or has it always kept them? American historians such as Philip May believe that Puritanism in the 18th century never permitted the development of a hedonist attitude toward death, and that the contemporary optimism goes back no further than the beginning of this century. Whether direct influence or repetition with a century's interval, the similarity is no less striking.

Romanticism is the reason that Père Lachaise no longer resembles Forest Lawn, the famous Los Angeles cemetery caricatured by Waugh. Romanticism distorted its features and the effects of Romanticism are still present in popular representations of death and in tomb worship. America, on the other hand, seems to have gone quickly through the period of Romanticism to rediscover intact the spirit of the Enlightenment, delayed by Puritanism. Puritanism in America might have had the same restraining influence that Romanticism had in Europe, but it yielded sooner and more rapidly, leaving the way clear for the not-yet-faded Enlightenment attitudes, the harbingers of modernity. One cannot help feeling that, in this area as in so many others (constitutional law, for instance), America is closer than Europe to the 18th century.

Thus, during the last third of a century, a major phenomenon has occurred that is only beginning to be perceived: death, that familiar friend, has disappeared from the language, its name has become taboo. In place of the many words and signs our ancestors had developed is a widespread anonymous grief. Literature, with the help of Malraux and Ionesco, is learning to give it back its old name, which has been erased from everyday use, from the spoken language, from social mores. In everyday life death, once so much talked about and so often depicted, has lost all positive meaning; it has become merely the opposite or reverse of what is actually seen, understood, spoken of.

This a profound change. Although it is true that during the early Middle Ages, and later among the common people, death occupied no more of a prominent place than it does now, it was absent not because of a taboo, as it is today, but because the extreme familiarity with death deadened its power. Then, in the 12th and 13th centuries, death became the overwhelming preoccupation, at least among clerics and the *litterati*. It came about in two stages, that is to say, it centered about two themes: the theme of the Last Judgment in the 12th and 13th centuries, and the theme of the art of dying in the 14th and 15th centuries. In the chamber of the dying man, depicted in the *artes moriendi,* the entire universe is united: the living of this world gathered about the bed, and the spirits of heaven and hell fighting over the soul of Moriens in the presence of Christ and all the heavenly host. The life of the dying man is compressed into this small space and this short moment, and, whatever kind of life it may be, it is then the center of the natural and supernatural world. Death is the place for the realization of self.

Moreover, we know that during the late Middle Ages man began to break away from the old collective representations, and individualism asserted itself in all its forms: religious, economic (the beginning of capitalism), cultural, etc. In my opinion, the most striking evidence of this individualism is the last will and testament. It turned into a kind of literary genre and became the individual's means of expression, the testimony to his self-realization. When it was reduced to playing a purely financial role, this signaled a decline, or at the very least a change. The advances in science, the assertion of the rights of man, the development of the bourgeoisie in the 18th century are all definite signs of an advanced stage of individualism; but they are the fruits of autumn, for, in the unnoticed privacy of daily life, man's self-determination was already being threatened, first by the restrictions of the family, then by his job or profession. The clear correspondence between the triumph over death and the triumph of the individual during the late Middle Ages makes one wonder whether a similar—but reverse—situation does not exist today between "the crisis of death" and the crisis of individuality.

CONTRIBUTORS

David E. Stannard is on the American Studies and History faculties of Yale University. The author of articles and reviews in various scholarly journals, he currently has two books in press—one on Puritanism and death, and one on the limits of psychoanalysis in historical explanation.

Jack Goody, director of the African Studies Centre, St. John's College, Cambridge, is the author of numerous books and articles including *Death, Property, and the Ancestors* (1962), and, most recently, *Comparative Studies in Kinship* (1969), and *Bridewealth and Dowry* (1973).

Mary Ann Meyers is a free-lance journalist and a Ph.D. candidate at the University of Pennsylvania. Her articles have appeared in a variety of publications, and in 1974 and 1975 she won feature writing awards presented by the Philadelphia chapter of Women-in-Communications. A contributing editor of *The Pennsylvania Gazette,* Miss Meyers has been an assistant to the president of the University of Pennsylvania.

Stanley French, Associate Professor of American History at the California State University at Northridge, is a specialist in American intellectual and social history of the nineteenth century.

Lewis O. Saum teaches in the History Department at the University of Washington. Currently at work on a study of the popular mind of pre-Civil War America, he is the author of *The Fur Trader and the Indian* (1965) and of articles in various scholarly journals.

Ann Douglas, currently on the English Department faculty at Columbia University, has previously taught at Princeton University and is the author of numerous articles on women and popular and intellectual thought in nineteenth century America. Her essay in this volume is a revised excerpt from a forthcoming book.

Patricia Fernández Kelly of Universidad Ibero-Americana has recently been appointed coordinator of the Art and Folklore Program of the Latin American Institute at Rutgers University. She is also lecturing at Jersey City State College on popular art and social theory. Her first book, *Arte del Pueblo de Mexico,* is in press.

Philippe Ariès of Maison Lafitte, France, is the author of numerous books and articles on a wide variety of subjects, including the internationally acclaimed *Centuries of Childhood* (1962). His 1973 lectures at the Johns Hopkins University Symposia in comparative History have recently been published as *Western Attitudes Toward Death* (1974). He is now completing a major study of the problem of death in Western thought since the Middle Ages.